DEMOCRATIC ILLUSION

Deliberative Democracy in Canadian Public Policy

The theory of deliberative democracy promotes the creation of systems of governance in which citizens actively exchange ideas, engage in debate, and create laws that are responsive to their interests and aspirations. While deliberative processes are being adopted in an increasing number of cases, decision-making power remains mostly in the hands of traditional elites.

In *Democratic Illusion*, Genevieve Fuji Johnson examines four representative examples: participatory budgeting in the Toronto Community Housing Corporation, Deliberative Polling by Nova Scotia Power Incorporated, a national consultation process by the Canadian Nuclear Waste Management Organization, and public consultations embedded in the development of official languages policies in Nunavut. In each case, measures that appeared to empower the public failed to challenge the status quo approach to either formulating or implementing policy.

Illuminating a critical gap between deliberative democratic theory and its applications, this timely and important study shows what needs to be done to ensure deliberative processes offer more than the illusion of democracy.

(Studies in Comparative Political Economy and Public Policy)

GENEVIEVE FUJI JOHNSON is an associate professor in the Department of Political Science at Simon Fraser University.

Studies in Comparative Political Economy and Public Policy

Editors: MICHAEL HOWLETT, DAVID LAYCOCK (Simon Fraser University), and STEPHEN MCBRIDE (McMaster University)

Studies in Comparative Political Economy and Public Policy is designed to showcase innovative approaches to political economy and public policy from a comparative perspective. While originating in Canada, the series will provide attractive offerings to a wide international audience, featuring studies with local, subnational, cross-national, and international empirical bases and theoretical frameworks.

Editorial Advisory Board

For a list of books published in the series, see page 183.

Democratic Illusion

Deliberative Democracy in Canadian Public Policy

GENEVIEVE FUJI JOHNSON

UNIVERSITY OF TORONTO PRESS
Toronto Buffalo London

© University of Toronto Press 2015
Toronto Buffalo London
www.utppublishing.com
Printed in the U.S.A.

ISBN 978-1-4426-4227-0 (cloth)
ISBN 978-1-4426-1124-5 (paper)

Printed on acid-free, 100% post-consumer recycled paper
with vegetable-based inks.

Library and Archives Canada Cataloguing in Publication

Johnson, Genevieve Fuji, author
Democratic illusion : deliberative democracy in Canadian public
policy / Genevieve Fuji Johnson.

(Studies in comparative political economy and public policy)
Includes bibliographical references and index.
ISBN 978-1-4426-4227-0 (bound) – ISBN 978-1-4426-1124-5 (pbk.)

1. Deliberative democracy – Canada – Case studies.   I. Title.
II. Series: Studies in comparative political economy and public policy

JL86.P64J64 2015   320.60971   C2015-900192-7

University of Toronto Press acknowledges the financial assistance to its
publishing program of the Canada Council for the Arts and the Ontario
Arts Council, an agency of the Government of Ontario.

  Canada Council   Conseil des Arts
for the Arts   du Canada

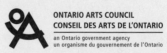 ONTARIO ARTS COUNCIL
CONSEIL DES ARTS DE L'ONTARIO
an Ontario government agency
un organisme du gouvernement de l'Ontario

University of Toronto Press acknowledges the financial support of the
Government of Canada through the Canada Book Fund for its publishing
activities.

This book has been published with the help of a grant from the Federation
for the Humanities and Social Sciences, through the Awards to Scholarly
Publications Program, using funds provided by the Social Sciences and
Humanities Research Council of Canada.

Contents

Acknowledgments vii

1 The Hope for and Illusion of Deliberative Democracy 3
   Roots and Ambitions 7
   The Substance of Procedure 12
   The Importance of Context 18

2 Participatory Budgeting and the Toronto Community
   Housing Corporation 24
   The Origins of Participatory Budgeting 26
   TCHC's Tenant Participation System 30
   Persisting Hierarchy and Circumscribed Participation 38

3 Deliberative Polling and Nova Scotia Power Incorporated 47
   The Basics of Deliberative Polling 49
   NSPI's Customer Energy Forums 55
   Prevailing Policy Requirements and Economic Interests 61

4 National Consultations and the Nuclear Waste
   Management Organization 70
   Canadian Nuclear Waste Management Policy 73
   NWMO's National Consultation Process 75
   Filtering Outputs and Diminishing Outcomes 86

5 Embedded Policy Consultations and Nunavut's
   Official Languages 92
   The Emergence of Nunavut 93

Nunavut's Embedded Policy Consultations   97
Implementation and the Passage of Time   110

6 Contextual Complexity and the Importance of Deliberative
   Democracy   117

*Epilogue: Interpretive Case-Study Research, Its Challenges
and Rewards*   126

Notes   129

Bibliography   158

Index   173

Acknowledgments

There are many people who made valuable contributions to this volume. Beverly Neufeld, in her capacity as a grants facilitator for the Faculty of Arts and Social Sciences, Simon Fraser University, spent countless hours providing comments on research grant applications for this project. It is not an overstatement to say that I owe my funding successes to her – successes that made this project possible. Of course, I should also acknowledge my gratitude for a Standard Research Grant (2008–2012) from the Social Sciences and Humanities Research Council of Canada (SSHRC). In addition, this book has been published with the help of a grant from the Federation for the Humanities and Social Sciences, through the Awards to Scholarly Publications Program, with funds provided by the SSHRC.

I am indebted to many research assistants, including Charlotte Calon, Julie MacDonald, Dina Dexter, Jonathan Craft, Josh Newman, Anna Vorobyova, Samuel Oliphant, Kerry Porth, and Daniel D. Guedes de Andrade. Their hard work has, at different times, included organizing research interviews, accompanying me on research trips, transcribing endless recordings, helping code transcripts and documents, proofreading multiple drafts, fact checking every reference, and generally keeping materials for four case studies reasonably organized. Sima Joshi-Koop was enormously helpful with the Nunavut official languages case, carefully identifying its parameters, conducting preliminary research, and drafting out a policy history that would become the basis of chapter 5. Mary Burns was also most helpful, providing meticulous research and editorial assistance throughout this project. Her dedication to it has never waned. I am extremely lucky to have had the support of all these bright, talented, and hardworking people.

Several colleagues provided much-needed guidance on the substance of this volume. I am thankful for the insights and feedback on specific chapters provided by Annis May Timpson, Graham White, Brendan Haley, Tsyoshi Kawasaki, Jade Larissa Schiff, and John Dryzek. Professor Dryzek along with Elaine Cristina dos Santos, Simon Niemeyer, and Carolyn Hendriks were welcoming and engaging hosts during a seven-week visit to the Centre for Deliberative Democracy and Global Governance at the Australian National University (now housed at the University of Canberra). Calvin Morrill, Jonathan Simon, Rosann Greenspan, and Meg Gentes were also very hospitable during my eight-month visit to the Center for the Study of Law and Society, University of California, Berkeley. My time spent at these centres was the most productive of my career so far.

Daniel Quinlan of the University of Toronto Press has been, as always, a wonderful acquisitions editor, striking a balance between efficiency and patience with my work. It continues to be a pleasure to work with him. I am grateful to the Press's anonymous readers, who provided generous comments seeking to nudge me towards greater clarity. I thank copy-editor John St James for his careful tweaks to the manuscript, managing editor Wayne Herrington, and Stephen Shapiro for his contributions to the marketing of the book.

I wish also to thank all the people who shared their insights with me in research interviews. The interviewees in each of my cases were most generous with their time and insights. I am very grateful for their contributions to this volume. Despite all the expert guidance I've received during this project, I'm well aware that there are lingering weaknesses. I take full responsibility for these.

Many thanks to numerous friends for stimulating thought and discussion: Michelle Bonner, Ellen Gutterman, Julie Simmons, Susan Brook, Tiffany Werth, Sylvia Smullen, and Kate Tremills. Melissa Williams remains an inspiration. Two friends with whom I share a beloved hobby, Scott Macdonald and Mannie Bondoc, continue to encourage me to dig deeper and push harder no matter how exhausted I may feel. I value their encouragement as many academic endeavours are psychologically and emotionally not unlike very long and gruelling bike rides up and down the mountainous terrain of Vancouver's north shore.

I must express my gratitude to my family. My husband Steve Dodge and stepdaughter Gabriela Maranhão Dodge were helpful beyond words, often asking the most basic but most clarifying questions. Their focus, determination, and brilliance in projects of their own inspire me.

I am thankful for all the support provided by the Dodge-Dillon family, as well as by the Kokubo-Gibbons-Johnson-Rosenbloom-Sakata-Izumi-Cable-White family. A special thank you to Paul Gibbons, who came up with the book's title in about fifteen seconds flat (when I had been agonizing over it for several months). Long-time family friend Denis Farley provided the evocative image for the cover of this volume (www.denisfarleyart.com). I owe him many thanks as well.

Finally, I wish to thank Sarah Hartley for carefully reading the whole volume and articulating constructive comments in a way that was critical but encouraging. I met Sarah in 1999, after Richard Simeon suggested that I meet another student in the University of Toronto's PhD program in political science who was also interested in interpretive policy analysis. For several months thereafter, Richard, Sarah, and myself would meet to discuss readings in non-positivist approaches to public policy. This experience set in motion similar research trajectories for Sarah and me, and we have continued our exchanges over the years. Richard, who passed away in 2013, was a brilliant scholar, but also a man with a great sensitivity to people and personalities. I will always be grateful to him for bringing key ideas and people into my life. I dedicate this book to his spirit of intellectual generosity.

DEMOCRATIC ILLUSION

Deliberative Democracy in Canadian Public Policy

Chapter One

The Hope for and Illusion of Deliberative Democracy

Deliberative democracy is a rich ideal. It invokes a democratic system of governance in which citizens[1] actively exchange ideas, engage in debate, and create laws responsive to their interests and aspirations. Canada appears to have good prospects for realizing interconnected sites, forums, and procedures informed by its central principles of citizen participation, inclusion, equality, reasoning, agreement, and empowerment. In this volume, I examine four such procedures. These are participatory budgeting within the Toronto Community Housing Corporation (TCHC), a set of Customer Energy Forums based on Deliberative Polling®[2] by Nova Scotia Power Incorporated (NPSI), an iterative national consultation process by the Canadian Nuclear Waste Management Organization (NWMO), and a series of public consultations embedded in the development of official languages policies in Nunavut.[3] I ask the following basic questions, posed some time ago by Maarten Hajer and Sven Kesselring, "What can we realistically expect from initiatives for enhanced participation in policy deliberation? What are the present functions of these practices, and how do these functions compare to the noble intentions of those who came up with the ideas?"[4] These questions inspire me to pursue the following four interrelated objectives: (1) To study cases of public policy that are most likely to be successful in approximating the deliberative ideal; (2) to evaluate these cases with reference to the deliberative democratic criteria of participatory inclusion, procedural equality, access to information, exchanges of reasons, orientations toward agreement, and empowerment in policy decisions and decision-making structures; (3) to account for their strengths and weaknesses by examining factors that characterize the context in which each is situated; and (4) to highlight structural conditions and design features that could optimize deliberative democratic procedures given limits imposed by contextual complexity.

When initially conceptualizing this project, I sought out success stories in contemporary public policy to understand how principles derived from or related to the ideal of deliberative democracy are being applied and what their implications are for a broader system of collective norm formation and decision making. The cases I bring together in this volume appealed to me because they were not "one-off" events, but appeared to mark genuine shifts in decision-making power away from traditional elites in government and corporations and toward a more inclusive constituency of individuals. They seemed to be strong cases for an empirical study of what was originally a highly idealized account of rendering ethically justifiable decisions that can have binding social and political force. Following John Parkinson, I take deliberative democracy to be an ideal that real-life procedures and institutions can only approximate, more or less.[5] These cases appeared to be robust approximations of an elusive ideal, with each having elements of deliberative democracy firmly rooted in policy processes. They appeared to exemplify the potential for democratization in what Mark Warren calls the "domain of governance."[6]

This appearance was deceiving. Indeed, an exploration of these cases focusing not only on their procedures but also on their contexts reveals troubling limitations. Probing their political, economic, and social contexts reveals that the ways in which procedures were implemented served in thwarting their deliberative democratic aims. How these policy areas developed, who set policy directions and parameters, and

Table 1　Case studies

Host	Topic	Procedure
Toronto Community Housing Corporation (TCHC)	Social housing issues in local community housing units	Participatory budgeting (2001–12)
Nova Scotia Power Incorporated (NSPI)	Electricity conservation and generation options in province of Nova Scotia	Deliberative Polls (2004, 2005, and 2009)
Nuclear Waste Management Organization (NWMO)	Nuclear waste management approaches for Canada	Iterative national consultation process (2002–5; 2008–10)
Government of Nunavut (GN)	Official languages and Inuit language protection in Territory of Nunavut	Embedded policy consultations (2000–12)

whose interests became dominant generated two kinds of problems. The first involved procedures and their *outputs*. Examining the procedures of each case, we see that they appeared to meet deliberative democratic principles. Taking a broader perspective, we see that their specific outputs for policy were curtailed. Outputs were either connected to subsequent policies in ways that were circumscribed or connected in ways that were filtered through the interests of the government department, agency, or corporation hosting the deliberations. Although there may have been valid reasons to circumscribe or filter, there was nonetheless a discrepancy between the ostensible aims of such procedures and the significance of their outputs for policy. The second involved more long-range *outcomes*. The procedures may have been empowering of participants in moments when they were discussing issues, exchanging reasons, and coming to conclusions, and they may have appeared empowering in providing institutionalized opportunities to contribute to collective decision making, but they turned out to be non-empowering in terms of outcomes that did not significantly challenge the status quo approach to formulating and implementing policy.

In each of the four cases, elites framed their procedures as a significant step in reshaping relations with their affected public. Elites created high expectations that their procedures represented a new approach to decision making – an approach that would enable participants to have a meaningful say in policy. Nonetheless, we learn from my study that, no matter how robust the procedures may be, if there is no elite willingness to empower them, they are essentially undemocratic. Perhaps worse, they are undemocratic while creating an illusion of democracy.

In the contextual details of these cases, we see how exercises in deliberative democracy can serve to uphold dominant interests, pre-existing power structures, hierarchical subcultures, and elitist approaches to policy. Context is critically important. Context shapes decision-making procedures and determines their significance. I try in this volume to identify and focus on specific and pertinent contextual elements including actors who frame, define, and present the topic for deliberation, and reasons why they do so. I also examine the general characteristics of those who participate in the procedures, basic motivations for why they participate, and mechanisms for how they come to participate. In addition, I examine the host entity's commitment, or its political will, to engage with members of its affected public, as well as its strategic and economic interests that may be at stake. More broadly, I probe the extent and implications of public pressure for greater inclusion and engagement that may be placed on the host. Finally, I explore aspects of the regulatory context, including existing policy requirements for public consultations or participation. All such factors contribute to contexts that create tensions between the reality of deliberative democratic procedures and their ideal ends.

Over the last three decades, theories of deliberative democracy, comprising nuanced procedural and substantive principles, have become a dominant – some would say the predominant – area of contemporary Western political thought.[7] These theories express not only ideal approaches to decision making but, more broadly, ideals for collective life, which encompass a vast range of interpersonal relationships, public procedures and forums, and social and political networks. Unlike many, if not most, areas of political thought, deliberative democracy has fed directly into principles informing public policy. From education to policing, urban planning, resource management, hazardous waste management, language protection, climate change mitigation and adaptation, and many more areas, elite actors who have typically driven policy processes appear to be drawing from this vibrant body of thought. Policy elites may not use the same language as political theorists, but it seems clear that many of the former find important resonance with ideas expounded upon by the latter.

Why is deliberative democracy such an important aim? Deliberative democratic procedures can contribute to the fair resolution of conflicts in and of policy by upholding principles related to the moral equality and freedom of individuals. These principles have been developed over a long and complex history. In democratic societies, it is now generally taken as a given that humans qua humans are born of equal moral worth and that, insofar as we respect and uphold the equality of other humans, we have equal rights to pursue a good life as we define it and not to be constrained arbitrarily in this pursuit. Deliberative democracy embodies these principles in terms of orientations, practices, and procedures aimed toward achieving mutually justifiable agreements that in turn provide the ethical basis for collective decisions. Deliberative democracy is conceptualized as protecting the rights of affected individuals by including them in processes that result in such decisions and by enabling their authorization of and consent to these decisions. Ideally, deliberative democratic procedures empower individuals by providing opportunities for their direct contribution to norms and policies and for their development of skills related to communication, argumentation, and persuasion.

From the perspective of real-world politics, deliberative democracy's value is highly contested. Although I believe that much of this scepticism

is misguided, I think that we should question why and how deliberative democratic principles are being implemented in specific contexts.
Why do they emerge from particular histories? How are decisions made
concerning recruiting participants, defining and framing topics, creating and disseminating information, and establishing linkages to policy?
What are their outputs for policy? What are their broader outcomes
for power relations within the policy area? Are the ethical principles
embodied in deliberative democracy being sought and realized in these
procedures? Or are more curtailed ends being served? Is deliberative
democracy, in fact, upholding material inequalities and hierarchical
power relations? Is it, paradoxically, serving non-deliberative ends?

For many years, we could not adequately respond to such questions
because of a lack of empirical studies. Recently, we've seen a rise in
case studies focusing on deliberative democratic procedures in areas of
policy.[8] These studies complement the vast literature on deliberative
democratic theory, revealing an important relationship between theoretical and empirical analyses. Theoretical examinations can clarify
goals, justify their ethical significance, and highlight the importance
of practical reforms to achieve them. While investigating normative
principles and aims, theorists should be responsive to historical, social,
cultural, economic, political, and institutional realities. In particular, we
should be vigilant in their efforts to identify exclusion, marginaliza-
tion, exploitation, and other forms of oppression that may be caused,
perpetuated, or masked by conceptual articulations of deliberative
democracy. To this end, empirical case studies can expose obstacles
in achieving deliberative democracy's aims of legitimacy, justice, and
empowerment. These studies also reveal possibilities, thus bolstering
optimism that the ideal can be approximated more rather than less. But
we should always be critical of how these studies are approached and
what suppositions underlie them. The deliberative ideal is so compelling that researchers may be prone to a "hope bias." In other words, we
may be prone to hoping too much to find something that is not in the
details of the case. Before turning to each of my case studies, I discuss
the development of deliberative democracy in both theory and practice.

Roots and Ambitions

In my view, deliberative democracy has its ancestry in ancient Athens.
At the height of Athenian democracy in the mid-fifth century BCE, during the so-called Periclean Age, most decisions relating to the affairs of

the *polis* were rendered by citizens in the *ekklesia*, or assembly, and the *boulé*, or cabinet. These bodies met weekly and more often during periods of crisis. I do not want to take an excessively romantic view of the Athenian *polis*, which was very hierarchical. Equality was understood within social strata and not across them. Freedom was enjoyed by the few. Those who were considered citizens were a small minority of the city's population. They were exclusively men, born into free Athenian families. Women were excluded from most, if not all, aspects of political life. This society, moreover, was based on the productive efforts of a large population of slaves and labourers. I do, however, want to express an appreciation for Athens's direct democracy,[9] in which space and time for public debates and discussion were central – although these were often dominated by rhetoric and oratory. As Robert Garland writes, the *demos* was "completely sovereign" and had "supreme judicial authority."[10] Citizens were expected to be active in the administration of the city, to articulate themselves publicly, and to vote in decisions affecting them.

Drawing from Plato, which may be highly idiosyncratic to my understanding of deliberative democracy, we can see the importance of examining oneself, one's beliefs, and those of others. Plato was no friend of democracy, especially post-399 BCE and the death of his mentor, Socrates, but his writings express the importance of dialogue in the pursuit of knowledge. In his dialogues, he uses wonderful imagery, interesting, thoughtful, and sometimes temperamental characters, and occasionally long poetic passages, all of which tend to raise rather than resolve questions, but the themes he develops concern the necessity of citizens exchanging and challenging reasons in order to free themselves from the opinions they hold uncritically. In this sense, Plato's works reminds us of the importance of responsibility to ourselves to try to understand what we need and why, and of responsibility to our fellow citizens to exchange ideas, debate reasons, and aim to reach resolution in an effort to govern ourselves legitimately and justly and to realize our full potential as human beings.

Much more commonly, deliberative democracy is understood to grow out of the Western Enlightenment tradition. From the seventeenth century, the tradition can be characterized by developments in and expansions of the notions of equality and freedom. In the writings of Thomas Hobbes and John Locke, we see certain qualified articulations of the equality of men – in the former, an equality to defend themselves; in the latter, an equality of moral worth. We also see an enlargement of the scope of freedom – from natural to civic and from self-defence to the pursuit of property. In many respects, these were limited theoretical developments. Many continued to be hemmed in by social and political convention. Many continued to be marginalized and not enfranchised. Many continued to be seen as less than fully human in the eyes of the social and political elite. Only in the late-nineteenth and into the mid-twentieth centuries were women in Western democracies recognized as having democratic, legal, and property rights equal to men's. But sexism as well as racism, colonialism, ableism, homophobia, transphobia, and deep material inequalities persist in the present, thus impeding the exercise of rights and realization of freedom for too many. Despite these realities, contemporary democracies extend, in principle, a wide set of constitutional rights and freedoms to a large citizenry. With the widening of the franchise, as well as with the rise of modernity (including population growth, urbanization, industrialization, and so on), came the ascendancy of representative democracy. John Stuart Mill lamented the disconnect between direct and representative democracy. As he wrote:

> There is no difficulty in showing that the ideally best form of government is that in which the sovereignty, or supreme controlling power in the last resort, is vested in the entire aggregate of the community; every citizen not only having a voice in the exercise of that ultimate sovereignty, but being at least occasionally, called on to take an actual part in the government, by the personal discharge of some public function, local or general.[11]

The vast majority of us cannot have a real voice in, take actual part in, or personally fulfil a prolonged public function. Most of us cannot participate in collective decision making in a sustained, involved, and meaningful way. Mill acknowledged this and concluded that "government must be representative."[12] Centuries later, even radical democrats recognize the need for, as Joshua Cohen and Archon Fung put it, a "system of competitive representation."[13]

Representative democratic government properly and justifiably exists on the basis of an agreement by its citizens. Citizens implicitly agree to transfer the exercise of their natural rights and freedoms to a government that seeks to uphold their civil rights and freedoms. This basis for representative democracy is reflected in the idea that citizens maintain the ultimate authority for collective decisions made on their behalf and that their government must be responsible and remain accountable to them. Citizens rightly expect their governments to represent their interests and defend their rights and freedoms from internal and external threats. They expect fair and transparent political procedures, access to information, protection of personal privacy, means to independent adjudication, impartial, efficient, and competent public administration, and an accountable and responsible government that submits to regular elections by a widely enfranchised citizenry.

Clearly, however, this form of democracy has its shortcomings. Government bureaucracies have grown in size, responsibilities, and functions. In many cases, bureaucracies have become impenetrable by the average citizen. They have become large, faceless entities often connected to citizens only through automated telephone messages and labyrinthine websites. Moreover, there is often a wide disconnect between members of the demos and their representatives. Representatives, for a range of reasons, are often unresponsive to the interests, concerns, and desires of their constituents. What's important to many citizens is frequently not incorporated into the policies that bind or affect them. In turn, voters can become apathetic and less inclined to exercise their democratic rights. They may also become mistrustful of politicians, which further dissuades them from participating in elections. As a consequence, voter turnout declines and popular mandates become questionable. In Canada's most recent federal election (2011), 61 per cent of eligible voters cast ballots, 40 per cent of which were for what resulted in a majority government. Thus, only approximately 24 per cent of the electorate voted for the current government. In Canada and beyond, many citizens feel disaffected by government and disengaged from politics.

Responsive representatives, regular and fair elections, and effective and efficient bureaucracies are among the virtues of government. Who has the time and expertise to make public decisions if not our professional politicians and bureaucrats? Who has the ethical justification to do so if not those either democratically elected or meritoriously appointed? Nonetheless, it is vital that citizens actively participate and be empowered in processes for collective governance and political life. Many areas of public policy are too important not to directly involve citizens, especially those who are immediately affected. Many areas associated with risk, uncertainty, diverse perspectives, opposing interests, and outright conflict call for broad public examination, discussion, and debate because the implications for existing and future generations are too great. Direct engagement involving the exchange of information and reasons toward generally acceptable agreements may be the only way to ensure that we authorize and consent to decisions concerning many important and complex issues. With Cohen and Fung, I believe we need a fuller and richer realization of democratic values through opportunities for "direct participatory deliberation" and assurances that those in power will be responsive.[14]

This conception of democracy – a conception prioritizing participation, deliberation, and empowerment – informs the normative argument of this book. Like many theorists working in this area, I envision an expansive system of deliberative democracy. Joshua Cohen argues that deliberative democracy is not "simply a form of politics."[15] Instead, it is "a framework of social and institutional conditions that facilitates free discussion among equal citizens – by providing favorable conditions for participation, association, and expression."[16] This discussion ties into the "authorization to exercise public power (and the exercise itself)" through institutional mechanisms that ensure the "responsiveness and accountability of political power to it through regular competitive elections, conditions of publicity, and legislative oversight, and so on."[17] Amy Gutmann and Dennis Thompson also advance a broad understanding of deliberative democracy. As they claim, there is a need for public deliberation toward provisionally justified agreements given that moral disagreement is widespread in societies.[18] For them, the scope of deliberative democracy encompasses "the land of everyday politics, where legislators, executives, administrators, and judges make and apply policies and laws, sometimes arguing among themselves, sometimes explaining themselves and listening to citizens, other times not."[19] This "middle democracy" includes "interest groups, civic associations, and schools, in which adults and children develop political understandings, sometimes arguing among themselves and listening to people with differing points of view, other times not."[20] Similarly, Seyla Benhabib develops a conception of deliberative democracy in broad terms, but she brings to the fore the connectivity among the parts.[21] Her deliberative democracy, conceptualized as a decentred public sphere, privileges

a plurality of modes of association in which all affected can have the right to articulate their point of view. These can range from political parties, to citizens' initiatives, to social movements, to voluntary associations, to consciousness-raising groups, and the like. *It is through the interlocking net of these multiple forms of associations, networks, and organizations that an anonymous "public conversation" results. It is central to the model of deliberative democracy that it privileges such a public sphere of mutually interlocking and overlapping networks and associations of deliberation, contestation, and argumentation.*[22]

More explicitly developing a system of deliberative democracy, Jane Mansbridge, James Bohman, Simone Chambers, Thomas Christiano, Archon Fung, John Parkinson, Dennis Thompson, and Mark Warren "recognize that most democracies are complex entities in which a wide variety of institutions, associations, and sites of contestation accomplish political work – including informal networks, the media, organized advocacy groups, schools, foundations, private and non-profit institutions, legislatures, executive agencies, and the courts."[23] They therefore "advocate what may be called a *systemic approach to deliberative democracy*."[24] They go on: "In allowing for the possibility of ratcheting up the scale and complexity of interrelations among the parts, this approach enables us to think about democratic decisions being taken in the context of a variety of deliberative venues and institutions, interacting together to produce a healthy deliberative system."[25]

Ideals of deliberative democracy invoke far-reaching changes to the ways in which democracies currently govern and to the material contexts in which they govern. Changes would include, for example, decentralizing agenda-setting and decision-making powers to involve a much wider range of participants. They would also entail profound attitudinal changes on the part of individuals, including traditional legislators, policy elites, stakeholders, technical experts, opinion leaders, and laypersons. Finally, they would involve a massive redistribution of social and economic resources to enable all to participate, deliberate, and make decisions on equal terms. Although a compelling theoretical alternative to representative democracy, deliberative democracy calls for radical changes that may or may not be realizable in practice.

The Substance of Procedure

While there is diversity among the writings on theories of deliberative democracy, many tend to converge on the central conceptual elements of inclusion, equality, information, reasoning, agreement, and empowerment. In my view, these elements constitute the core ideals of deliberative democracy.

The principle of inclusion derives from the intuition that all humans who are governed, bound, or seriously affected by a policy have a claim to be involved – directly or indirectly – in the processes of its development and implementation.[26] Proponents of deliberative democracy maintain that, where our interests and desires are at stake in a policy decision, we ought to be included in processes concerning that decision. More specifically, we ought to have a say, or an opportunity to have a say, in the decision. Another kind of inclusion refers less directly to humans as humans and more to our specific interests, perspectives, and epistemologies. Arguably, deliberative exercises should include members or representatives of pertinent social, cultural, sub-cultural, political, economic, and environmental communities, organizations, and groups in order to incorporate their particular viewpoints and wisdom. For example, religious communities may have ways of understanding a problem, the context in which it is situated, and possible solutions to it that differ from secular understandings but that are both reasonable and important. Indigenous peoples, similarly, may have views that differ fundamentally from colonial/settler perspectives and that cannot be made to meet dominant standards of inquiry and knowledge. The same can be said for all those in entrenched marginalized and stigmatized positions. For Iris Marion Young, such views, insights, testimonies, and arguments should not be excluded. Rather they should be included, and those that prevail in informed, considered, and critical exchanges should be incorporated into decisions.[27] Together, these two dimensions of inclusion hold that all of us should have opportunities to participate in deliberations on decisions that bind or affect us and, moreover, that all perspectives and epistemologies relevant to the topic, or expressing an interest or stake in the topic, should be brought into such deliberations.

In a closely related vein, the deliberative democratic principle of procedural equality is based on the intuition that all humans are moral equals and, as such, all should have opportunities to contribute to rendering decisions that govern us. These opportunities should be equal in the principles, practices, and procedures of decision making. We should have equal time to voice ourselves; no one should be able to dominate the direction, tenor, or substance of deliberation. All of us should have equal opportunities to articulate, develop, and defend viewpoints, raise and respond to questions, and ask for further clarification. In addition to procedural equality, all should have the resources to enable equal and meaningful participation and deliberation. Access to information is critical to deliberative exchanges, and all should have equal access to information based on the best available scientific, social scientific, and humanistic research and writing. We should also have access to a wide range of knowledge based on lived experiences such as insights from oral traditions, Indigenous traditional knowledge, and marginalized or stigmatized communities. Deliberative democracy also has implications for the accessibility of information technologies. These technologies play an important role in the dissemination and discussion of ideas, hypotheses, theories, and narratives. The Internet, electronic databases, computer apps, and the like can be powerful resources that should be accessible to all of us. Access to information and information technologies implies educational opportunities to develop critical thinking, logical argumentation, competence in math and sciences, and compassion for others. Indeed, James Bohman argues that citizens must be capable of "adequate political functioning" in order to be fully included in collective deliberation.[28] As he writes, "only a capability-based account articulates an ideal of political equality that is appropriate to the high demands made on citizens in deliberative democracy."[29]

Theorists also take degrees of material or structural equality as necessary for deliberative democracy. Cohen makes a strong case for a certain material equality to sever "the fate of citizens from the differences of social position, natural endowment, and good fortune that distinguish citizens."[30] Material inequalities, related to, for example, income, housing, education, health, job security, food security, flexibility of time, and access to childcare – inequalities that are profoundly gendered and racialized – can impede equal and meaningful participation. It can be hard to think, reason, and articulate yourself in the context of deliberative processes when you're preoccupied with the realities of making sure your family is safe, fed, and engaged, all while you are on a tight budget. Without addressing these kinds of inequality, many will find it too difficult to participate adequately and communicate freely in deliberative processes.

Reason giving, receiving, and considering are also central to deliberative democracy. Gutmann and Thompson refer to a reasoning that is characterized by a particular understanding of reciprocity. Reciprocity occurs when "a citizen offers reasons that can be accepted by others who are similarly motivated to finds reasons that can be accepted by others."[31] It involves genuine attempts to appreciate a wide diversity of perspectives and to search for, exchange, and discuss reasons that can be acceptable to all as equal and free citizens. Similarly, according to Mansbridge et al., participants in deliberation "advance 'considerations' that others 'can accept' – considerations that are 'compelling' and 'persuasive' to others and that 'can be justified to people who reasonably disagree with them.'"[32] This reasoning entails an openness to assessing views, interests, and arguments, including one's own, and, where warranted, revising them. Such a process toward mutual justification may not be smooth or definitive. As Gutmann and Thompson point out,

"Some reasons that can be accepted in this sense are often not in fact accepted because the social and political conditions are not favorable to the practice of reciprocity."[33] Contestation always looms. It may even be desirable. For John Dryzek, contestation can increase reflection, stimulate deeper discussion, and contribute to a shared understanding.[34] It can spur participants into either developing their arguments more fully and advancing them more forcefully or deciding to modify, even abandon, them in light of stronger and more convincing arguments. In a similar vein, Christian Rostbøll argues that deliberative democracy should involve the contestation of beliefs that we as individuals and as societies hold dear.[35] For Rostbøll, deliberative democracy is a form of critical theory and set of practices that serve to enable citizens to challenge the status quo and bring about social and political change.

Despite our appreciation for contestation, deliberative democrats emphasize the importance of processes that give rise to expressions of an agreement or shared interest. As Dryzek and Simon Niemeyer point out, to many contemporary political theorists, "consensus remains the gold standard of political justification."[36] Over the years, however, theorists have increasingly distanced themselves from this standard.[37] For Gutmann and Thompson, participants should deliberate in a way that accommodates and respects differences until they reach a provisionally justified agreement.[38] Bohman emphasizes the principle of deliberative majority agreement.[39] As he writes, actual conditions of deliberation should ensure that there is *ongoing cooperation with others* of different minds,"[40] that laws are the outcome of fair and inclusive participatory processes, and that deliberative majorities are understood as the source of sovereign power. Jorge Valadez also writes about the importance of accommodation, mutual respect, and continuous deliberation and argues that participants should engage in deliberative processes that facilitate compromises by which all can abide.[41] His moral compromises are similar to Cass Sunstein's "incompletely theorized agreements."[42] For Sunstein, deliberators do not need to agree on all the reasons for a particular decision but only on those necessary to make that decision.

Taking a complementary perspective, Niemeyer and Dryzek claim that deliberation should result in a "meta-consensus," which is an agreement about the nature of the issue at hand.[43] In their words:

This occurs because deliberation requires that individuals transcend private concerns and that they engage with competing views, taking them into account as part of their evaluations. To the extent this occurs, deliberation should produce agreement on the domain of relevant reasons or considerations (involving both beliefs and values) that ought to be taken into account, and on the character of the choices to be made. But it does not require agreement on the veracity of particular beliefs, or ranking of values, still less unanimity on what should be done.[44]

As Niemeyer and Dryzek put it, "Although deliberation should not make concrete claims about making the 'right' decision, it can legitimately claim superiority to the extent that individuals have taken into account all the relevant considerations determined by meta-consensus."[45] In processes of deliberation, both agreements and disagreements are in play, but what is important is the consideration and discussion of relevant reasons for a given decision. Finally, for James Fishkin, the aim of deliberative procedures – Deliberative Polls, in particular – is to identify the range of views among participants with respect to specific issues and the patterns in how these views develop over the process of deliberation.[46] These findings may be taken as indicators of support, or lack thereof, for a shared interest, which may (or may not) serve in modifying, bolstering, or justifying a policy decision taken by government or by a corporation, agency, or organization. Clearly, there is diversity among political theorists concerning the nature of agreements implied by deliberative democratic ideals, but all tend to converge on the importance of informed and well-reasoned expressions of shared interests made by free and equal individuals in inclusive and equal procedures.

Many theorists claim that deliberative democracy best articulates the appropriate standards for achieving the social, economic, and environmental justice and democratic legitimacy of public norms and policies.[47] In line with this thinking, I make the assumption that, to the extent that deliberative democratic criteria are met, the outputs of these procedures will more likely accord with principles of justice and will have a strong claim to legitimacy. Beyond greater justice and legitimacy, another critical aim of deliberative democracy is empowerment.[48] Fung defines empowerment as the "expectation that citizens' participation and deliberation will directly affect public action."[49]

More specifically, in my view, democratic empowerment refers to the capacities, capabilities, and opportunities of individuals to shape the policies that either bind or affect them. Empowerment encompasses the personal skills, social and political resources, and procedural and institutional opportunities necessary to directly influence policy. It is helpful to understand empowerment in terms of two dimensions:

individual and institutional. In the individual dimension, deliberative empowerment includes agency (i.e., an ability to act according one's reasoning), autonomy (i.e., an ability to act according to one's reasonable conception of the good), political literacy and skills (i.e., an ability to understand and articulate political ideas and problems, work through issues, advance interests, and resolve conflict), and social capital (i.e., interpersonal networks, based on shared public values and trust, and facilitated by lines of communication). In the institutional dimension, empowerment includes opportunities for individuals to participate in inclusive, equitable, transparent procedures and institutions for developing and implementing public policies and assurances that elected officials will be responsive to these inputs. Ultimately, deliberative empowerment involves a disruption of pre-existing power structures and relations in policy areas. It involves genuine, systematic shifts in decision-making power away from elite policymakers and toward members of affected publics.

Of course, I recognize that not all public consultation or participation processes are intended to empower per se. But those based on principles of or related to deliberative democracy create an expectation that the views of participants will be at least minimally incorporated into the policy of the host organization, agency, or department. Where we see this kind of framing, we have good reason to evaluate the procedures with reference to their specific opportunities for participants to contribute directly to policy and to transform power structures. After all, as Stephen Elstub points out, if "collective deliberation is not linked to decision-making then the fact participants' preferences are more prudent seems irrelevant, better decisions will not be made, and decision-making procedures will not be fairer."[50] While these claims may be true, empowerment remains a lofty end – especially lofty in policy contexts characterized by entrenched power relations between policy elites and affected publics. The empowerment of citizens, as well as the achievement of greater justice and legitimacy, may be as elusive as the realization of deliberative democracy itself.

Table 2 Deliberative democratic criteria

- Participatory inclusion
- Procedural equality and access to information
- Mutual reason giving and receiving
- General agreement or shared interests
- Empowerment

The Importance of Context

Policy elites do not typically employ the term "deliberative democracy." Instead, their language is that of public engagement, participation, or collaboration. Nonetheless, when one examines their procedures, it becomes evident that they approximate principles that are associated with, directly or indirectly, deliberative democracy. This broad trend in public policy appears to involve a shift away from more elitist models of representative government in which citizens effectively authorize their elected officials to draw advice from technical experts and industry stakeholders to formulate and implement public policies. The trend suggests a movement toward a model of democracy in which citizens are put on equal footing with experts, stakeholders, and civil servants, and play a more direct role in policy processes.

Within the past decade, theorists and practitioners of deliberative democracy have started systematically to study such processes. To date, the findings are mixed. Those who report generally positive experiences of deliberative democracy tend to focus on the development of participants' capacities for reason and knowledge in these processes. For instance, Jason Barabas finds that participants in a deliberative forum on social security reform in Arizona increased their understanding of the policy area.[51] Based on his study of pre- and post-deliberative surveys of participants, he found that deliberation softens strongly held views, alters opinions, and increases knowledge. In deliberation, he writes, citizens discard their "inaccurate factual perceptions as well as rigidly held political views."[52] Perhaps most interestingly, Barabas finds that deliberative participants learned to become more open-minded.[53] He is quick to point out, however, that his study is limited to two cases of deliberation in one policy area. Robert Goodin and Dryzek also highlight positive impacts of mini-publics, which in their view are small-scale, deliberative forums that are broadly representative.[54] They point to evidence from consensus conferences, Deliberative Polls, and town meetings demonstrating the potential to achieve public engagement in policymaking. They find that mini-publics can produce informed recommendations to elected lawmakers, stimulate public debate, legitimate public policy, provide a sense of empowerment to the public, and function as a mechanism for popular oversight. Goodin and Dryzek note that their study is selective, intended to map out and illustrate democratic possibilities. Elstub also identifies successful experiments in deliberative democracy.[55] As he writes, there is "extensive empirical evidence available from unpartisan deliberative forums like citizens' juries and deliberative opinion polls that indicates citizens have the competence to address complicated issues, that participants will change their preferences in light of reasons and information and that they can arrive at compromised decisions."[56] Increasingly, he notes, there are studies documenting the benefits of deliberative democracy, including the generation of public reasons, individual autonomy, and publicly binding decisions that are true, well justified, or commensurate with the just and the good. Hendrik Wagenaar finds other positive effects of deliberative democracy for public policy.[57] Examining the case of legalizing brothels in the Netherlands, Wagenaar finds that deliberative democratic procedures can be a good way to negotiate sustainable policy. In his case study, these procedures enabled the successful implementation of a new policy in a difficult area. More recently, John Gastil and Katherine Knobloch confirm many of these positive findings.[58] In their evaluation of two sets of Citizens Initiative Reviews in Oregon in 2010 and 2012 respectively, they find that participants consistently engaged in high-quality deliberation on a range of proposed policies and that the citizens' statements resulting from the reviews served to inform state-wide voters as they cast ballots for these initiatives. The analyses by Gastil, Knobloch, and their colleagues demonstrate the political feasibility of intensive deliberation and voters' appreciation for neutral information statements written by their peers.[59]

Numerous researchers present more mixed findings. For example, Vibeke Normann Andersen and Kasper M. Hansen studied a Danish National Deliberative Poll on the single European currency.[60] During this poll, the 364 participants engaged with each other and with experts in discussions about the implications of a single currency for Denmark, which remains a divisive topic. The results of the poll were in favour of Denmark's participation in a single currency, whereas the results of the national referendum were against it. Andersen and Hansen found that the deliberation produced considerable changes in political opinions, an increase in the level of knowledge, an improved ability to form reasoned opinions, and a mutual understanding on the subject matter. However, they also found that self-interest and domination persisted among the participants. Andersen and Hansen conclude that the theory of deliberative democracy needs to be further elaborated so that it better reflects the persistence of interests and power in "real-life" politics. As they write, "Too little focus has been placed on interest and power in deliberative processes."[61]

Several researchers have found that experiments in deliberative democracy are often primarily strategic. Carolyn Hendriks examines the participation of interest organizations in citizen forums in four cases and finds that, although these forums pose "fundamental challenges to the way most interest organizations conceptualize 'the public' and democracy, in the end most decide to participate in or at least support citizen's deliberations."[62] They do so, she argues, for strategic purposes, when there is an "opportunity to improve public relations and promote trust, distribute information and market products, sell and legitimize expertise, or advocate for a particular cause."[63] More troubling, Paul Maginn finds that the "Dialogue with the City" initiative in Perth, Australia, was biased toward the government's political intentions, and while structured to give the appearance of encouraging dialogue, it did not actually allow any of the participants to have an impact on policy.[64] Yannis Papadopoulos and Philippe Warin warn that both participatory and deliberative democratic experiments can be sophisticated public-relations manoeuvres by governments that wish to appear committed to public involvement in decision making.[65] These experiments can allow "rulers to show that they are willing not only to deal with crucial issues, but also to associate the 'profane' in decision making."[66] As Archon Fung and Erik Olin Wright argue, the likelihood that deliberative democratic "institutional designs will generate desired effects depends significantly upon the balances of power between actors engaged ... and, in particular, the configurations of non-deliberative power that constitute the terrain upon which structured deliberation" occurs.[67]

A number of researchers are turning to contextual factors in search of explanations for these diverse findings. The sentiment driving this research is that deliberative democratic procedures are inherently political and cannot be isolated from the broader political context. Andrea Cornwall calls for closer attention to be paid to politics and political culture when assessing deliberative democratic procedures.[68] Based on her study of a municipal health council in Brazil, she highlights the importance of examining the "political culture/cultures of politics; the significance of contention and contestation; and party politics."[69] Leonardo Avritzer, in his research on participatory and deliberative governance in Brazil, notes that two contextual factors contributed to creating a cultural and political context in which participatory budgeting could flourish.[70] The first of these factors was the process of democratization. In the late-1970s to the mid-1980s, "neighborhood associations blossomed as part of the general reaction to authoritarianism."[71] The second factor was the new constitution of 1988, which enshrined forms of and arenas for public participation. Avritzer writes that "Porto Alegre stands out from the whole of the rest of Brazil in terms of the degree to which it took advantage of this legal infrastructure."[72] He finds that the conditions accounting for the emergence of participatory budgeting in this city are unique to its characteristics. Celina Souza, also noting that participatory policies have been adopted in Brazil with varying results, finds that contextual factors play a large role in the success or failure of exercises in participatory budgeting.[73] Based on a nation-wide survey documenting participatory budgeting in a number of jurisdictions, she argues that the success of participatory budgeting depends on

> several factors, such as a) the kind of political party that implements it; b) society's level of organization, mobilization and politicization; c) socio-economic features and population size; d) the administration's technical skills and management capacity; e) the government's commitment; f) the financial situation of the municipality; and g) the method adopted to establish the relationship between the government and the community.[74]

In this volume, I contribute to this literature linking contexts, procedures, and their significance for the formulation and implementation of policy and the distribution of decision-making power. I examine the cases of social housing in Toronto, energy policy in Nova Scotia, nuclear waste management policy in Canada, and official languages policy in Nunavut. These cases meet basic deliberative democratic criteria. Moreover, they appear to be incorporated into existing procedures for policy decision making. They are more than single events, appearing to be a shift in governance from elite democracy toward more direct, participatory, and deliberative democracy. I ask critical questions concerning the framing and importance of the topic, characteristics of participants, commitment of elites, presence of public pressure, details of the regulatory framework and policy requirements, and interests, aims, and constraints of the host entity. How do these contextual factors influence the design of these procedures? How do these factors bear upon their meaning and significance? What are their implications for policy decisions and decision-making power, if any?

To respond to these questions, I draw from various types of materials and engage with them from an interpretive policy perspective. I try to understand the meaning of events transpiring in policy areas from

Table 3 Contextual factors

- Framing and importance of topic of deliberation
- Characteristics of participants in deliberation
- Elite commitment to public consultation, participation, and deliberation
- Public pressure for consultation, participation, and deliberation
- Policy requirements for public consultation and participation
- Predominant economic and strategic interests, aims, and constraints

---

the position of the actors directly involved.[75] My aim is to understand how these meanings shape or constitute procedures, their outputs, and outcomes. While being explicit that this is a project in interpretation, I believe it is important to point out that my study is research driven, empirically oriented, and highly detailed. For each case, I sought out a comprehensive range of materials and carefully analysed them.

I conducted sets of lengthy semi-structured interviews in 2005, 2007, 2008, 2010, and 2011 with a range of actors broadly reflective of the interests and perspectives in each case. I conducted two sets of interviews in each policy area. The first included in-depth interviews; the second included follow-up interviews. Interviews involved open-ended questions. All interviews began with a list of identical questions and progressed into questions more specific to the interviewee. In each policy area, I interviewed individuals who represented, formally or informally, the following sectors, organizations, or people: government, business, environmental, religious, Aboriginal, deliberative host, organizer/facilitator, or participant. I also analysed primary policy documents, including those regulating the area. In addition, I examined extensive official policy documents designed and disseminated by the host concerning the procedures and their outputs and outcomes. Moreover, I studied official public submissions where they existed. Finally, I examined numerous reports that either emerged from or spoke directly to the cases. In these materials, I located different perspectives, identified idiosyncratic meanings, and traced common themes. This enabled me to articulate plausible explanations for both the strengths and limitations of these procedures. In a brief epilogue to this book, I discuss some of the challenges (and rewards) associated with this kind of case-intensive research.

I chose the cases in this volume because of their apparent strengths in meeting deliberative democratic criteria. This made a comparison not only possible but also fruitful. In each case, elites appeared to express a genuine commitment and willingness to include public participation in their decision-making processes. They invested substantial amounts of money into designing and running these processes, which took place over the course of several years. In each, we see key institutional features informed by principles of or related to deliberative democracy and attempts to realize deliberative democratic orientations toward mutual reasoning and a general agreement or shared interest. Moreover, participants in each case valued their experiences and felt they were meaningful.

Examining such instantiations of deliberative democracy, especially where these appear sustained and institutionalized, deepens our understanding of the distance between existing procedures and a prospective system of deliberative democratic governance. This study tells us a great deal about the current procedural and institutional potential for a larger deliberative whole. Each case had mixed results for policy decisions and little, if any, impact on the configuration of decision-making power in the policy area. This suggests broader forces at play, in terms of both the structure of political institutions and the *ethos* of politics. Decision making in these areas has historically taken place within very hierarchical structures. Traditional policy actors may be too habituated to entrenched decision-making models. This habituation, enforced by contextual factors, may have thwarted the potential for a sustained shift in procedures and power. Is deliberative democracy, even more or less approximated, too ambitious for current policy contexts? Is a broader deliberative system beyond the reach of contemporary societies? Are existing practices, procedures, institutions, and networks in the name of deliberative democracy mere illusions?

Chapter Two

Participatory Budgeting and the Toronto Community Housing Corporation

The Toronto Community Housing Corporation (TCHC) was the first public housing provider in North America to develop a set of procedures to engage residents in participatory budgeting. In 2001, the Metro Toronto Housing Corporation and the Toronto Housing Company, the two social housing companies that would come to form the TCHC, initiated participatory budgeting among their residents as a fundamental component of their "Community Based Business Planning" process. This spirit of resident[1] or tenant involvement in budgetary decision making was carried over into the TCHC, which was established in 2002. In this case, we see what appears to be an excellent example of real-life deliberative democracy that was participatory and empowered. We see what seems to be a set of robust procedures that were based on a genuine commitment of all those involved to enable residents to make decisions concerning their homes and communities. However, at some time between the advent of the TCHC's Tenant Participation System and its decline in 2012 this commitment appears to have been attenuated.

From the start, members of the TCHC's board of directors, as well as many of its management and staff members, appeared committed to realizing principles of resident participation in planning and to devising, implementing, and maintaining institutionalized ways of bringing residents into these decision-making processes. Despite this commitment, the TCHC's system for resident participation evolved in terms of a tension between procedural success and substantive shortcomings. From one perspective, it was a model of inclusive and fair decision-making procedures that were based on principles related to deliberative democracy. The system was not only meaningful to residents but also empowering of them, granting them regular opportunities to participate in planning projects for their buildings. The outputs of these procedures fed directly into decisions authorized and implemented by TCHC management and staff.

However, from another perspective, focusing on these procedures as they were situated within the broader context of the TCHC, we see troubling limitations. Ultimately, decision making within the TCHC remained primarily an elite and hierarchical activity. Its management model continued to have a distinctively "top-down" tenor, with senior management in the corporate head office, middle managers in local offices, and residents dispersed among local communities across the city. Residents in any given TCHC Community Housing Unit (CHU) were essentially isolated from residents in other CHUs, having few institutionalized opportunities to engage in cross-community dialogues. Resident participation, moreover, was confined to the distribution of limited funds for highly localized projects. From a contextualized perspective, resident participation appears to have been a tool used by management to justify funding certain basic maintenance and security projects over others – when all such projects were arguably in need of funding. This participation system, while realizing certain principles of deliberative democracy, did not ultimately contribute to a shift from an elite model to a more empowered model in the corporation's decision-making processes.

In 2010, rumours emerged concerning an ethos of mismanagement within the corporation. These rumours suggested the predominance of individual economic interests, a sense of individual entitlement, and mishandling of funds by individual TCHC management and staff members. In March 2011, in the wake of two very critical reports by the auditor general of the City of Toronto, the TCHC's board of directors was dissolved and its CEO was let go.[2] One of the reports identified "significant concerns with the extent and nature of staff related expenses" and a "greater concern" with "a culture at the TCHC which allows such expense to occur."[3] The other documented a series of contracts not being properly tendered.[4] In the following year, the auditor general released an additional report that articulated similar findings with respect to a TCHC subsidiary.[5] In 2012, the TCHC lost government funding equalling 75 per cent of its budget for capital repairs and 80 per cent of its allocation for participatory budgeting.[6] In 2013, the budget for participatory budgeting was partially reinstated to an allocation of $5 million,[7] only about 56 per cent of its annual allocation of $9 million for 2003–8.[8] This is relevant because it presents us with a different perspective on the significance of the resident participation system.

Taking a wide-angle look at the TCHC, we see a corporation that seemed to embrace resident participation in its planning and budgeting *as well as* a corporation that seemed to allow patterns of questionable expenditure and procurement practices.

In this chapter, I examine the TCHC's participation system, including its participatory budgeting. This examination includes both a detailed description of the procedures and an evaluation of them vis-à-vis criteria of deliberative democracy. I then broaden my analysis to include contextual factors at play within the TCHC as a corporation but also as a collectivity of communities. This wider view highlights paradoxes of outputs and outcomes, which can be explained by the range of topics and issues for deliberation, the general characteristics of participants in deliberations, expressions of elite commitment to resident participation, public pressure and policy requirements for resident participation, and economic and material interests of members of the TCHC's management and staff. Before turning to this case, I discuss the origins of participatory budgeting in southern Brazil, which highlights the strengths of participatory budgeting in that context but also raises a cautionary flag concerning its transfer to other contexts.

The Origins of Participatory Budgeting

Participatory budgeting originated in southern Brazil in the late 1980s and has since spread across the country and world. In the 1990s, individuals working at the Metro Toronto Housing Corporation and the Toronto Housing Company were inspired by participatory budgeting and decided to implement it as a way of addressing a palpable sense of alienation among their residents.[9] Shortly after a trip to the city of Porto Alegre, they decided to draw from a "best practices" model that had taken shape in the city.[10] This model was introduced into the TCHC's predecessor companies and then developed by TCHC staff and residents. Participatory budgeting within social housing communities in Toronto was one of the first experiments of its kind in Canada and the United States.

Participatory budgeting in Brazil emerged out of a specific social, economic, and political context. This context was characterized by widespread efforts to re-democratize political practices and institutions in the wake of a military dictatorship that took place between 1964 and 1985. There was growing activism, mobilization, and organization as the Workers' Party became increasingly popular at the municipal level in the early 1980s.[11] Andreas Novy and Bernhard Leubolt write that in Porto Alegre, and in the rest of the country, citizens in impoverished districts began to demand greater investment in urban infrastructure and services.[12] They also sought greater autonomy in their neighbourhood initiatives.[13] Their assertions were sometimes expressed in high-profile protests, demonstrations, and roadblocks. Citizens were not only mobilized but also savvy, linking their demands to those for civil rights more broadly understood. In this way, they fused local issues to the political aspirations of the country and continent. In 1988, the Workers' Party came to power in Porto Alegre with, as Graham Smith puts it, "an explicit pro-poor commitment."[14] In the following year, the new ruling party established participatory budgeting in the city.

The Workers' Party initiated participatory budgeting in order to empower citizens with respect to public decisions that immediately affected them, such as those concerning the allocation of funds for schools, roads, water, sewers, health care, and social welfare. Participatory budgeting has since provided the procedures and institutions for their direct public participation, and their election of delegates and councillors to participate on their behalf, in decisions concerning a portion of municipal budgets for capital expenditures. Today, it remains a collective effort to set spending priorities and redistribute public resources more equitably within a given community. It aims to enable citizens to develop, implement, and evaluate policies for realizing shared goals related to projects in their communities. The results of participatory budgeting processes are generally incorporated into the community's overall budgetary agenda. Although the municipal council retains the legal authority to reject budget proposals, in practice, it has never changed the outputs of participatory budgeting.[15] Novy and Leubolt write that the "replacement of clientelism with open and transparent discussion is one of the main reasons for the high legitimacy of [participatory budgeting]."[16] Over the years, distributable resources for participatory budgeting in Porto Alegre have grown from 3.2 per cent in 1989 to 11.2 per cent in 1990, and 17.5 per cent in 1991.[17] Currently, district and thematic popular assemblies determine the distribution of about 10 per cent of the budget.[18] According to Yves Cabannes, "100% of the budget is considered participatory, because the Participatory Budget Council (COP [*Conselho do Orçamento Participativo*] in Portuguese), made up of elected delegates, examines and comments on the complete budget (before it is sent to the Municipal Council)."[19] He goes on: "The part debated in assemblies in which all citizens participate equals 100% of the resources available for investment, which varies year to year and is more than 10% of the total budget."[20]

Participatory budgeting, as conceptualized and practised in Brazil, is founded on several normative principles similar to those of deliberative democracy. In principle, participatory budgeting is a process and system providing for the inclusion and equality of all who wish to participate in collective decision making. It rests on the idea that all who could be directly affected by collectively binding decisions should have a right to participate in their processes as equals. In addition, participatory budgeting is based on the idea that participants should meet in regular public forums and adhere to certain rules such as those relating to procedural equality, access to information, and reasoned discourse towards a shared interest or common good. Principles of participation on inclusive and equal terms extend to the making as well as revising of such procedural rules. Participants should develop proposals to distribute resources according to substantive criteria that they have conceived and to technical, economic, and legal criteria that recognized experts in these areas have devised. These criteria should also be revisited and revised by participants in the budgetary cycle.

The participatory budgeting process in Porto Alegre is both complex and extensive.[21] It begins with informal, local meetings organized by the previous year's councillors and delegates to mobilize residents and prospective representatives.[22] Such preparatory or planning meetings take place among local residents without the participation of the municipal government. Their objective is to get a sense of the aims and priorities of individual citizens, grass-roots movements, and community organizations. These meetings also serve to initiate community mobilization and involvement, and to select district delegates to attend the popular assemblies. Since 2001, there has been one round of popular assemblies in each of the districts as well as a simultaneous round of popular assemblies for the whole city on thematic areas, such as the environment, transportation and traffic, education, leisure, and culture, health and social welfare, economic development and taxation, and city organization and urban development.[23] The thematic popular assemblies develop broad guidelines, long-term plans, priorities for the following year, and policies for the whole city. During the popular assemblies in the districts, municipal officials present general information about the current budget as well as information about the budget and investment plan adopted the previous year.[24] The regional budget forums and thematic forums play consulting functions and act as intermediaries between these district and thematic assemblies and the COP, as well the municipal administrative units. Delegates from these forums and the COP work together to develop city-wide priorities.

The COP is the main participatory institution, meeting regularly in winter and spring (i.e., August to December).[25] Its membership consists of two elected budget councillors from each region, two from each thematic area, and one representative from the union of neighbourhood associations, plus two non-voting representatives from the municipal government.[26] The COP makes plans and proposals for, as well as oversees, the entire municipal budget. It also reviews the participatory budgeting constitution and its general and technical criteria. Members of the COP become familiar with municipal finances, examine and rank regional and thematic priorities emerging from the forums for the current year, and discuss and establish the general criteria for resource allocation for the following budgetary year. The COP develops and votes on the investment plan for the coming year, which includes a detailed list of priorities encompassing specific allocations of resources for every region and thematic area. The investment plan is then submitted to the municipal executive, which becomes responsible for its ratification and implementation. The COP is then responsible for overseeing the development and realization of the priorities set out in the plan. Finally, the COP is responsible for defining the general criteria for the ranking of priorities and allocation of funds for the following participatory budgeting cycle.

Participatory budgeting in Porto Alegre is the result of a democratic evolution. Novy and Leubolt write that participatory budgeting "has never been understood as a completed finalized concept, but as one that was to develop through conflicts, as a step-by-step institutionalisation of popular participation in local politics, combined with on-going participant-oriented evaluation and modification of the process."[27] Since its inception, there have been several variations of participatory budgeting implemented in over 130 Brazilian cities.[28] Cabannes writes that at least three hundred cities across the world have "adopted this method of public administration."[29] As Brian Wampler writes, there "is no precise or exact model for participatory budgeting programs," as they are "structured in response to the particular political, social, and economic environment of each city or state."[30] Smith is somewhat cautionary about the transferability of participatory budgeting to other jurisdictions. In his words, with "an understanding of the extent to which PB in Porto Alegre realizes democratic goods," we have "the opportunity to draw lessons on the extent to which the design has been and could be effectively transferred and developed in other locations."[31] But not all designs "that claim to be PB stand up to close scrutiny."[32] It is not clear that the TCHC's participatory budgeting process ultimately stands up to such scrutiny. Indeed, there is good reason to be cautious of designs implemented from the top down according to parameters set by elites, no matter how well intentioned they may be.

TCHC's Tenant Participation System

With the amalgamation of its predecessor companies, the TCHC emerged as the largest social housing provider in Canada and one of the largest in North America, with approximately 164,000 residents in roughly 58,500 households.[33] Its portfolio includes more than 2200 buildings.[34] Employing about 1400 staff, the TCHC is incorporated as a non-profit, share-capital corporation and has as its sole shareholder the City of Toronto. The TCHC operates at arm's length from the City and is responsible for managing assets of about $6 billion.[35] In 2012, its revenues were approximately $650 million.[36] Roughly half of the TCHC's annual revenues are from government subsidies and half from residential and commercial rent payments. Its board of directors, which includes city councillors, residents of the TCHC, and citizens who are unaffiliated with the TCHC, oversees the company's management and is accountable to the City.[37] The board presents to the City its business plan, annual reports, and financial statements. Its meetings, which are held regularly, are open to the public when no confidential item is being discussed. In addition to the board, the TCHC executive includes the CEO and a general manager, as well as chief operating, chief financial, chief development, and chief administrative officers.[38] The TCHC's operational structure was originally organized into twenty-seven fairly autonomous community housing units. CHUs contained at least one building but varied in geographical size. From 2001 through 2008, each CHU had a manager, supervisor, and health officer. In 2008/9, the TCHC launched a major restructuring of the organization and management of its housing units. The twenty-seven CHUs have been replaced with thirteen operating units.[39]

In the early days of the TCHC, members of its board, management, and staff sought to develop and implement a participation system in which residents could play an ongoing role in the decision making of the corporations and its communities.[40] Their aim was to create a formal participation system that would complement more informal resident activities and gatherings, and that would be integral to the corporation's community management and budget planning.[41] This formal participation system would include elected tenant representatives and councils, elected tenant representation on the board, participatory community business-planning processes, and a social investment fund for TCHC communities. Drawing from their experiences with the TCHC's social housing predecessors, and inspired by the success in Porto Alegre, management and staff worked with residents to design this system, making participatory budgeting its centrepiece. Although collaborating with residents, TCHC elites established the parameters and drove the design process.

The TCHC and Porto Alegre are very different sites for participatory budgeting. In addition to having vastly different political histories and cultures, the former is a corporation, while the latter is a municipality. The TCHC's process was not nearly as large in terms of numbers of participants nor as complex in terms of meetings and assemblies when compared to the Porto Alegre. Nor were its institutions and procedures as developed and comprehensive. The TCHC had nothing similar to the COP, popular assemblies, forums, or administrative bodies of Port Alegre. The TCHC had much fewer funds and much less autonomy in the distribution of those funds. Even relative to the size of its budget, the TCHC's participatory budgeting was much smaller than that of Porto Alegre. From 2002/3 to 2008/9 the funds allocated each year to the Tenant Participation System ($9 million) amounted to about 1.5 per cent of the TCHC's total annual budget, which in 2009 was approximately $600 million.[42]

Nonetheless, some basic similarities exist between the two cases. For instance, the nature of the topics for discussion and deliberation were similar in both cases. As with residents of Porto Alegre, those of the TCHC were concerned with addressing immediate infrastructure priorities. They sought to distribute funds to projects that, if realized, would directly increase their standard of living and sense of well-being. Through the participatory system, TCHC residents were enabled to make decisions concerning needed repairs to their buildings and desired improvements to their common areas. These projects were comparable to building houses and schools and paving roads – projects proposed and undertaken in Porto Alegre – in that they were improvements to the status quo experiences of day-to-day living. In particular, they were improvements in the daily lives of individuals who were not economically privileged and who lived in materially impoverished areas. Indeed, participants in the budgetary cycles of the TCHC and Porto Alegre were similar in that they tended to come from lower income brackets (at least as participants did in the initial years of participatory budgeting in Porto Alegre). The average annual income per TCHC resident was approximately $15,400,[43] which amounts to roughly half of the average income across the country. Both groups of participants were highly motivated to address issues of immediate concern to them.

Procedurally, certain features of the TCHC's Tenant Participation System were similar to Porto Alegre's participatory budgeting, although they were radically scaled down and highly circumscribed. These included ongoing local meetings, elected local representatives, and elected delegates to participate in a city-wide allocation forum. Both cases, moreover, were characterized by participatory inclusion and collective deliberation.

During the TCHC's first participatory business planning and budgeting cycle, residents allocated $18 million in funds over two years to 237 capital projects.[44] In total, there were over 6000 participants in this cycle.[45] During 2003 and 2004, residents, staff, and management of the TCHC formed a Tenant Advisory Committee to refine the process. This committee served general steering and oversight functions, developing and implementing clearer substantive criteria for the distribution of funds. For subsequent budget cycles, 2004 through 2008, the TCHC set aside $9 million in capital funds.[46] This portion of TCHC's capital budget was distributed among its twenty-seven CHUs for resident decision making each year. Sixty per cent of the $9 million was distributed to the CHUs based on their size. Another 20 per cent was split equally across the CHUs. These funds were distributed within each CHU on the basis of decisions made primarily by tenants and elected tenant representatives. Tenants and their representatives, in consultation with local TCHC staff members, established priorities during regular inclusive and democratic meetings. The remaining 20 per cent, that is, $1.8 million, was distributed on the basis of decisions made collectively by residents from all twenty-seven CHUs, during one-day, city-wide allocation forums (also known as "1.8 Days" or Allocation Days). In both of these processes of distribution, residents were responsible for deliberating and deciding on the capital needs and spending priorities of their CHU.

Residents would begin each budgetary cycle with fall planning meetings in their building or complex of buildings with local TCHC staff, including the CHU manager and community health officer. The purpose of these meetings was to identify and prioritize capital projects for specific buildings or complexes. During these meetings, TCHC staff would provide information, advice, and support with respect to prospective projects. They would also try to ensure that an accurate record was kept for each meeting, for instance, of members present, decisions made, and conflicts of interest declared. After discussion and debate, residents would use either secret ballots or dots on a flip chart to collectively rank the projects. The top five priorities from each building or complex would then be presented to the CHU tenant council. In these meetings, residents would also elect representatives to sit on their tenant council for a term of three years.

Each council was mandated by TCHC management "to provide a forum for Tenant Representatives, Toronto Community Housing staff, and community service providers to communicate and exchange ideas" towards the end of developing the annual business plan.[47] Each council would thus facilitate discussions to address existing issues, set future priorities, allocate resources, and make decisions for their local communities. The number of units in the building or complex would determine the number of representatives on any given council; there would be one representative for up to 250 units, two representatives for 251 to 500 units, and an additional representative for each additional 250 units.[48] The size of councils varied among the CHUs. According to an evaluation of the Tenant Participation System, in 2005 the largest council had twenty-two representatives and the smallest had seven.[49] This study also found that two CHUs had no representatives. Each council had the right to add council members to ensure residents were represented equitably. Some councils would add residents to ensure the inclusion of people belonging to certain identifiable minority groups such as youths, seniors, and speakers of a particular language. Council elections were sometimes very large, with more than 700 candidates running in 200 contested elections across the city.[50] Election campaigns would take place over at least a month, during which time candidates would pitch their platforms to voters. These campaigns would include canvassing, distributing posters and flyers, and hosting all-candidate meetings. This system of resident representation and participation within a social housing organization or corporation was unique in Canada and possibly the United States.

In principle, each CHU council would meet regularly to deliberate on all the projects within its community. Councillors would rank the priorities from the buildings and complexes across their entire CHU. They would identify projects that could be covered by the CHU's existing resources (that is, from its portion of the $7.2 million) and select one that could be funded from the $1.8 million. With respect to the latter, each council would then prepare a project proposal to present at the 1.8 Day. CHU representatives and staff would develop a draft budget for its project and submit it to the TCHC's Application Review Committee, which included both TCHC residents and staff. This committee would review each proposed budget to ensure that it contained appropriate quotes, clearly identified the scope and nature of the project, and did not contravene building codes or other policies related to health and safety. Also during this stage, each council would elect delegates to attend the Inter-Community Housing Unit (ICHU) forum, which would deliberate collectively on allocating the $1.8 million. Approximately five delegates from each CHU would attend the 1.8 Day.

CHU representatives and staff would then prepare to present their project to the ICHU forum. On the day itself, delegates from each CHU would make their presentation to the forum. Their proposals would also be available in poster format, kept on display. To help the ICHU delegates with their decision making, TCHC staff would seek to ensure that each was given background information on all of the projects submitted. They would also distribute a list of each CHU's priorities with estimated costs. According to the procedural rules, delegates would consider not only the merits of each project but also the needs of all the CHUs. ICHU delegates would deliberate among themselves. Delegates would distribute their votes (between ten and fifteen per delegate, depending on the year) for their preferred projects, excluding the project from their own CHU. Based on the results of the vote, the delegates would make recommendations for the projects that should be funded. The precise number of recommended projects would depend on the size of their individual budgets. These recommendations would be submitted to the TCHC's CEO, who would finalize the list of projects to receive funding and forward the final budget to the TCHC's board of directors for approval. The decisions made during 1.8 Days, as well as those made during CHU council meetings, were generally implemented by the TCHC. Its CEO and board seldom overrode the participatory process, especially as both residents and staff became better at communicating with each other in the development of proposed projects. As Penny Milton, a former board member, put it, this would happen only where a project was "absolutely not doable or contravene[d] building codes."[51]

Once the board finalized the budget, a monitoring committee in each CHU, also made up of staff and residents, would oversee the implementation of its projects and financial status.

The TCHC's system had impressive features that could be understood in terms of principles related to the deliberative democratic ideal. The strongest evidence of this is found with respect to the principle of inclusion. As Gail Johnson, former community health consultant at the TCHC, put it, the "theory is that every one of the 164,000 tenants should have the opportunity to participate."[52] All tenants could run for CHU representative or ICHU delegate, and all could participate on various committees, including the Tenant Advisory Committee and the Application Review Committee. To this end, the TCHC put great efforts into publicizing elections, council meetings, and 1.8 Days. According to Ken Thompson, former manager of community health at the TCHC, "We've got extensive messaging out there saying if you want to [participate] you can."[53]

The TCHC was fairly successful in involving its residents in its participatory system, which was no straightforward task. Generally, TCHC residents face a number of challenges to integration and participation in their communities. Many are recent immigrants, single parents, elderly, or disabled. Some residents are more transient, staying only for short or medium terms within the TCHC. Others are more long-term, with families having lived in the community for more than a generation. Collectively, residents speak over a hundred different languages, observe an array of religions, and belong to a wide range of recreational groups. Through various means, including door-to-door visits, TCHC staff sought to achieve a high degree of inclusion in the resident participation system. Some of the specific ways in which staff attempted to address logistical barriers to participation included reimbursing participants for day-care and transportation costs and providing lunches and snacks. In buildings with historically low rates of attendance, staff would set up flipcharts in the lobbies so that residents could record their views at their convenience.

Despite the challenges, there is evidence that participants in CHU meetings and 1.8 Days reflected the general diversity of the broader TCHC community.[54] In terms of the numbers of participants, it is difficult to be specific. In 2005, there was a total of 319 tenant representatives.[55] In 2007, there were 383.[56] In 2009, approximately 335 delegates participated in the Allocation Days.[57] Voter turnout for the elections of tenant representatives in 2010, which involved a new stratum of youth representatives, was 21 per cent of youth residents and 31 per cent of all eligible residents.[58] However, based on their direct observations of the TCHC's process, Josh Lerner and Estair Van Wagner point out that participation was not always on equal terms. As they write, if "deliberations are not well structured and facilitated, they can reproduce class and knowledge hierarchies, by enabling those with more power and greater linguistic or technical skills to control discussions."[59] Nonetheless, there is evidence that TCHC staff consistently attempted to ensure that the perspectives of residents were voiced and concerns weighted equally during meetings.[60] There is also evidence suggesting that residents viewed the procedures for participation and, specifically, for participatory budgeting, as fair.[61] Results from a 2006 evaluation of the resident participation system suggest that most residents regarded procedures as fair and that "very few" residents raised concerns about them.[62] In a 2009 evaluation, over 90 per cent of 140 tenant delegates felt that decisions rendered in the system were fair, "even though many of them did not receive funding."[63]

The TCHC's participatory budgeting process also provided for fairly equal access to information concerning the development, evaluation, and implementation of projects. Funds were allocated to each CHU for educational and training opportunities for residents and their representatives to build their individual capacities for participation and leadership. Although a number of CHU managers and residents expressed a need for more of these kinds of opportunities, some CHU councils made use of these funds to develop effective communication, conflict management, and budget preparation skills.[64] In addition, according to Johnson, the TCHC had "a process where every tenant representative" could have a computer and Internet access.[65] As mentioned earlier, members of CHU councils would work with TCHC staff in preparing the draft budget for their proposed capital projects. TCHC staff would support representatives in identifying priorities and developing proposals. They would use visual aids, incorporating colours, pictures, and symbols to enable residents to communicate across languages. There was an effort to ensure that interpreters were available for residents attending building, CHU, and ICHU meetings. As noted in the 2006 evaluation, however, interpreters "were usually not available at meetings" and information about meetings was not posted in all the languages spoken in buildings.[66] In the 2009 evaluation, this concern to ensure that information about meetings be in multiple languages was echoed.[67] This evaluation also found that respondents wanted more information, as well as time, for their meetings.[68] A serious issue was raised that residents were not provided with information regarding how much money they could allocate to projects through their CHU council meetings.[69]

Another important feature of the TCHC's Tenant Participation System was local transparency and accountability. After allocation decisions were made in either council meetings or the ICHU forum, CHU plans would in principle be posted in each building. These plans, placed in lobbies so that residents could see them, would list each project's allocated funds, costs, and completion date. According to TCHC bylaws, CHU managers were required to give their CHU council monthly updates on the progress of the capital projects. Council members, in turn, were required to update the residents in their buildings about the status of the capital plans in each building. Despite the existence of the bylaws, there was room for improvement in this area. According to the 2006 evaluation, residents and managers "indicated a need for improved communication between staff and tenants."[70] Here, again, this concern was echoed in the 2009 evaluation.[71]

There is stronger evidence suggesting that residents focused their deliberations on a shared or collective interest. Residents in most CHUs aimed to develop, propose, and implement projects intended to benefit the community housing unit as a whole. This was done in informal and formal meetings of residents and their representatives. Meetings within each CHU to distribute the community's allocated funds were generally more amenable to cooperation and collective deliberation. According to the 2009 evaluation, more than 70 per cent of respondents felt that identified priorities reflected the discussions in the council meetings.[72] Although the process of the Allocation Days was more competitive, it nonetheless encouraged deliberation among residents, councillors, and delegates concerning both the strengths and necessity of the projects. Lerner and Van Wagner note that most participants initially focused on their own interests, but over the course of deliberations came to appreciate the needs of others.[73] Generally, they write, participants developed "greater mutual understanding, trust, and reciprocity."[74] Indeed, there are many examples of CHUs competing for funding for similar projects, but seeking ways to share the funds or conceding to the CHU most in need.[75] As a former TCHC board member put it, there is "a sense of 'We can share, we don't have to beat on each other for a slice of pie that is never enough.'"[76]

On the whole, the TCHC's Tenant Participation System realized principles of deliberative democracy. In important ways, the system achieved inclusion, procedural equality, access to information, and mutual reason giving and sharing. Participants considered not merely their own but also the interests of others, and sought agreement with each other on proposed projects. Their decisions were tied directly to budgetary decisions that would be authorized by TCHC senior management. Projects conceptualized and agreed to by participants were consistently implemented by the TCHC. Participants' collective preferences and priorities became those of the TCHC. In this case, we see no obvious limitations of output. If we were to focus only on procedures, resident participation at the TCHC is a success story. While a far cry from the Porto Alegre model, the TCHC's system was more than participatory budgeting in name only.

Persisting Hierarchy and Circumscribed Participation

By stepping back from an examination of the procedures to consider more broadly the context in which they were embedded, we see a disconnection between the TCHC's Tenant Participation System and the ultimate decision-making power within the corporation. Decision-making power remained configured in terms of a hierarchy, with TCHC elites at the top, CHU staff in the middle, and residents at the bottom. Why is this problematic? Isn't it important for an organization to maintain control over its resources, especially when they derive from the underprivileged (i.e., rent from tenants) and the public purse (i.e., subsidies from government)? The TCHC is a very large organization, and this hierarchy and control can facilitate clear channels of accountability. The disjuncture between the TCHC's participation system and its management structure is problematic because it arguably served not only to bolster the existing configuration of power but also to uphold the material privileges with which this power is associated. As one resident put it, the system was "smoke and mirrors."[77] From this perspective, it may have obscured, as well as diverted attention away from, questionable practices by some TCHC management and staff with respect to expenditures and procurements.

Moreover, the participation system can be understood to have shifted responsibilities to residents that rightfully belonged to management. It can, in particular, be seen as a means of distributing the burdens of basic maintenance to TCHC residents. Many proposed projects were both very important and in dire need of funding. The 2006 evaluation found that such projects included the installation of security equipment (e.g., cameras, locking systems, and lighting), replacement of aging and leaky windows, development of community gardens and playgrounds, and creation or improvement of public spaces.[78] In 2009, residents made allocations to the following projects, most of which could be best described as basic maintenance and repairs.

- Garden beautification, 123 Sackville St (Queen and Parliament) – $5000
- Playground improvements, Blake Boultbee (Gerrard and Pape) – $25,000
- New hallway tiles, Kennedy-Dundalk (Ellesmere and Kennedy) – $90,000
- Additional security cameras, Finch-Brahms (Finch and Brahms) – $30,000
- Paint common areas, Warden Woods (Danforth and Warden) – $40,000
- Gym renovations, Scarlett Manor (Lawrence West and Scarlett) – $50,000
- New kitchen cupboards, Thistletown (Martingrove and Albion) – $55,000
- New bathroom vanities, Jane-Yewtree (Jane and Finch) – $50,000
- Computer resource centre, Swansea Mews (Queensway and Windermere) – $25,000[79]

While gym, playground, and garden improvements, as well as the installation of computers, may have been empowering, providing residents with infrastructure to enrich their lives, floor, kitchen, and bathroom repairs were issues of basic sanitation. Any other landlord would be on the hook for, if not identifying the problem, then at least laying out the scope of the work, finding contractors, and paying for the repairs.

The 2006 evaluation found that maintenance and security had become the overwhelming concerns expressed by tenants.[80] The 2009 evaluation also found evidence of residents feeling frustrated by being limited to funds primarily for these kinds of projects.[81] They felt that they had shouldered enough of the responsibility for capital repairs and upgrades and had done enough "fixing."[82] As stated by a staff member in the evaluation,

> You get priorities that really shouldn't be there – things like fixing a boiler or roof are essentially things that the property manager should have repaired anyway, and shouldn't be things that the tenants put forward

as their number one thing. And so they put it forward, and then you have all this negotiation and explaining that this should be funded somewhere else. And tenants say, "Well, you're not funding it through anything else."[83]

Taking a broad look at the TCHC's properties, we see that many were, and continue to be, in run-down conditions. Numerous media reports exist on the dilapidated conditions of TCHC buildings. The City of Toronto has reported that the "significant capital repair challenges facing TCH are well known."[84] As an employee of the TCHC stated in 2008, the corporation has "a capital deficit of 300 million ... That number goes up every year that we don't fix it because more things start to go. We have units that cost so much to put into a state of liveability ... You're talking about housing in Toronto that people can't access because we can't bring it to a liveable level. It costs $100,000 for a unit ... so that someone can rent it."[85] And, as the City of Toronto disclosed in March 2013, the "current TCH capital repair backlog exceeds $750 million. TCH estimates that without new investments the capital repair backlog will continue to grow by some $100 million annually."[86]

Despite the desires of residents, TCHC management maintained the circumscribed scope and structure of the participation system. Frustration among residents concerning the limitations of the system may have impacted on their levels of participation. The 2006 evaluation found that, although twenty-one CHUs reported high tenant and tenant council participation, tenants in three CHUs indicated that they did not participate because "they felt there were insufficient resources to address the issues of their CHU."[87] Tenants and staff from four CHUs with high participation "also acknowledged the insufficiency of funds available, but felt it was important to have a say in the ways in which limited resources were allocated."[88] The 2009 evaluation found consistent concerns regarding low levels of participation.[89] It found, furthermore, that while most CHUs had councils, many buildings did not have representatives.[90]

The participation system was limited not just in terms of distributable resources but also in terms of participatory institutions. The TCHC's Tenant Participation System was largely compartmentalized, existing primarily within as opposed to across CHUs. Aside from the 1.8 Days, residents in any given CHU had few opportunities to meet and engage with residents from other community housing units. Residents expressed a desire for a city-wide council and corresponding communication network, but TCHC management was resistant to creating these mechanisms.[91] Residents talked about their desire for a "third level" of governance, beyond building meetings and CHU councils, that would include representatives from each CHU and that would meet regularly. Without these institutional basics, they faced obstacles to organizing among themselves and pushing for greater decision-making power within the TCHC. A feeling expressed was that, while the Tenant Participation System "looks good" in reports, TCHC elites were "afraid that the tenants have too much power" and wanted to limit it.[92]

What accounts for the contradictions in the TCHC's participatory system, which appeared to meet principles of deliberative democracy and yet produced limited outcomes? Contextual factors, including the general characteristics of resident participants, elite commitment to their participation, public pressure for participation, and policy requirements provide an explanation for the strengths of the system. Looking at the participants, we see committed and motivated individuals who made direct contributions to the system's merits. This is not surprising, as participants were self-selected, choosing to involve themselves in decision making for their immediate neighbourhoods. Some were new Canadians, some were economically marginalized, and some had never had opportunities to influence, let alone make decisions for, a wider collectivity. Through this system, they were given possibilities to contribute to projects in their buildings and communities that were important to them. Beyond becoming very knowledgeable about local needs, participants acquired valuable experience and skills to develop and advocate for projects and to work with others to reach agreements on which ones ought to be funded. Participants were motivated, knowledgeable, and skilled. They had a vested interested in having an effective participation system and making it work for the long term. Many CHU council members and ICHU delegates remained actively involved in the Tenant Participation System for several consecutive years.

Many TCHC staff, management, and board members, moreover, expressed what appeared to be a genuine normative commitment to resident participation. According to Derek Ballantyne, a former CEO of the TCHC, he and his management team wanted to move away from a more traditional form of public housing, based on a hierarchical and paternalistic model of service delivery.[93] Ballantyne articulated a strong concern for low-income tenants in relation to a large institutional landlord. He spoke of the importance of "home" to self-identity and to individual empowerment. Low-income tenants were, in his words, "the most disempowered." "They have a sense of lack of control over their home space. They don't have a choice to go anywhere else. If you come to that realization, it is not a big leap to want to create systems of tenant engagement."[94] Members of the TCHC board of directors also expressed a commitment to resident participation and empowerment. A former TCHC board member, Penny Milton, stated that the TCHC tenant participatory system is based on "a philosophical stance," whereby, "as a corporation, we were clear about the differences between consultation, participation, and decision making. The bigger goal is that the community should be involved in making decisions that affect housing, health, and well-being. We have visions of community-level governance."[95] TCHC staff echoed this commitment.[96] As a CHU manager put it, everyone, "top down, believes in [the Tenant Participation System] ... Key people believe it, and they look to cultivate it."[97] Indeed, the TCHC channelled substantial resources into the system. In many ways, its identity as an organization was based on it, which distinguished the corporation from other social housing providers in North America.

Nonetheless, it is important to examine the context from which this commitment emerged, which was one characterized by both bottom-up and top-down pressure for greater resident participation. In terms of the former, social housing providers in Toronto in the 1990s faced significant pressure from their residents for increased involvement in the decisions affecting their communities. Specifically, residents wanted more direct say in the decisions that affected them.[98] As Lerner and Van Wagner write, residents of both Metro Toronto Housing and Toronto Housing "were asking for greater participation in budget decisions and more control over how funds were spent."[99] When the TCHC was formed in 2002, residents saw an opportunity for greater decision-making power and insisted not only that the new housing company maintain existing but also develop new channels of participation.[100] As a member of the TCHC management staff put it, residents had gained experience in collective decision making within the former social housing organizations and demanded more direct participation when the TCHC was formed.[101] This pressure likely fed into the development of an elite commitment to greater resident participation and was likely a part of the motivation to formalize participatory business planning within the TCHC.

The TCHC's Tenant Participation System was also prompted by provincial and municipal policy. The Social Housing Reform Act of 2000 was introduced to govern the transfer of funding and administering social housing programs from the Ontario government to municipalities. According to Ballantyne, when the Province amalgamated and decentralized social housing in Toronto, it provided the TCHC with a clear mandate "to produce quality housing at a reasonable cost; but it also included in the mandate an intent to engage with communities."[102] This mandate included a number of objectives. Chief among these was the implementation of a community management model that makes operational decisions at the local level. For Ballantyne, it was clear that the mandate implied not merely consultation, but a re-conceptualization of the relationship between the social housing provider and its tenants. Indeed, he understood both the nature and extent of the existing policy requirements specific to the TCHC and its Tenant Participation System. The Social Housing Reform Act stipulates the following with respect to tenant participation:

8.1   Tenant Participation
    8.1.1   Prior to September 30, 2002, *TCHC* and the *tenants* will develop a democratic system of active tenant participation and involvement that will:
        (a)   provide a tenant council structure or similar organization;
        (b)   provide for tenant input for decisions at the corporate and local levels;
        (c)   provide for tenant input for setting local spending priorities and service levels;
        (d)   be based on the best practices current systems in place in *MTHC* and *THC*; and
        (e)   include a process to identify two *tenants* to be proposed for appointment to the *Board*.[103]

The act spells out the requirement of "active tenant participation" and tenant councils based on practices of the TCHC's predecessors. The act requires tenant input at both the local and corporate levels, as well as input on local priorities. The TCHC's system essentially meets these requirements.

The motivation for the participation system was embedded in a particular context characterized by not only resident pressure and policy requirement but also the interests and aims of the TCHC. From this angle, salient contextual factors appear to have been the economic interests and strategic aims of the TCHC in light of significant budget cuts in the 1990s and into the 2000s. During this time, the Province of Ontario and the City of Toronto were cutting budgets. As Lerner and Wagner write, the Metro Toronto Housing Corporation and Toronto Housing Company were facing "new funding cuts, due to the provincial government's downloading of responsibility for social housing and the municipality's reductions in social programs funding."[104] They add: "The companies' capital budgets were shrinking quickly, and staff and management chose to involve tenants in the process of making difficult decisions about capital investments."[105]

TCHC staff, management, and board members were likely well aware of the economic constraints associated with being a social housing provider in this context. With the amalgamation came the establishment of the TCHC as the largest social housing provider in Canada, owning and operating close to 60,000 aging units. The combination of the size of the TCHC's property holdings and its capital deficit may have resulted in additional pressure to consult and engage with residents to ensure that its policies and programs would be cost effective and stable.[106] Decentralizing decision making may have enabled TCHC management and staff to make and implement difficult decisions concerning a portion of its capital budget given scarce resources and to do so with a rationale provided directly by its residents. The TCHC may have therefore placed responsibility for making decisions about the allocation of limited resources for capital development in the hands of residents. Their participation may have been a way of directly assessing priorities, as well as justifying the allocation of resources to some projects while not to others. After all, residents had an immediate understanding of infrastructure priorities and often of how best to meet these priorities. As one CHU manager stated, "Tenant participation is crucial … We don't have enough money to do all the capital repairs that are required." The manager continued, "I would be very alienated from the tenant population if I didn't use a community management plan [including] principles of participatory democracy and if I didn't engage tenants in addressing community safety concerns on an ongoing basis."[107] As another CHU manager put it, this push towards increased tenant participation was "also to our benefit. Under that old paradigm – i.e., the parent-dependent paradigm – we were providing things we shouldn't have been. When people live within your walls in social housing, you become like their mayor. You provide fire protection, garbage pickup, and security. It's not sustainable."[108] From this perspective, it is not surprising that the TCHC would develop procedures for resident participation and participatory budgeting that were procedurally inclusive and fair but limited in terms of both funds and power.

Taking an even broader look at the management culture of the TCHC, we see that an institutionalized shift in power was unlikely – unlikely perhaps all along, but almost certainly in recent years. Instead, a decision-making process that was both hierarchical and opaque may have been more in line with the interests of some TCHC management and staff. As mentioned at the outset of this chapter, in 2010, official reports concerning questionable individual practices started to emerge. An auditor general's report of December 2010, released by the City of Toronto, exposed serious issues with the number and nature of staff expenses.[109] Among the numerous expenditures were Christmas dinners associated with net expenditures of $53,500 in 2008 and $40,000 in 2009, a planning session at a local spa, including lunch, pedicures and manicures, staff training and development, a four-hour boat cruise, and an offsite planning session in Muskoka, a holiday region north of Toronto. There were also expenditures at a number of golf courses outside Toronto, gifts from the upscale Holt Renfrew store totalling $1000, and entertainment at a restaurant totalling almost $5000. Based on these findings, the auditor general expressed a greater concern with the culture that allowed such expenditures to occur.[110] They may have been appropriate for private, for-profit corporations; but for a social housing corporation, such expenditures were highly inappropriate. Moreover, the report identified serious problems with the filing of expense claims. For example, the individual who incurred the expense for the $5000 dinner approved the expenditure and provided neither a documented reason for it nor a record of who attended.[111] The only supporting document was a copy of a credit card slip.

The report also cites a general lack of due diligence in terms of managing expense reimbursements from third parties. In addition, it articulates concerns derived from internal reports about the use of purchasing cards. As the report states, if "TCHC's expense claim approval process had been working effectively, we would have expected many of the instances of non-compliance to be addressed."[112] The report concludes that discontinuing such expenditures has the "potential to save at least $200,000 on an annual basis."[113] Two additional reports – one also dated December 2010 and the other December 2011 – were critical of procurement practices.[114] The former found that procurement policies and procedures were not being followed by TCHC management and staff, and the latter found that such policies and procedures were not being followed by a TCHC subsidiary. According to the earlier report on procurement, many of the issues identified by the auditor general "were either a result of decisions made by management or were undertaken with the concurrence of management," and "senior management commitment" was needed to improve the procurement process.[115]

The TCHC's Tenant Participation System, including its participatory budgeting, was embedded in the corporation's management structure and culture – a structure and culture that raise serious concerns about the commitment to empowering residents. Questionable management practices may not have directly impacted on the participation system in its day-to-day functioning. However, they may partially explain why the system was ultimately limited in the size of its budgetary allocation and why it lacked a more robust city-wide participatory infrastructure. Arguably, some in TCHC management may have sought to maintain control over the vast majority of funds for capital expenditures, and all of its funds for operations, in order not to risk disrupting what had become status quo practices. Empowering residents with more significant decision-making authority could have exposed such practices, and could have served in putting an end to them. As a TCHC resident put it, "You would think that a social housing company would follow proper procedure ... but the problem is that they're making money, and we're still sitting ducks."[116]

This case reveals contradictions involving procedures that appeared to be based on principles related to deliberative democracy and their significance for decision-making power held by the TCHC. Certain contextual pressures from residents and the provincial government, and the motivation of residents to ameliorate living conditions in their communities, feed into an explanation concerning the strengths of the TCHC's participation system. Again, it is important to point out that management and staff also appeared to be genuinely committed to this system. But their commitment seems to have had its limitations. Other factors, including a large capital deficit, a broader ethos of questionable management practices, and a sense of individual entitlement, may contribute to explaining the limited scope of this system. Ultimately, these stronger contextual forces may have thwarted aims for greater resident empowerment.

Chapter Three

Deliberative Polling and Nova Scotia Power Incorporated

Nova Scotia's energy policy has been the site of an important deliberative experiment: Canada's first Deliberative Poll.[1] For decades, the generating capacity of the province's primary electricity producer and supplier, Nova Scotia Power Incorporated (NSPI), formerly a Crown corporation, was based almost exclusively on oil and coal. Between 1979 and 1993, the provincial government spent $1.2 billion to convert an oil-fired generating unit to a coal-fired one, to build new coal-fired units, and to install the necessary transmission infrastructure.[2] In 2006, coal accounted for 80 per cent of the electricity produced by NSPI.[3] Two years later, an article in *Corporate Knights* claimed that NSPI's parent company, Emera, was one of the highest carbon emitters in Canada.[4] In 2009, the province's Department of Energy stated that "Nova Scotians rank with some of the highest consumers of energy in the world."[5] Over several years, moving away from coal and toward other options has been critical for both NSPI and the province. The utility has made impressive inroads. Coal now accounts for 59 per cent of the electricity that NSPI generates; natural gas provides 21 per cent, and renewable sources provide 18 per cent.[6] Energy efficiency has also in recent years become an important part of the generation scenario. Approximately 4 per cent of Nova Scotia's electricity now comes from saved megawatt hours that would have been produced without efficiency programs.[7] This ongoing movement away from coal is, of course, good for the health of the environment and people of Nova Scotia (and beyond). But it has created and will continue to create certain economic burdens for citizens, corporations, and the government of the province.

NSPI management elites knew that they were facing very difficult challenges going into the twenty-first century. They knew that they would need to raise the rates charged to Nova Scotians in order to pay for programs to decrease electricity consumption and to offset some of the costs of developing technology and infrastructure to increase electricity generation from renewables. Both demand-side (i.e., the conservation of electricity) and supply-side (i.e., the generation of electricity) management would require increased funds, at least in the short term. In addition to raising rates, NSPI would also have to encourage its customers to change their electricity consumption behaviour. Rate increases and behaviour changes would present obvious challenges. The Utility and Review Board of Nova Scotia (UARB) would have to approve proposed rate increases; customers would have to be agreeable to proposed changes. Success in both areas would require careful planning and policy development. NSPI elites were impressed by the Deliberative Polling that had taken place in energy policy in the United States and saw it as a potentially important way of tapping into not merely the "top-of-the-head" opinions but rather the more considered perspectives of their customers. They decided to experiment with such polling as a source of guidance for their policy changes.

In November 2004, NSPI held Canada's first Deliberative Poll, based on James Fishkin's methodology.[8] NSPI elites found this poll, or Customer Energy Forum, so insightful that they would hold smaller forums in 2005 and 2009.[9] Similarly to participatory budgeting within the TCHC, NSPI's forums largely realized procedural principles of deliberative democracy. The procedures facilitated inclusive, fair, informed, and well-reasoned deliberation and, in some respects, resulted in a greater degree of convergence of views than had existed previously. Moreover, participants in these polls consistently claimed that their experiences were meaningful to them. With three polls in five years, NSPI appeared to have made a commitment to these periodic deliberative forums, and seemed to have implemented a consistent strategy for involving members of its affected publics in its decision-making processes. Although Deliberative Polls are generally not intended to empower participants directly in decision making, NSPI made it clear that it wanted to bring Nova Scotians into its energy planning for the future and that the forums would provide foundations for that planning.

Despite these claims, it is difficult to see a relationship between NSPI's hosting these polls and its planning for the supply of and demand for electricity in the province. While the outputs of the polling and the decisions of NSPI were generally congruent, they were disconnected in the sequencing of events involved in developing plans. Indeed, the outputs were consistent with initiatives that the utility had already been putting in place. The polls may have served as a "check-in" with a representative sample of Nova Scotians regarding NSPI's policy changes. But the utility's decisions concerning these changes were based more directly on elite stakeholder negotiations, economic reasoning, regulatory directives, and policy requirements. The polls played a very minor role relative to closed-door negotiations within a context of increasingly strict regulatory requirements.

In this case, contradictions lie in the procedures and their outputs being democratically deliberative but policy decisions falling short of this standard. On the one hand, we see the three Customer Energy Forums appearing to represent a trend in energy planning to include the informed views of Nova Scotians. On the other, we see that the forums were fundamentally limited in shifting decision-making power away from the exclusive domain of government, corporations, and selected stakeholders. The forums, especially as a series, had the potential to facilitate the informed and meaningful engagement of citizens with respect to energy issues and to tie this engagement to policy decisions. They did not fulfil this potential. While they may have provided participants with an opportunity to learn about and deliberate on issues, with respect to their longer-range outcome, these forums were ultimately non-empowering.

Why would NSPI elites decide to implement the methodology and procedures of Deliberative Polling? Why would NSPI invest a great deal of time, energy, and money into hosting three of these deliberative events if they would not ultimately feed into its decision making? What ends did they serve? This case further highlights the importance of looking beyond deliberative democratic procedures and examining their broader context. As we will see, contextual factors provide an explanation as to why NSPI's forums were largely insignificant for both the substance of policies and exercise of policy power. Before turning to an examination of this case, I provide an overview of Deliberative Polling, which is *itself* characterized by contradictions.

The Basics of Deliberative Polling

James Fishkin was motivated to devise and develop Deliberative Polling during the US presidential primary campaign of 1988.[10] Through this polling, he hoped to address certain concerns with democracy in America. These concerns were with what he perceived as superficial campaigns in small and unrepresentative states, such as Iowa and New Hampshire, which had the potential of determining the presidential race. He found the process lacking in both representativeness and thoughtfulness, and wanted to address these deficiencies. He thus developed a set of procedures for democratic deliberation involving a random sample of citizens constituting a microcosm of the broader citizenry. According to specific procedural guidelines, members of this microcosm would meet over the course of one or two days, engage with experts, deliberate among themselves, develop their understanding, and express their views. Ideally, participants in these polls would receive balanced background information on the issues, listen to a diversity of expert opinions, deliberate in small moderated groups, and raise questions and make comments in plenary sessions.

Deliberative Polling is a distinctive approach to public participation for two reasons. First, its design derives directly from an ideal of deliberative democracy. As Fishkin states, "For years, political theorists around the world have been talking about deliberative democracy but, in theory, in a very general way, and it has often been dismissed as something impractical, something purely theoretical. [Deliberative Polling] is a practical method that can easily be instituted in many different public policy contexts."[11] Deliberative Polling is a set of procedures intended specifically to realize certain principles of moral equality, mutual reasoning, and informed deliberation. According to Fishkin and Cynthia Farrar, it combines the values of political equality and deliberation.[12] Participants are understood to be morally equal, and their equality is upheld and realized through procedurally fair rules and access to information. Moreover, they claim that it facilitates more robust arguments by ensuring engagement with countervailing views. They also contend that it provides participants with reasonably accurate information relevant to the issues at stake. In addition, they maintain that it encourages participants to make decisions on the basis of having examined arguments, counterarguments, and a diversity of viewpoints. According to Fishkin and Farrar,

Balance is the hallmark of the briefing materials, the panels of experts, and the training of the moderators. Every effort is made to provide the participants with accurate information, which is usually reviewed by an advisory group ... Organizers also create an atmosphere of mutual respect · so that participants will be interested in deciding the issue on its merits. Random sampling, when effective, produces a diversity of viewpoints and backgrounds. When it works well, the deliberative polling process requires citizens to take their real differences into account, sidesteps the distorting power of special interests, and mitigates polarization among the participants.[13]

The second way in which this polling is distinctive is that it is a form of both public engagement and consultation. Engagement is maximized by the specifics of the procedures, including the small-group discussions, plenary sessions, and duration of the event. These characteristics enable participants not only to develop their knowledge about a topic but also to bond with each other, which serves in enhancing the deliberative experience.

Engagement is also facilitated by what Deliberative Polls do not require, that is, that participants reach an agreement (let alone a consensus). Instead of requiring that participants seek either a basic agreement or a more demanding consensus, the polls are geared toward surveying their opinions as they develop over exchanges among themselves and with experts. This design feature serves to alleviate some of the pressure that participants may experience to modify their views in order to reach an agreement or consensus. It enables participants to become familiar with views that might compete with their own, and to deliberate collectively on the beliefs and reasons supporting this range of views, but ultimately to come to conclusions as relatively autonomous individuals. It minimizes, in other words, the potentially coercive implications of a requirement to concur with a collectivity. If participants change their perspectives over the course of deliberation, as they typically do, these changes are more likely the result of being persuaded by reasoned arguments. These changes may or may not be voiced by participants during the plenary or small-group sessions, but they are recorded in pre- and post-deliberation surveys administered to them as individuals. While this feature enhances the prospects for the engagement of autonomous participants, it is a drift away from one of the central aims of deliberative democracy as initially conceived, which is to establish a mutually justifiable position shared among participants that provides the ethical foundation for a collectively binding decision. It effectively prioritizes the polling of individuals over the deliberation of the collectivity toward a mutually justifiable position. From a purely instrumental perspective, Deliberative Polling is a well-designed tool for determining informed and considered public opinion. It is not surprising that it has been employed as such.

The first nation-wide Deliberative Poll in the United States was the January 1996 National Issues Convention, which featured presidential aspirants and broadcast coverage on PBS. Since then, numerous Deliberative Polls have taken place across the United States and in a range of other countries, including the United Kingdom, Denmark, Bulgaria, Australia, China, and Japan.[14] Many have been conducted on behalf of governments at the national level on topics such as the monarchy, membership in the European Union, adoption of the Euro, reconciliation with Indigenous Peoples, democratic reform, foreign policy, the family, economics, and energy. Many more have been hosted by a range of entities, including community groups, municipal governments, public utilities, and energy corporations, and have focused on a variety of local or regional issues.

The organization hosting the poll – that is, the organization in whose name, for whose purposes, and on whose tab the poll is being conducted – sets the budget for the poll, chooses the topic for deliberation, enlists experts to provide guidance, and hires outside parties to organize and run the poll. Well in advance of the poll, the host organization works with consultants (e.g., consultants from Public Decision Partnership) associated with Fishkin's Center for Deliberative Democracy based at Stanford University. The organization then hires a public opinion firm to recruit participants via random-digit dialling. Sometimes targeted phone calls complement random dialling to encourage the participation of those who may least likely attend. Participants tend to approximate the larger target population in both demographics and attitudes. They tend, however, to be skewed toward English speakers who are older, better educated, and more politically active.[15] Participants tend typically to have landlines, spend time at home, and be willing to talk to pollsters.[16] They are paid an honorarium and have their travel, accommodation, and meal expenses covered.

Before each poll, participants receive background information on the issues to be discussed. In principle, this background information is comprehensive and well balanced, based on the input of a range of experts in the particular area. As part of the drafting process, this informational material is peer reviewed. Participants are expected to have read these materials prior to the meetings. Before the deliberative meetings, they are administered a pre-deliberation survey relevant to the issues. The administration of this survey sometimes takes place during the recruitment telephone call, and sometimes when participants arrive at the event.

Although there is variation among them, all of these events include small-group discussions as well as plenary sessions. As Fishkin and Farrar state, these sessions are run by moderators who are trained in the "specific approach embodied in the Deliberative Poll, particularly on remaining neutral and not imparting information; encouraging broad participation; and refraining from promoting consensus among participants."[17] Moderators do not restrict what participants say or what kind of speech they use; they are not required to focus discussion on a common good.[18] They actively encourage input from all participants and systematically canvass the "various perspectives and concerns identified in the background materials and represented by individual group members."[19] During the plenary sessions, participants have the opportunity to ask questions of expert panels. During the small-group deliberations, ideally among eighteen participants, they have access to a resource person, who is available to answer questions of fact. In principle, participants reflect on, and exchange reasons and arguments about, what they have learned from the background materials and panels in the plenary session. At the end of the event, participants complete a survey similar to the pre-event survey. Sometimes, the events are televised to encourage a broader public discussion on the topic. Sometimes, participants are given specific opportunities to express their views directly to policymakers.

To highlight the polls' potential for contributing to a robust democratic culture, Fishkin and Farrar discuss annual Deliberative Polls in and around New Haven, Connecticut, that are part of the By the People Citizen Deliberations project.[20] This project was designed to build infrastructure for local deliberation and to link local interests to a national and international context, partnering with public television stations, civic groups, community foundations, and colleges and universities to convene and broadcast simultaneous deliberations.[21] These particular polls are a good example of the role such polls can play in developing more democratically engaged communities. They can provide opportunities for citizens to come together publicly to discuss issues of concern, enabling them to debate and deliberate on substantive issues while also developing and deepening social bonds and honing individual skills of communication.[22] As Fishkin and Farrar state, these polls are "good for democracy in that the participants come away from the process with a greatly increased sense of efficacy and engagement."[23] Those who participate in them are more likely to continue learning and participating than those who do not.[24] Moreover, the "voice of the people revealed by these exercises is motivated by information and mutual understanding and is more likely to be collectively coherent and reflectively stable."[25]

From this perspective, these polls are excellent contributions to the realization of deliberative democracy.

Deliberative Polls have a much more pragmatic use. A rationale for holding one is frequently to gain insight into public opinion both before and after deliberation on given issues. In some respects, it is to understand how opinions might develop in circumstances of fairness, information, and deliberation. Standard forms of polling provide a sense of what members of the public think "off the top of their heads." Fishkin's polling can yield an understanding of views that may be representative of those of members of the broader public were they better informed and directly engaged. Thus, both governments and corporations have resorted to this kind of polling to acquire greater knowledge of public opinions and how they might evolve if they became more informed and deliberative.

Specifically, Deliberative Polls have been employed in the context of energy policy in a number of US states. Texas, in particular, stands out. In the late1990s, eight energy corporations used the method to determine what energy options their customers preferred "to meet future electric requirements."[26] Ron Lehr, Will Guild, Dennis Thomas, and Blair Swezey note that participants changed their opinions substantially based on the information they gained during these polls.[27] They write that these polls demonstrated that "customers were concerned about the environment, and that they preferred renewable energy and energy efficiency resource options more than the fossil fuel alternatives."[28] These results were unanticipated by the utilities and their regulators, and both entities "changed their level of interest in and commitment to renewables and efficiency as a result of what they heard from customers."[29] In the words of Lehr and his colleagues,

> Subsequent to the Deliberative Polls, utilities and independent suppliers have made substantial investments in new renewable energy-based generation projects. And, in 1999, the Texas Legislature included a renewable portfolio standard in the state's electricity restructuring law. All told, more than 1,000 MW of new renewables capacity has been developed in Texas since the Deliberative Polling events. The important contribution of the Deliberative Polls was to provide a measurement of what is important to those most affected by energy resource decisions – the public.[30]

Deliberative Polling can encourage the engagement of a collectivity, and it can also facilitate the informed public opinion polling of individuals.

It can contribute to community building, but it can also serve the interests of corporations in by enabling them to tap into the willingness to pay of their customers. In the case of NSPI, its Customer Energy Forums appear to have been exercises that served both ends. But, in this context, they deviated somewhat from polls in jurisdictions where the sequencing of events involved in developing plans and policies is more conducive to participatory and deliberative democratic inputs.

NSPI's Customer Energy Forums

In 1992, Nova Scotia Power Incorporated bought the assets of Nova Scotia Power Corporation, a Crown corporation created two decades earlier to generate electricity for the province. NSPI is a wholly-owned subsidiary of Emera Inc., a for-profit shareholder-owned company based in Halifax. Both NSPI and Emera trade on the Toronto Stock Exchange. NSPI is regulated under the Public Utilities Act and by the Nova Scotia Utility and Review Board. According to the act, NSPI is allowed only to earn a limited return on its equity each year – a limit the specifics of which are determined by the UARB. For example, for 2013, the utility was permitted a ceiling of 9.25 per cent for its return on equity.[31] When it has exceeded this limit, as it did in 2010, it has provided its customers with a rebate.[32] Employing 1700 people and serving 500,000 customers, the utility provides 95 per cent of electricity generation, transmission, and distribution province wide.[33] It has 2453 megawatts of generating capacity from coal, oil, natural gas, hydro, tidal, wind, and biomass.[34] NSPI operates coal power, natural gas/oil, and biomass plants, as well as oil burning combustion turbines, single wind turbines, wind farms, a tidal station, and hydro stations.

In the early 2000s, NSPI elites felt out of touch with Nova Scotians and desired a better understanding of their views on energy options, especially with respect to heightening environmental, and thus economic, challenges.[35] When members of NSPI's management were pondering ways of consulting with Nova Scotians, they decided to host a Deliberative Poll. As in the case of the TCHC, elites at NSPI expressed a commitment to a novel approach, derived from another jurisdiction, to involving members of their affected public in their planning. As with the TCHC and its participatory budgeting, NSPI's choice of Deliberative Polling appeared to be a commitment not merely to consultation but also to engagement.

NSPI's 2004 Customer Energy Forum involved a sample of 135 of the utility's customers.[36] The design and process of the forum were overseen by the Public Decision Partnership, and in particular Guild, Lehr, and Thomas,[37] all of whom had experience with Deliberative Polling in energy policy in Texas, Nebraska, and Vermont. Similarly to the Deliberative Polls in these states, NSPI's forum involved a random sample of the utility's customers and sought their informed opinions on energy planning. In particular, its objective was to determine informed opinions on options involving fossil fuel, renewables, and conservation. The expressed aim was to involve Nova Scotians in developing NSPI's future energy plan.[38] Like participants in other Deliberative Polls, participants in NSPI's 2004 forum were asked neither to reach an agreement nor to make final policy decisions. Instead, they were instructed to talk about their individual values and preferences in terms of energy options for the province. As put in the *Customer Energy Forum Guidebook*, considered together, "individual opinions of this forum's participants will provide a reasonable picture of what all NSPI customers would say if it were possible to ask each of them the same questions."[39] The guidance provided would be "taken very seriously" and "will become a basic element" in the utility's planning process.[40] As Ralph Tedesco, former Chief Operating Officer of NSPI, stated: "It's essential we reach out and engage our customers and stakeholders. We want to find out what strikes them as reasonable. We want to balance reliable, inexpensive and clean energy. Nova Scotians are capable of addressing that. Our commitment is to listen to what they say and factor it into our planning."[41]

As with the Customer Energy Forums of 2005 and 2009, NSPI paid for and convened this forum, hiring independent parties to design and run it. In most respects, the process operated independently of the utility. Public Decision Partnership provided oversight on the design and process. Corporate Research Associates, a local public opinion research firm, conducted participant recruitment. Both Corporate Research Associates and MT&L Public Relations Limited provided moderators for the small groups. Potential participants were selected through random dialling to NSPI's customers. Eight hundred and fifty-two were administered a telephone survey and, from this group, 135 were invited to participate in the event.[42] This sample was statistically representative of NSPI's residential customers. As Guild, Lehr, and Thomas write, the "demographics of those who participated in the larger pre-event survey were checked against the demographics of those who participated in the event."[43] In general, the demographics of the two groups and their attitudes on key questions were very similar.

The forum participants were all residents of Nova Scotia, which is a relatively small province in its geography and population. With an area of approximately 55,000 square kilometres, it is the second smallest province in Canada. In 2003 – a year before the first forum – the population of the province was estimated to be 936,025.[44] Participants were well informed and prepared for the forum, perhaps because of their general knowledge of NSPI in its historical and primary role in generating and distributing electricity in Nova Scotia. Since its beginning in 1972 as a Crown corporation, through its transformation to a private company, NSPI has been the principal electrical utility in the province. Virtually every resident and business based in the province is directly affected by NSPI. There appears to be a sense that NSPI is a fundamental part of the Nova Scotian community. Participants in the forum may have been motivated to make contributions to the utility's planning knowing full well that it would impact their lives, with or without their input. They may have also had a sense of responsibility to members of their provincial community to try to address challenges associated with transitioning away from coal and toward more sustainable electricity consumption and generation options. As Guild, Lehr, and Thomas write, the "Nova Scotia sample participants came to the forum well prepared with a higher percentage having studied the materials than seen in similar events."[45] They go on: "The sample was very serious, studied hard, and thought about the options."[46]

Participants completed a survey before the event and a similar one following it. They received an honorarium of $150 and were offered a hotel room and meal vouchers. Those travelling from a distance were reimbursed for their expenses. When participants arrived at the forum, they registered and received name tags. They were welcomed in a plenary session by Emera's then chief executive officer, Chris Huskilson, and provided with a brief overview of the forum's procedures by Ron Lehr. Following this introduction, they were assigned randomly to small groups of approximately fifteen people. A moderator led each small group through a discussion of the issues, which had been outlined in the background materials sent out to participants. Over the course of a day and a half, participants alternated between small group and large group sessions, where participants posed questions to panels of experts and advocates. Lehr led the large group sessions, while the local moderators led the small ones. The entire process was open to the press and observers and was videotaped by the Canadian Broadcasting Corporation. On the face of it, the process met important criteria of the deliberative democratic ideal.

While participation in the forum was based on invitation, it was inclusive in that its participants were statistically representative of Nova Scotians. Again, the forum's sample was broadly representative of NSPI's wider customer base in both demographics and basic attitudes. According to Guild, Lehr, and Thomas, in terms of the results of the Deliberative Poll, the confidence limits for the forum were plus or minus 10 per cent at 95 per cent.[47] Thus, 95 per cent of the time, "if all NSPI customers were asked the same questions, their responses would not vary by more than ±10%."[48]

The poll was also inclusive of views and interests represented on its advisory committee and expert panels. NSPI convened an advisory committee comprising fifteen people, each representing different perspectives and interests (such as government, business, consumers, seniors, and environmental and charitable organizations).[49] The committee's responsibility was to frame the issues to be deliberated, develop relevant background materials (in particular, the *Guidebook*), and oversee the design of survey questions and appointment of expert panels. Its responsibility was to ensure that the process was fair and that the materials and surveys were balanced. While there were some concerns that the committee was not inclusive of low-income Nova Scotians and thus did not represent their interests,[50] there was general agreement that it was inclusive and representative of most of the interests in the province and that the *Guidebook* developed by the committee was comprehensive and well balanced.[51] Indeed, with respect to the information materials developed by the committee, 81 per cent of participants thought that they were "mostly balanced."[52] The committee also appointed three panels of experts to make presentations and respond to questions during the plenary sessions. These panels were inclusive in the sense of generally reflecting major perspectives on the various energy generation and management options. These included a broad range of perspectives, including those from the Nova Scotia Department of Energy, Ecology Action Centre, Electricity Consumers Alliance of Nova Scotia, Luscar Limited, Canadian Federation of Independent Business, Renewable Energy Services, RBC Dominion Securities, Sierra Club, United Way, Cape Breton District Health Authority, and NSPI.[53]

NSPI's forum was based on certain principles of equality of procedure. Moderators were instructed to try to ensure that deliberations were characterized by an atmosphere of mutual respect and that all participants had opportunities to voice issues, make points, or ask questions. During the plenary sessions, all participants had opportunities to ask the expert panels questions on the different options. During the small-group discussions, independent moderators sought to ensure the participation of all group members.[54] On the whole, there is evidence to suggest that the deliberative event was generally perceived as procedurally fair.[55] When asked if the forum was biased toward one side or the other, or if it was fair, with 1 indicating "very fair" and 10 indicating "very biased," 32 per cent responded with a 1, 19% with a 2, 8% with a 3, 6% with a 4, and 4% with a 5.[56] Twenty-eight per cent gave it a ranking between 6 and 10.[57]

There was also a certain equality in terms of access to information. Approximately four weeks before the forum, all participants received the forum's guidebook containing background information developed by the advisory committee on energy generation, energy and conservation options, and economic and environmental factors in Nova Scotia. In addition, it contained information about NSPI, its current and projected generation needs, the Nova Scotia energy strategy, fossil fuel, renewable, and conservation options, and fixed and variable costs associated with generating and distributing as well as conserving electricity. As Bruce Cameron, of the Nova Scotia Department of Energy, stated: "At the core of the Deliberative Polling exercise, you're trying to inform people."[58] According to Cameron, that "is why it was important that the advisory group agreed that these were the issues and this was the information that [participants] needed to have."[59]

Throughout the event, participants could ask moderators to obtain more factual information pertaining to relevant issues and options. Participants could also pose questions and make comments to the panels of experts and advocates. These opportunities helped participants understand the complexity of energy policy in the context of environmental and economic constraints. They helped participants comprehend the key issues, trade-offs, and costs of different energy options, and develop considered opinions about these issues.

There is also evidence suggesting that there were appeals to public reasoning and an orientation toward a shared interest.[60] According to an NSPI employee, participants had a wide range of different views, but ultimately reached broad agreement on the need for more renewable energy, lower emissions from existing power plants, and greater energy efficiency in their own homes and businesses.[61] The results of the post-deliberation survey indicate an increase over the pre-deliberation survey in the percentage of those who rated certain factors in the delivery of electricity at 7 and above on a scale of 10, with 10 being "extremely important."[62] This was the case with limiting greenhouse gases, where there was an approximate 10 per cent increase in the percentage of those who ranked it at 7 and above. The importance of ensuring enough electricity and limiting pollutants also increased in percentage but only marginally. However, with respect to the importance of keeping stable electric costs, ensuring lowest costs, and creating jobs, there was a drop in the percentage of respondents ranking their importance at 7 or above, suggesting less convergence in the post-deliberative survey. In addition, with respect to the general distribution among participants in the post-deliberation survey of ratings between 7 and 10, there was less convergence. Nonetheless, in their consideration of the generation and delivery of electricity, participants in the post-deliberation survey ranked environmental factors generally higher than economic ones, with more than 90 per cent of them viewing limiting greenhouse gases as important.[63] When forced to rank all these factors, participants placed limiting pollutants at the top, followed by limiting greenhouse gases and ensuring enough electricity.[64] Participants ranked stable electric costs strongly, but 10–20 points behind these factors.[65] According to Guild and colleagues, when "asked if NSP should only meet federal and provincial requirements in the production of electricity as a means to produce electricity as inexpensively as possible" or "go beyond the current requirements to reduce pollution or greenhouse gases, even if that meant higher bills, the response to go beyond was three to one at 73%, with 26% saying meet current requirements."[66] Participants also converged on high rankings for renewable energy and conservation and on the lowest ranking for oil. Between 82 and 84 per cent of participants indicated a willingness to pay higher rates for renewable sources of energy and for conservation and efficiency programs.[67] Finally, on the whole, participants viewed the forum favourably. Guild, Lehr, and Thomas note that participants gave the forum high marks: "On a scale of 1 to 10, with 1 being a waste of time and 10 being an extremely valuable experience, the average ranking was 9.4."[68] Indeed, NSPI's forum was impressive in terms of realizing inclusion, procedural equality, access to information, a kind of public reasoning, and an articulation of shared interests.

Nonetheless, it is difficult to discern the impact of the outputs of the forum on NSPI's policies concerning the supply and demand of electricity in the province and thus difficult to discern the significance of this poll for decision making concerning energy options in Nova Scotia. Deliberative Polling can be a mechanism enabling participants to contribute to shaping policies that bind them. Even in an advisory role, the potential of Deliberative Polls is to transform the relationship between citizens and officials charged with the authority and responsibility to make or implement binding public decisions. Its potential for empowerment is especially strong since there is evidence that participants' perspectives, views, and arguments become better informed, which in turn can translate into better-informed planning and policy. But this case suggests that outputs of NSPI's Customer Energy Forum of 2004 did not feed directly into its decisions and that the outcome of this poll, as well as those of 2005 and 2009, in shifting decision making away from an elite model and toward a more inclusive one did not ensue. If the forums had an impact on NSPI's policy decisions, and if they had an impact on changing elite attitudes to decision making, it was diffuse and indirect.

Prevailing Policy Requirements and Economic Interests

The results of NSPI's 2004 Customer Energy Forum expressed the desires of participants to see NSPI implement programs for energy conservation and increase its electrical generation from renewable sources. They also expressed a willingness of participants to pay more to offset the costs of these options.[69] In June 2005, NSPI released a statement announcing a second forum, scheduled for the fall, that would focus exclusively on demand-side management planning. In addition, this statement indicated that, based on its initial forum, NSPI was proposing to the UARB an investment of $5 million in conservation programs.[70]

With respect to demand-side management, there appears to be a loose relationship between the 2004 forum and NSPI's decisions to create more programs. NSPI could have proposed a much more robust conservation plan, especially in light of the results of the poll. Indeed, NSPI's proposal to the UARB was generally seen as lacking in detail and inadequately developed.[71] The UARB would in 2006 approve only $550,000 in additional funds to enable NSPI to hire consultants to assist in developing its plan.[72] This ruling effectively directed NSPI back to the drawing board. For two years, NSPI would develop its plan, holding negotiations with selected stakeholders. In January 2008, NSPI filed a new conservation and efficiency proposal to the UARB.[73] Included were expenditures for conservation and efficiency programs of up to

$2.6 million in 2008, as well as increased spending each year through 2010.[74] Under the settlement agreement that was announced in April 2008, NSPI was to "invest $12.9 million over the next two years on programs that provide assistance to specific customer groups for reducing energy consumption."[75]

Although NSPI was clearly responding to feedback, it is difficult to know whose was more decisive – that of NSPI's consultants, stakeholder meetings, or Customer Energy Forums. It is very possible that the consultant reports and stakeholder negotiations had much greater influence than the engagement with a broader customer base. What is clear is that there was an initial Customer Energy Forum in 2004 and a second in 2005, both of which yielded consistent messages concerning a strong desire for greater electricity conservation and efficiency, but that it was not until 2008 that NSPI filed a comprehensive demand-side management plan. Intervening events occurred, including an unfavourable ruling by the UARB and closed-door stakeholder meetings. Another factor may have been a slow evolution within NSPI from understanding energy efficiency as a good customer-relations strategy to viewing it as economically rational. This development may have brought about gradual change, with NSPI remaining reluctant to bringing on more energy conservation programs too quickly. Doing so may have conflicted with overriding shareholder interests. In 2009, the provincial government created Efficiency Nova Scotia, "an arm's-length non-profit corporation, to better manage the use of electricity,"[76] which served in addressing this perceived or real conflict.

It is even more difficult to discern the impact of NSPI's forums on its plans for increasing its output of electricity derived from renewable sources. When looking to the broader context, we see that policy requirement most likely played a prevailing role in NSPI's subsequent diversification. The 2000s saw a flurry of activity in Nova Scotia's energy policy. In 2001, the provincial government articulated a comprehensive energy strategy, which included the objectives of increasing electricity from renewable sources, reducing greenhouse gas emissions, and understanding the environmental impacts of energy development.[77] According to the strategy, the government would create policies to encourage renewable energy from independent power producers (IPPs).[78] The government and NSPI would also create short-term voluntary targets for IPP renewable generation totalling 2.5 per cent of NSPI's current generating capacity. Over three years, both the government and NSPI would monitor progress toward these targets and then establish a longer-term "mandatory renewable energy portfolio standard."[79] In 2007, the Government of Nova Scotia set ambitious targets "for generating more electricity from renewable sources, as well as setting the first and only hard caps on greenhouse gas emissions in North America."[80] Nova Scotia's *Renewable Energy Standard*, which came into effect in that year, states that for each of the calendar years of 2010, 2011, and 2012, NSPI, along with all other load-serving entities, must supply its "customers with renewable low-impact electricity produced by renewable low-impact electricity generation facilities operated by independent power producers in an amount equal to or greater than 5% of the total amount of electricity supplied to its customers."[81] This percentage would increase to 10 per cent for 2013, at which time NSPI would be mandated to provide electricity from its own renewable sources.[82] In April 2010, the provincial government articulated clear requirements for electricity generated from renewable sources: 25% by 2015 and 40% by 2020.[83] In October 2010, the provincial government announced amendments to the *Renewable Energy Standard* entailing more specific requirements for 2013 through 2020.[84]

NSPI has responded consistently to these requirements. In 2005, NSPI added 100 megawatts of renewable energy to the grid. In 2007, it announced that it was negotiating contracts with independent producers for 240 megawatts of renewable energy.[85] That year, NSPI would also announce that it had awarded purchase agreements to a number of wind projects for a total of 246 megawatts.[86] By 2012, NSPI was generating 18 per cent of its electricity from renewables, just shy of the provincial target of 18.5 per cent for 2013.[87] Since the renewable energy requirements came into effect, NSPI has exceeded them.

In this sense, the outputs of the forums seemed to have informed NSPI's planning. As stated by an employee of NSPI, the 2004 forum was significant "because it really set us on path with some confidence to say, 'We are going to do more renewable supply.'"[88] The 2004 poll, as well as the subsequent ones, may have provided NSPI management with the confidence to more aggressively bring on renewable energy sources. However, a number of commentators perceived the polls as having little impact on NSPI's immediate and longer-term plans for increasing its electricity supply from renewable sources.[89] According to an employee of the Nova Scotia Department of Energy, the forums were "fantastic … but NSP is putting more wind power out because it's a government requirement and the same holds for their demand-side management programs."[90] Realistically, provincial policy had much more impact on NSPI's plans for both demand-side and supply-side management.[91]

In this case, we see interesting contradictions. NSPI invested time and money into the Deliberative Polls, carefully choosing this methodology.[92] NSPI's polls achieved basic requirements of deliberative democracy, and yielded informed and reasonable opinions. Participants in these polls experienced meaningful moments of deliberation. Yet the outputs of the polls do not appear to have been directly connected to the planning and policy decisions of the utility. Were it not for the regulator and regulations in this policy area, it remains questionable whether or not NSPI would have acted on the polls. We also see ambiguities in the significance of the polls for decision-making power in this policy area. Again, NSPI elites expressed a commitment to this form of customer engagement and held three polls between 2004 and 2009. To my knowledge, no other utility in Canada has held a Deliberative Poll, let alone three. Nonetheless, NSPI management has continued to uphold status quo approaches to decision making, responding to the UARB, provincial requirements, and selected stakeholders. Despite this series of polls, there has been a continuation of elite-centred decision making in NSPI's planning.

Both deliberative and non-deliberative qualities characterized NSPI's planning processes. Potentially empowering procedures were present, but ultimately they had non-empowering implications. As in the case of the TCHC, the contextual details – those relating to participants, elite commitment, public pressure, policy requirements, economic interests, and strategic considerations – provide us with some insight into the puzzles involving both the strengths and weaknesses of NSPI's Customer Energy Forums.

With respect to the general characteristics, participants in NSPI's forums were highly motivated to address issues related to curbing carbon emissions and diversifying away from coal-fired plants. They took their participation in these polls, and their assumed role in NSPI's planning, seriously. Again, Nova Scotia is a relatively small province, and NSPI has played a direct role in providing electricity to its residents. Nova Scotians were and continue to be aware of the prospects of higher electricity rates, the need to incorporate more renewable energy sources, and the imperative to curb electricity consumption. These polls may have represented to them opportunities to contribute to determining their energy future. NSPI elites were also committed to the process of Deliberative Polling. As stated by an NSPI employee, the company "wanted to bring the voice of the customer ... in a meaningful way, where the executives would understand that society was changing and ... try to anticipate that change, incorporate it, and move with it."[93] As another employee of NSPI stated, "There was an increasing demand for energy from the public. There was an increasing demand for environmental stewardship from the public. There was increasing demand to keep costs down ... So, there was a lot of public pressure."[94] NSPI elites genuinely wanted to get a clear idea of what their customers wanted and were willing to pay.[95] But NSPI management had to make decisions that were in the interests of both its customers as well as its shareholders – interests that were potentially divergent.

Participants and elites were both committed to Deliberative Polling. But they may have been committed to differing dimensions of this kind of polling. Participants likely wanted to be involved in a collective exercise that would contribute to energy planning for their province. Elites were arguably more interested in tapping into the informed opinions of their customers. This elite commitment may have stemmed from a particular context, in which economic and strategic considerations were salient against a backdrop of strict policy and regulatory requirements.

Indeed, plans for both conservation and renewables will be very expensive for NSPI in the short term. Increasing its portfolio of renewable energy sources, in particular, will be both complicated and costly in terms of capital expenditures. Similarly to the move from oil to coal in the 1980s, the current diversification is requiring enormous resources. Tidal and wind sources of energy, both being developed by NSPI, will require further investment in research and development as well as in generation, transmission, and distribution infrastructure. Virtually every major actor in this policy area in Nova Scotia is aware of the economic, social, and political challenges facing NSPI in diversifying its electricity supply, including the huge costs of upgrading the generation and transmission systems and shutting down existing coal-fired plants.[96] As an NSPI employee put it, this is "probably the biggest challenge that this organization will ever have."[97] As Brendan Haley (formerly of the Ecology Action Centre) states regarding the transition toward aggressive levels of renewable energy, well above the wind targets currently in place:

NSPI's system is not set up to complement renewables. The problem is with the load capabilities of the transmission grid ... We can do renewables only to a certain point, because we can fire up and down our hydro or we can fire up and down our natural gas, depending on how the wind is blowing at a certain time of day. But we can't fire up and down coal like that. So, if we bring on more renewables, then we're going to be in trouble with our transmission system ... And that is really the issue: are we willing to pay the extra costs of upgrading the system, building transmission lines, or building natural gas plants, or connecting hydro outside of the jurisdiction, or doing energy storing technologies.[98]

This challenge likely motivated NSPI management to conduct its polls in an attempt not only to sample but also to inform a selection of Nova Scotians on possible responses.[99] Given the relationship between diversifying the energy portfolio and what are, at least upfront, enormous capital expenditures that would translate into higher energy costs, NSPI elites may have wanted both to probe informed public opinion and to disseminate information concerning these trade-offs. NSPI has encountered much public contention regarding their rate increases. Deliberative Polls, with their success in energy policy in the United States, may have been seen as a useful mechanism through which NSPI could inform a representative sample of its customer base about the difficulties of diversification and thus mitigate some of the potential pushback. As an employee of the Nova Scotia Department of Energy put it, the "stakeholders have very definitive needs and desires. They tend to be experts in their fields ... What we struggle with in government is that we deal with these issues every day and forget that the general public doesn't. Educating a sample of people before asking them these very important and inclusive questions is fantastic way to develop policy."[100] In the words of one NSPI employee, the "whole idea behind Deliberative Polling is to ask your customers, 'What should we do?' ... You get a much clearer and better answer if you first educate and inform your participants."[101]

Perhaps cynically, the polls may have also been an endeavour to improve public relations.[102] As a privatized corporation, with what is essentially a monopoly in the generation and transmission of electricity in Nova Scotia, NSPI is often viewed with suspicion by its customers.[103] As a commentator on energy issues in Nova Scotia expressed, "There's an understanding that [NSPI] is a bad company and no good for the environment ... People don't understand how expensive and hard it is to be good to the environment."[104] Accordingly, he claimed, one reason for NSPI's polls was to "lay out all the issues for people," to inform them of the difficulties that the corporation faces, and to "show people how hard it is to be environmentally conscious and to diversify away from coal."[105] An overarching objective may have been to bolster the image of the utility in what were and continue to be challenging times. While not directly contributing to its planning, NSPI's polls served certain pragmatic purposes. While participants in them were very minor players in NSPI's planning, the polls may have played an important PR role in enabling the utility to meet provincial requirements.

The context in which NSPI implemented Deliberative Polling gives rise to multiple paradoxes. On the one hand, the polls appear to be a serious effort to realize certain aspects of deliberative democracy. On the other, they had little, if any, impact on decisions, which is an important end of deliberative democracy. Deliberative Polling, even on an advisory basis, can enable members of affected publics to have direct input into the decisions that affect them. It can serve in providing a more open and inclusive approach to rendering such decisions, and can shift decision making away from the exclusive domain of traditional policy elites. However, certain aspects of their procedural design may make such forums less conducive to deliberation and more conducive to polling. The procedural design of these forums can facilitate quality collective deliberation, but it can also prioritize the polling of individuals. These forums can facilitate informed perspectives, but they can also be reduced to a tool for measuring willingness to pay. In addition, as we've seen in this case, they can serve an important educative function. They can be used, when well publicized and broadcasted, as a conduit for delivering important information and encouraging individual and collective reflection on this information. But they can also be employed to sway affected publics favourably toward policy changes, the decisions for which have already been taken. Which aspect of Deliberative Polling prevails depends in large part on the broader policy context.

This case raises interesting questions concerning the legitimacy of the outputs of these kinds of forums vis-à-vis those of more traditional legislative processes. The outputs of NSPI's forums were superseded by provincial policy, but they were generally consistent with the values embodied in that policy. Had they been at odds, which should have prevailed? The response is not obvious given the statistical representativeness of these forums and their expression of informed opinions of a sample of citizens. In terms of the representation of interests in decisions and the soundness of those decisions, it's not obvious that policy formulated largely by selected stakeholders and bureaucratic officials should dominate. Deliberative Polls can reinforce the legitimacy of existing policies but, importantly, they can and perhaps should challenge them. Despite their potential, however, insofar as they remain external to decision-making processes, these forums will likely have limited influence on public policy. They are likely to remain hemmed in by traditional policy actors, procedures, and institutions.

With respect to energy policy in Nova Scotia and NSPI's hand in developing and implementing that policy, we see that Deliberative Polling was a refined tool for tapping into the considered opinions of consumers concerning more environmental but also more expensive energy options. In this context, it was a mechanism for gauging what consumers want and how much they would pay for it on reflection. There is nothing inherently wrong with using such a mechanism in policy processes. Polling is an appropriate tool in policy development. To the extent that Fishkin's polling yields informed opinions, it may be a very desirable tool. It becomes problematic, however, if it is used as a public relations instrument that is presented as an important way of reaching out to, engaging with, and taking seriously an affected public, but that results in little policy guidance let alone policy impact. In this case, it was not used to transform the relationship between citizens and NSPI. Instead, Deliberative Polling was an exercise in deliberative democracy but was not geared toward realizing the aims of deliberative democracy.

Since its inception close to twenty-five years ago, Deliberative Polling has spread across the globe and into many areas of public policy. From studying other cases, we can derive important insights into how and toward what ends it has been implemented. I close this chapter with some brief insights from Japan, as it continues to recover from the 2011 tsunami off the coast of Fukushima and the meltdown of reactors at the Daiichi Nuclear Power Plant. That country's recent experience with Deliberative Polling in the area of energy policy and the role of nuclear generation suggests further limitations of these procedures and asserts the importance of a broader deliberative context. In the summer of 2012, the Japanese government held a Deliberative Poll on the country's energy options for the future. The event involved approximately 300 participants from a larger sample of roughly 6800 respondents to the telephone survey conducted in advance. The results of the poll were expected to inform the development of Japan's energy policy by the government.[106] In an editorial, the *Asahi Shimbun* expressed scepticism and argued that this kind of polling is but a single part of what should be a larger system of public deliberation. Ideally, this system would be tied directly to processes of policy formulation and implementation. According to the newspaper, "Gauging the trend of public opinion should not be the only purpose of having a popular discussion forum of this nature. It is just as important to create a system that makes people feel they are part of the nation's policymaking process."[107]

Chapter Four

National Consultations and the Nuclear Waste Management Organization[1]

The Nuclear Waste Management Organization (NWMO) was established in 2002 by Canada's three nuclear energy corporations (i.e., Ontario Power Generation [OPG], Hydro-Québec [H-Q], and New Brunswick Power[2] [NBP]) and Atomic Energy of Canada Limited (AECL) as a private, not-for-profit entity regulated by the federal government. As directed by the Nuclear Fuel Waste Act, the NWMO became responsible for studying waste management options for Canada's growing stockpile of irradiated nuclear fuel bundles (including on-site storage, centralized storage, and deep geological disposal), proposing to the federal government its preferred option, and implementing the option chosen by government. Soon after its establishment, the NWMO launched what would become a three-year, $24 million, national consultation process to assess management and disposal options for used nuclear fuel bundles (often referred to as either high-level radioactive waste or, simply, nuclear waste) from Canada's nuclear energy reactors.[3] The expressed aim of this process was to develop collaboratively with Canadians an option that would be "socially acceptable, technically sound, environmentally responsible, and economically feasible."[4] Designed, funded, and overseen by the NWMO, the process included more than 150 information, consultation, and participatory events organized over four phases. During each phase, NWMO management and staff focused these events, which they characterized as dialogues, on a key decision related to the long-term waste management and disposal of Canada's nuclear waste. At the end of each phase, the NWMO publicly released a discussion document encapsulating the overall results of the dialogues. The document was then the focus of the next phase of dialogues, which sought validation of the previous decision and direction on the subsequent decision. In 2005, at the end of the fourth phase of the study, the NWMO released its final report and recommendations.

Prima facie, this process was impressive in the number of participants and events, the length of time over which it took place, its iterative-phased and multi-event design, procedural fairness, and access to information. The outputs of the NWMO's process included wide agreement among participants that the waste management and disposal options needed to be technically sound, socially acceptable, and environmentally responsible and that opportunities had to be created for Canadians to participate in the selection and implementation of the preferred option. However, it also highlighted historical divisions among participants about the place of nuclear energy within Canada's energy policy. Participants consistently articulated a deep concern about the need for a broad public discussion and deliberation on the place of nuclear energy in Canada's electricity generating portfolio – a concern that was acknowledged in the NWMO's final report but not explicitly incorporated into its recommendations. Although a discussion of energy policy was beyond the official remit of the NWMO's consultation process, given the relationship between the continued use of nuclear energy and Canada's growing inventory of nuclear waste, the NWMO could have incorporated these concerns into its recommendation.

The NWMO's recommendation for "adaptive phased management," which was accepted in 2007 by the federal government, comprises onsite storage, centralized storage, and deep geological disposal. It is to be implemented over a protracted time frame and includes an incremental decision-making process, ongoing oversight and monitoring, and waste retrievability. The approach is intended to be somewhat flexible with respect to both social and political decisions as well as technical developments. Generally, the consultation process yielded support for the recommendation.[5] There were, however, important dissenters, such as participants in a roundtable organized by the Trudeau Foundation and the Sierra Club of Canada and members of the United Church of Canada.[6] Aboriginal organizations also expressed concern with the recommendation.[7] It thus seems that the input of important policy actors, such as members of civil society organizations and Aboriginal nations with specific perspectives and interests at stake, was limited in the NWMO's recommendation. As the NWMO moves into developing policy to implement adaptive phased management, its decision-making processes may ultimately revert to a more explicitly elitist model. While involving a collaborative process of developing an approach to site selection,[8] while seeking to find a site in an informed, willing host community, while articulating expectations and requirements about what it means to be "willing and informed," and while holding regional information sessions[9] and "open houses" in prospective host communities,[10] the model may result in prioritizing the insights of officials within the NWMO and of local politicians and civil servants.

This story plays out as a process that was presented as a sustained dialogue among NWMO elites, stakeholder groups, and members of the Canadian public, but that was in fact circumscribed by the federal government and directly mediated by the NWMO. Despite this process containing multiple procedures that were clearly deliberative, the NWMO's ultimate recommendation was made in non-deliberative ways. In other words, it was made by elites who appear to have prioritized their interests in pursuing deep geological disposal, couched in terms of adaptive phased management, over those of certain participants and stakeholders in their national consultation process. The process may have been an endeavour to secure a veneer of public acceptance of the NWMO's predetermined preference for the long-term management and disposal of nuclear waste. As opposed to transforming the relationship between the nuclear energy industry and the broader Canadian public, as the national consultation process seemed initially to promise, the outcomes of this process may have served merely to uphold the priorities of industry elites.

Adaptive phased management will involve siting and building a centralized nuclear waste management facility, transporting the waste to and depositing it in the facility, and eventually decommissioning the facility. Designed to occur over the course of more than a century, adaptive phased management will have as its endpoint "a repository deep underground in a suitable rock formation"[11] – a repository that, it is worth noting, is in significant ways indistinguishable from conceptual plans for deep geological disposal developed by AECL in the 1980s. The repository will be continuously monitored and have features allowing for waste retrieval. The NWMO claims that the plan is intended to facilitate adaptations based on the democratic inputs of affected communities and developments in technological knowledge among networks of scientists and engineers. But, as the organization moves ahead in its process to find a suitable site for the facility, there may be a narrowing of discussions to those between NWMO elites and community officials of prospective host communities. While there is language of collaboration with members of the public toward establishing informed willingness to host the facility,[12] and language of the adaptability of the waste management and disposal plan, there may be a reversion to elite negotiations concerning a determined endpoint, although it is too early to tell definitively. What we can tell is that there is an increasingly pronounced acknowledgment by the NWMO that new nuclear generators are likely to be built, but no corresponding call for a public dialogue on nuclear energy.

Once again, we see two sides of a deliberative democratic process – one side represents an appearance of deliberative democratic practices; the other represents the reality of the ways in which these practices occur and the ends toward which they are geared. Throughout the NWMO's consultation process, it consistently used the language of "developing plans, policies and processes collaboratively with Canadians,"[13] and its consultative and participatory dialogues appeared to serve these aims. However, the process was very much NWMO-driven and its outputs were ultimately NWMO-controlled. An industry-elite approach has always dominated this policy area. From this angle, it is not surprising that the NWMO's consultation process did little to shift decision making concerning the long-term management and disposal of Canada's nuclear waste and little to transform power relations between elites and the public. Before turning to a discussion of the consultation process and its implications, I present an outline of nuclear waste management policy in Canada.

Canadian Nuclear Waste Management Policy

Canada generates about 15 per cent of its electricity from nuclear reactors.[14] It has a total of twenty-two nuclear power reactors, the vast majority of which are located in Ontario and produce almost 50 per cent of the province's electricity. New Brunswick operates one reactor. Quebec operated one reactor, but permanently shut it down in December 2012. In 2005, at the end of the NWMO's national consultation process, the total stockpile of used fuel bundles in Canada was approximately two million. According to the NWMO, "We expect to have about 3.7 million bundles if each of the electricity generating nuclear reactors has an average operating life of 40 years."[15]

Canadian nuclear waste management policy has its origins in the mid-1960s. Those involved in decisions concerning the development and implementation of this policy were elite officials, scientists, and engineers in the federal Department of Energy, Mines, and Resources (EMR) (now Natural Resources Canada [NRCan]), AECL, the Atomic Energy Control Board (AECB) (now the Canadian Nuclear Safety Commission [CNSC]), and nuclear energy corporations. Since the early 1970s, these elites have identified deep geological disposal as their preference for Canada's nuclear waste. In 1972, a committee made up of officials from AECL, Ontario Hydro (OPG's predecessor), and H-Q concluded that disposal of Canada's nuclear waste was "most promising" in "geological media."[16] In 1974, discussions between EMR and AECL led to research focused on "plutonic rock in the Ontario portion of the Canadian Shield."[17] The authors of a 1977 report for EMR, having surveyed various management and disposal options, including launching the waste into outer space, recommended burying it in the Canadian Shield.[18] The following year, the Governments of Canada and Ontario accepted this recommendation and established the Canadian Nuclear Fuel Waste Management Program.[19] This program directed AECL, with the assistance of Ontario Hydro, to develop non-site-specific, conceptual plans for deep geological disposal in the Canadian Shield.[20] According to plans that emerged in the late 1980s, waste from CANDU reactors or solidified high-level wastes from reprocessing would be sealed in containers designed to last at least five hundred years.[21] These containers would be placed in rooms in a disposal vault or in boreholes drilled in the rooms, which themselves would be 500 to 1000 metres below the surface.[22] Each container of waste would be surrounded by a buffer, and each room would be sealed with backfill. The vault would also be sealed. All tunnels, shafts, and exploration boreholes would ultimately be sealed so that the disposal facility would not depend on institutional controls.

In the fall of 1989, the federal minister of the environment appointed Blair Seaborn as chair of a panel to examine AECL and Ontario Hydro's concept of deep geological disposal under the auspices of the federal Environmental Assessment and Review Process (later subsumed by the Canadian Environmental Assessment Agency [CEAA]). The terms of reference directed the panel to examine the social, economic, and environmental implications of the proposed concept.[23] In the 1990s, the panel held public hearings across the country that focused on societal issues and safety concerns associated with the concept. In 1998, the panel released a carefully worded report seeking to capture the competing views articulated during the hearings. In this report, the panel concluded that, from a technical perspective, the safety of the AECL concept had been demonstrated for its stage of development, "but from a social perspective," it had not.[24] It also concluded that the concept did not have the broad public support or acceptability required for the development of a nuclear waste management facility in Canada.[25] The panel recommended that the federal government establish a nuclear waste management agency at "arm's length" from the utilities and AECL to run a comprehensive public participation process for assessing a wider range of nuclear waste management options.[26] The panel called for "broad Canadian public participation," an "on-going and interactive process between citizens and the [organization]," and a "two-way system" of information and communication between the public and the waste management agency.[27]

The federal government's 1998 official response to the Seaborn panel was not nearly as nuanced. It noted that AECL's concept had been deemed to be safe from a technical perspective,[28] but made no mention that it had not been deemed safe from a social perspective. The response also directed OPG, H-Q, NBP, and AECL to establish a nuclear waste management organization and to appoint its staff, board of directors, and advisory council. This response provided the foundations for Canada's Nuclear Fuel Waste Act, which came into force four years later.[29] The act mandated policy and oversight roles for the federal government, and operations and financial roles for the nuclear energy corporations and AECL. Essentially, the nuclear energy industry became responsible for establishing the NWMO. In turn, the NWMO became responsible for studying technical waste management options, proposing to the federal government its preferred option, and implementing the option chosen by parliament. The NWMO would report to a board and obtain advice from a council, but members of the industry would appoint both of these bodies. Although the strong language of an independent agency and public participation was lost in it, the act did require the NWMO to hold national consultations.

NWMO's National Consultation Process

In 2002, the NWMO launched its national consultation process toward the end of identifying a safe and acceptable waste management option. Over the course of the next three years, the NWMO would examine a total of four options: (1) The concept for deep geological disposal in the Canadian Shield; (2) above-ground storage at nuclear reactor sites; (3) above- or below-ground storage at a centralized facility; and

(4) adaptive phased management. According to the NWMO, the process was designed to incorporate the values, interests, and principles held by Canadians into the decision making of the organization.[30] In this sense, it appeared to represent a distinctive turn in policy formulation away from a closed-door, elite-centred process and toward a more open, inclusive, and participatory process.

The NWMO designed the three-year process over four phases, during each of which it focused on a key decision. The NWMO hired "third parties," that is, think tanks, civil-society organizations, and consulting firms specializing in public consultations and participatory approaches to decision making. While the NWMO achieved some independence from its consultation process through these organizations and firms, and while these third parties sought to uphold deliberative democratic principles, the NWMO nonetheless maintained control. The NWMO was ultimately responsible for framing, organizing, and funding the process, establishing and phrasing the general consultation questions, interpreting the results of each consultation event, and formulating a policy recommendation to the federal government. After each consultation event, the third party would report its findings to the NWMO. NWMO management and staff would sift through, organize, and analyse all these materials. The NWMO would then publicly release a discussion document encapsulating its interpretation of the over-all results of the phase. This document would summarize the decision and outline its rationale. The document would then be the focus for the following phase. Throughout the entire process, the NWMO's website was updated to include not only all the background papers, reports, and discussion documents but also public submissions.

From one vantage point, the NWMO's national consultation process appears to have been based on principles of deliberative democracy – principles of inclusion, equality, reasoning, and general agreement or shared interest. The NWMO began its consultation process with the ostensible recognition that all Canadian citizens could be affected by this policy and thus have a certain claim to participate in its development.[31] The process incorporated a range of events and forums in an attempt to include a wide spectrum of participants. For example, the NWMO commissioned the Canadian Policy Research Networks (CPRN) to facilitate exchanges among a statistically representative sample of the Canadian electorate.[32] Taking place across the country, these events brought together more than 450 individuals with views on nuclear energy generally consistent with those of the broader population.

The NWMO also commissioned stakeholder forums to incorporate more defined views and specific interests. The NWMO hired DPRA Canada, for instance, to run a national stakeholder dialogue. Seeking to ensure that this group of participants was inclusive of the array of interests at stake, DPRA chose participants from a comprehensive set of categories (such as local/municipal governments, educational/ academic actors, cultural/faith-based organizations, labour unions, industry/economic associations, consumer adovcates, environmental groups, healthcare workers, and young people).[33] A year later, Hardy Stevenson reconvened many of these stakeholders.[34] Where they were unable to include the same participants, they employed DPRA's template to ensure the inclusion of relevant interests. In the summer of 2005, Stratos brought together a number of these same stakeholders, as well as other participants in the consultation process, for dialogues on the NWMO's draft report.[35] All these forums were premised on principles of respect for the equality of participants and their points of view. Facilitators sought to ensure that participants had an equal voice in deliberations and equal access to information.

The NWMO also organized round-table discussions to solicit input from different epistemological perspectives. In September 2003, it appointed an ethics round table including individuals from a diverse range of professional and academic backgrounds.[36] The round table included not only academics in the disciplines of philosophy, medicine, business, and political science, but also public figures with perspectives informed by Aboriginal traditional knowledge and Christianity. The NWMO also commissioned a workshop with experts in the technical aspects of nuclear waste management,[37] another with experts from business, industry, non-governmental organizations, and the public sector,[38] and another with Aboriginal people, nuclear workers, environmentalists, academics, and members of religious organizations.[39] The NWMO also sought input from Aboriginal organizations. Given its fiduciary responsibilities, NRCan entered into an agreement with national Aboriginal organizations to carry out dialogues.[40] The NWMO then made specific arrangements with the Assembly of First Nations, the Congress of Aboriginal Peoples, the Inuit Tapirrit Kanatami, the Métis National Council, the Native Women's Association of Canada, and the Pauktuutit Inuit Women's Association.[41] The objectives of these dialogues were to build more effective working relationships and to improve the capacity of Aboriginal peoples to participate more effectively in nuclear waste management policy. Other objectives were to understand Aboriginal perspectives on the technical options and to include Aboriginal ideas, insights, wisdom, and values in the NWMO's final recommendation to government.

Aside from forums with invited participants, the NWMO commissioned DPRA to organize public information sessions. The NWMO, with DPRA, held more than 120 public information and discussion session in over 30 locations across Canada.[42] These sessions were widely advertised in local papers and on local radio. Mayors, provincial MPPs/MLAs, and federal MPs were contacted to encourage greater attendance among their constituents. These sessions served an educative function, providing opportunities for the public to learn about the NWMO's work. Each session was followed by a facilitated discussion.

Taking all these forums into account, many participants and observers felt that the NWMO's process was inclusive of actors, interests, and perspectives.[43] From a different vantage point, however, many felt that it was not inclusive enough. For example, a nuclear industry spokesperson felt that, because many of the dialogues were by invitation, they excluded certain individuals and organizations from participating.[44] This position was echoed by non-governmental organizations[45] and by independent observers.[46] The most serious challenge to its inclusiveness was the narrow focus of the process. Mary Lou Harley, who was participating on behalf of the United Church of Canada in this process, claimed that topics concerning the impacts of different possibilities for the future of nuclear energy were excluded "despite the fact that they were repeatedly introduced by different participants at different exercises."[47] These topics were excluded despite their importance for determining the acceptability of a waste management option. Participants in and commentators on the consultation process raised this concern consistently.

We also see dualistic characteristics in the NWMO's attempts to achieve equality in procedures and equal access to information. Many dialogues were premised on principles of respect for the equality of participants and their points of view.[48] Participants had access to a wealth of information, including more than sixty peer-reviewed papers from a variety of disciplines, methodologies, and ideologies.[49] Where they could not access the NWMO's website, they could request hard copies from the organization. Efforts were also made to bring in independent specialists to provide overviews of the technical, social, and ethical issues characterizing nuclear waste management. The CPRN reported that 91 per cent of their participants agreed that there was sufficient opportunity to contribute and participate.[50] Harley, who participated in a number of dialogues, stated that "good facilitators countered the problem [of inequalities among participants] by making a point of valuing the input of each person ...; they made an effort to draw back into discussion anyone who seemed intimidated and together they generally kept the discussion moving over the bumps."[51] Dave Hardy, principal at Hardy Stevenson and Associates, also spoke of the efforts of facilitators to ensure that participants had an equal voice.[52]

However, there is evidence that participants' perspectives were not weighted equally. There were many accounts of how views were dismissed and excluded from the NWMO's assessment framework and recommendation.[53] Aboriginal nations took serious issue with the lack of equality. Although the national and regional Aboriginal organizations designed, organized, and ran their own dialogues, they expressly noted that these dialogues did not constitute formal Aboriginal consultations.[54] Aboriginal nations were not provided with sufficient time and funding to participate on an equal footing with the NWMO. Aboriginal participants also noted that the information on the website was inaccessible logistically and linguistically.[55] From this perspective, the NWMO's process did not treat Aboriginals as equal participants.[56]

Access to information also varied. For example, 85 per cent of CPRN's participants agreed that its workbook was clear and contained relevant and useful information.[57] Yet, only 51 per cent felt that the information package sent in advance was helpful.[58] Hardy stated that participants in his dialogues had well-balanced information and had access to the NWMO's website.[59] Thomas Berger, who was asked by the NWMO to comment on the consultation process, also claimed that the materials were generally well balanced.[60] A member of the NWMO's advisory council also commented on the quality of the materials.[61] Nonetheless, there were notable criticisms. Harley noted that "at most dialogues, the presentation of the hazards of waste was minimal and sometimes misrepresented."[62] According to Anna Stanley, Richard Kuhn, and Brenda Murphy, the NWMO in their information presentations, discussion documents, and official reports minimized hazards associated with nuclear waste, its transportation, management, and disposal.[63]

Findings of deliberative reasoning in the NWMO's forums were also mixed. Many were explicitly premised on principles of meaningful dialogue, all speaking to a certain ideal of reasoning.[64] For example, the CPRN designed its forums to enable participants to work through initial opinions and to reach broader and deeper understandings of nuclear waste management approaches.[65] The initial stage of each forum involved participants completing a questionnaire to rate their level of agreement with waste management scenarios. Upon reviewing with the facilitators the procedural rules of the forum, which they were clear to point out were not to be understood as rules of debate, participants broke out into smaller groups. In these groups, participants deliberated among themselves on the characteristics that they would most want to see in a waste management approach. Participants then reconvened in plenary session, where each group reported on the results of its discussion. The same process was initiated again, with small groups deliberating on the tradeoffs that they would be prepared to make in the implementation of their desired approach. The plenary reconvened to identify overarching commonalities and divergences. At the end of the day, participants were asked to rate their level of agreement with the vision they had collectively developed. Other forums were not as successful with this kind of collective reasoning. There were many accounts that participants maintained their historically entrenched positions and launched boisterous attacks on opposing positions. As Hardy notes, participants often walked away with their fundamental positions unchanged.[66]

A number of the NWMO's forums yielded significant common ground. For example, there was general agreement among participants in a workshop on the technical aspects of nuclear fuel waste management. Participants shared the view that on-site storage for the next fifty years was inevitable, even if the government opted for centralized permanent disposal.[67] They also shared the opinion that storage and disposal were not necessarily distinct, but rather stages of an approach to permanent disposal allowing for flexibility and retrievability.[68] There was also significant convergence among participants in the CPRN's dialogues.[69] Participants in these forums concurred that safety for both existing and future generations was paramount, and that it was the responsibility of existing generations to ensure safety be attained. In addition, they agreed on the merits of an adaptable and flexible management approach incorporating new knowledge and technologies. Furthermore, participants concurred on the need for accountability and transparency, and called for "real engagement of experts, citizens, communities, and other stakeholders before any decision is made" concerning a waste management option.[70] In a post-dialogue questionnaire, 77 per cent of participants supported a waste management scenario incorporating these concerns.[71] Agreement also emerged from the national and regional stakeholders dialogues. Stakeholders in DPRA Canada's dialogue coalesced on the view that used nuclear fuel was a significant risk to human health and the environment and that it needed to be safely managed for a long time.[72] They also voiced a common theme concerning the importance of a "neutral third party to oversee the development and implementation of the management approach."[73] They generally agreed, moreover, that the waste management option must be socially acceptable and that there should be opportunities for interested Canadian to be involved in the process of selecting and implementing this option.[74] However, these dialogues also highlighted long-standing divisions among stakeholders about the place of nuclear energy within Canada's energy policy.[75] Many participants argued that the waste from existing reactors should define the extent of the management problem. Others contended that there should be planning for a higher inventory of waste. The former position called for the end of nuclear generation, while the latter was more favourable to it. As expressed by DPRA, "On this point, there was no agreement among participants and two strong opposing views were expressed."[76]

In 2005, the NWMO released its draft study report and, after additional consultation, its final study report. The reports recommended adaptive phased management, characterizing this approach as an amalgam of on-site storage, centralized storage, and deep geological containment implemented over a protracted time frame. In principle, this approach incorporates a step-by-step decision-making process, ongoing monitoring, and retrievability.[77] According to the NWMO, the key attributes of this system include adaptive decision making, optional shallow storage at the central site, continuous monitoring, provisions for retrievability, and "citizen engagement."[78] The ultimate aim of adaptive phased management is "centralized containment and isolation of used nuclear fuel in an appropriate geological formation."[79] Generally, many observers expressed support for the recommendation, claiming that the organization captured and addressed primary concerns articulated by participants.[80] According to Stratos, a "large majority" of participants in its stakeholder round tables expressed "comfort with the recommendation."[81] Participants were "nearly universal" in backing continuous monitoring over extended periods of time.[82] There was also wide participant support for sustained citizen engagement, public education, and community decision making.[83] Moreover, there was wide support for the NWMO's recommendation that a deep geological repository be "sited only in a willing host community."[84]

There was, however, very strong criticism of both the recommendation for adaptive phased management and the process by which it developed this recommendation. With respect to the process, Stanley, Kuhn, and Murphy claim that the NWMO was unjustifiably selective in its incorporation of "the vast amount of material they collected" over the consultation process, not shedding light on the criteria or methodology used to filter that material.[85] Aboriginal nations and organizations were also very critical. As a staff member of the Assembly of First Nations stated, the NWMO drew from its dialogues with Aboriginal peoples only what supported its recommendation.[86] The Congress of Aboriginal Peoples noted that the "Aboriginal concerns, priorities, and values" embodied in the recommendation were merely the interpretations of the NWMO and did not represent their views.[87] Members of Inuit, Metis, and First Nations organizations felt that they did not participate in real consultation, that their Aboriginal and treaty rights were not upheld, and that their cultures and languages were not respected in either the NWMO's process or its recommendation.[88]

Others participants also voiced criticism of the NWMO's recommendation for adaptive phased management. According to Dave Martin of Greenpeace and Brennain Lloyd of Nuclear Waste Watch, this approach was "the worst of all worlds," effectively giving a green light to continued on-site storage, transportation to and storage at an above-ground site, and deep geological disposal.[89] Most participants in a round table organized by the Trudeau Foundation and the Sierra Club of Canada expressed a lack of support for the recommendation for similar reasons.[90] The United Church of Canada also raised a number of concerns.[91] Many of these more critical actors argued for continued on-site storage pending a public discussion, deliberation, and debate on the role of nuclear energy. For these individuals, nuclear energy generation is associated with risks of too high a magnitude. A nuclear waste management and disposal plan could serve in justifying the perpetuation of this very risky form of generation. From this perspective, not only addressing the problem of a safe and acceptable plan but also discussing the phasing out of nuclear energy were critically important. For many participants in the process, important concerns related to identifying a limit on the waste to be managed and disposed and to having a wider public discussion on the status of nuclear energy in Canadian energy policy were not incorporated into the NWMO's reports and, crucially, into its final report. To its credit, the NWMO acknowledged some of these concerns in its final report.[92] In this report, it stated that concerns about nuclear energy be "the subject of their own assessment and public process."[93] To date, the NWMO has made no further mention of the importance of a public discussion on this topic in its annual reports, although the organization has noted that this is still contentious.[94] The NWMO has also acknowledged the likelihood of additional nuclear reactors.[95]

In addition, critics argued that the NWMO's adaptive phased management approach did not differ substantively from AECL's concept for deep geological disposal.[96] Although the NWMO sought to distinguish its adaptive phased management from this concept, the two approaches are fundamentally similar. Both have deep geological burial in stable rock formations, on environmentally sound and economically feasible terms, as their endpoint. Both have options for the retrievability of the nuclear waste. Both are similar in their phased approach. Indeed, adaptive phased management could be understood as deep geological disposal mapped out on a realistic timeline. If the latter were to be implemented, taking into consideration technical, logistical, and political constraints, its plan would likely look very similar to the former. Finding a centralized and permanent site for the deep geological burial of Canada's high-level radioactive waste, constructing this facility, having it licensed, and transporting waste to it would not only require a phased approach but also extensive consultations and negotiations among the NWMO, regulators, and affected communities.

This line of critique raises serious questions with respect to the adaptability of the NWMO's plan. NWMO's final report of 2005 states that adaptive phased management allows for "sequential decision making on whether, when, and how fast used nuclear fuel is moved to a final disposition."[97] But, in a table entitled "Engagement as an Input to Decision-Making," it states that once a site has been chosen, a decision will be made on "whether or not to construct central shallow underground storage," "when to begin transportation of used fuel from the reactor sites to the central site," "when to construct the deep geological repository," and "when to close the deep repository."[98] Decision points all appear to move toward deep geological disposal. All except one is a question not of "whether" but of "when" to move toward deep geological disposal. The only "whether" question concerns interim centralized storage, which could itself be understood as a "when" question. If the host community opts for centralized storage, it will effectively delay deep geological containment. If it does not, it expedites the progression toward the deep repository. According to the NWMO's annual general report of 2011, the ninth and final step in the process for finding a suitable site is the "construction and operation of the deep geological repository and associated facilities."[99] Accordingly, "Operation will begin after an operating license is obtained from regulatory authorities," and the "NWMO will continue to work in partnership with the host community in order to ensure the commitments to the community are addressed throughout the entire lifetime of the project."[100] The language of this report is more definitive than adaptive.

Having its recommendations for adaptive phased management accepted in 2007, the NWMO spent two years developing a process for selecting a site appropriate for a nuclear waste management facility.[101] According to the NWMO, this process was developed with the collaboration of a "broad cross-section of Canadians" from 2008 through 2010.[102] In the words of the NWMO, the "site selection process was designed to reflect the ideas, experience, and best advice of those who participated in dialogues and who shared their thoughts on what an open, transparent, fair, and inclusive process for making this decision would include."[103] As of the time of writing, the jurisdictions of Arran-Elderslie (ON), Blind River (ON), Brockton (ON), Creighton (SK), Ear Falls (ON), Elliot Lake (ON), English River First Nation (SK), Hornepayne (ON), Huron-Kinloss (ON), Ignace (ON), the North Shore (ON), Pinehouse (SK), Saugeen Shores (ON), Schreiber (ON), South Bruce (ON), Spanish (ON), and Wawa (ON) had participated in this siting process and formally requested a feasibility study.[104]

Although described as open, inclusive, and adaptive, the siting process is characterized by a shift away from consultations with Canadians generally and toward negotiations with specific communities. Perhaps of greater concern is the way in which the NWMO's process has moved from an emphasis on engagement with and consultation of Canadians to negotiations between NWMO elites and authorities in prospective host communities. In fairness, it must be pointed out that the NWMO has held community information sessions and open houses, and it has been clear that a host community has to demonstrate informed willingness. Moreover, the NWMO has articulated basic criteria to demonstrate this willingness. In its words:

In order to ensure that the project is implemented in partnership with the community, and before the regulatory approvals process initiated, the NWMO will require a formal expression of willingness from the community ... This is expected to include a formal expression of interest from an accountable decision-making body, supported by a compelling demonstration of willingness among those living in the local area. The NWMO will encourage any community interested in hosting this project to engage citizens in assessing interest in the project at multiple points [and ensure] the involvement of a broad cross-section of citizens. Resources will be provided by the NWMO for this purpose.[105]

But, in a list of "key activities" in the siting process, the NWMO refers to the engagement of citizens only once.[106] Moreover, it is vague in its reference to this kind of engagement. Conversely, engagement with "accountable authorities" is referenced ten times.[107] There have been numerous media reports out of these communities that, while interest in hosting a nuclear waste facility may have originated with local politicians and while municipal councils have formally invited the NWMO to conduct initial studies, there is much division regarding the possibility of hosting a deep nuclear facility.[108] There has been concern about the "secrecy" under which negotiations between NWMO elite and local politicians have taken place,[109] and there have been local protests.[110] In the years between the NWMO's national consultation and the development of its siting process, there appears to have been a narrowing of its engagement activities that purportedly feed into its decision making.

The NWMO's national consultation process went an impressive way toward meeting basic elements of deliberative democracy. While not completely fulfilling those requirements, the process was impressive. It appeared to represent a movement away from the status quo approach to developing nuclear waste management policy in Canada. It was more open, transparent, and democratic than any other process in this policy area.

Yet the outputs of the process appear to have had limited substantive impact on the organization's recommendation to the federal government and, ultimately, on the ensuing policy. The organization's recommendation and the government's acceptance of it were partially at odds with the process's outputs. Again, many involved in this process expressed an imperative for a national dialogue on the status of nuclear energy in Canada *before* forging ahead with long-term plans for the management and disposal of nuclear waste. Many expressed concern that adaptive phased management did not differ substantially from earlier articulations of deep geological disposal and believed that the uncertainty and risks associated with this approach were too great. These positions were not incorporated into the NWMO's recommendation despite its proclamations concerning the merits of its national consultation process. From this angle, the process may have served only to garner a veneer of public acceptance for a predetermined plan while silencing critics. Although the NWMO spent millions of dollars, and employed a wealth of expertise, this process may ultimately have little impact on the historically dominant approach to decision making in this area. Whether or not there is a shift in power relations depends in large part on how the site-selection process is implemented over the course of the next few years.

Filtering Outputs and Diminishing Outcomes

An assessment of the NWMO's national consultation process in terms of principles of deliberative democracy is mixed. It was procedurally inclusive, but certain views were excluded from the NWMO's recommendation to the federal government. It was based on certain principles of procedural equality, but key perspectives were not equally considered by the NWMO or incorporated into its recommendation. The NWMO made publicly available a wealth of balanced and pertinent information but it could have been more explicit in explaining the rationale for its decisions, including to not recommend a national dialogue on nuclear energy in Canada's energy policy. When one considers the history of decision making in the policy area of nuclear waste management, this process seemed to represent an important democratic shift. The process appeared to have been a much more open, inclusive, and democratically empowering approach to policy development than had ever been seen. Yet the NWMO's process was seriously limited. Although it yielded outputs that were informed, considered, and based on reason, the more critical of these were not incorporated into the recommendations. This case like the others in this volume begs multiple questions. Perhaps most significantly for the prospects of realizing elements of deliberative democracy in policy procedures, what accounts for these strengths and limitations?

The broader policy context in which the NWMO's consultation process took shape provides plausible explanations. Its strengths and weaknesses grow out of a long history revolving around deeply contentious policy issues – issues that invoke both the horrors of war and the hope of prosperity – and involving very committed actors – actors who had become deeply invested in this policy area. Nuclear energy and waste management have been and likely always will be exceedingly controversial topics and many actors have deeply held views about them. The NWMO's process provided a venue for such actors to express their views and to try to influence policy decisions. Although national in scope, the process centred in Ontario, and many of the most vocal participants were from that province. Ontario is the epicentre of Canada's nuclear energy industry, with twenty of the country's twenty-two nuclear energy reactors located there. Canada's approximately two million used nuclear fuel bundles, each with a uranium mass of about 19 kilograms, are in storage at reactor sites located in the province.[111] Most of this waste sits within a 250-kilometre radius of Toronto. Needless to say, many participants were highly motivated to participate in the NWMO's planning for the management of this waste. NWMO elites were also highly committed to developing and running a robust consultation process. Elizabeth Dowdeswell, former president of the NWMO, seemed to articulate a genuine belief that all Canadians have a stake in nuclear waste management policy and should be involved in its formulation and implementation.[112] According to Dowdeswell, the NWMO wanted to provide a wide cross-section of Canadians with opportunities to be involved.[113] Others playing a lead role in the NWMO's consultation process echoed this commitment. As an NWMO employee put it, an attempt was made to be inclusive of all interested parties.[114] Again, the iterative and multi-event design of the process, transpiring over three years, was impressive.

Similarly to elite commitment in the cases of the TCHC and NSPI, this commitment was situated within and shaped by a context marked by entrenched economic interests. The NWMO, an organization formed by the major actors in Canada's nuclear energy industry, has always had an interest in developing and implementing a realistic plan for deep geological disposal. Even before the NWMO existed, core members of this policy community understood that developing a waste disposal system was critical for reasons related to curbing social, environmental, and economic risks but also for the success of the nuclear energy industry in Canada and beyond. The nuclear generation of electricity creates highly radioactive waste but, insofar as these wastes can be safely and economically contained, this form of generation can have certain benefits over others, especially those that emit carbon. Address the problem of its waste, and nuclear generation becomes an appealing source of electricity. Although no country is currently operating a deep geological disposal system for used fuel from civilian reactors, there is a broad international agreement concerning its conceptual and technical viability.

From this perspective, we can see a possible explanation for why NWMO elites chose not to incorporate into their recommendation a plan for a broader public discussion on nuclear energy before moving forward with adaptive phased management, and why adaptive phased management is tied directly to deep geological disposal. Again, the focus of the NWMO's consultation process was intended by government to be on nuclear waste not energy policy. However, the scope and nature of the nuclear waste problem is fundamentally connected to the generation of nuclear electricity. Nuclear generating capacity determines how much waste needs to be managed. For many participants in the process, nuclear generation and nuclear waste management should be treated as links in a chain.

From the point of view of NWMO elites, a public discussion on nuclear energy may run the risk of contributing to political pressure to reduce or phase out nuclear energy, which could cause an enormous loss of revenue for OPG and NBP (Quebec has already phased out nuclear energy). This pressure could also have ramifications for AECL, a Crown corporation that not only conducts research in nuclear technologies but also markets CANDU reactors worldwide. Making a recommendation for a waste management plan while remaining non-committal on the amount of waste to be managed would enable Canada's nuclear energy industry not only to grow domestically (there has been talk of building new reactors in Ontario and Alberta), but also potentially to become a leader on the international stage. In addition to CANDU reactors, Canada could potentially become an exporter of expertise and technologies related to deep geological disposal systems, for which there could be multiple international markets. These prospects, in part, depend on success at home. To implement such a system in Canada would require broad public acceptance of it. Such public acceptance would be critical for the siting, constructing, and operating of a nuclear waste facility and repository for, without it, there could strong opposition, which could result in serious disruptions to these processes. Thus, it seems that the strategic interests of the nuclear energy industry were in play in the context from which the NWMO's consultation process emerged.

From as far back as the early 1970s, the industry has faced public pressure to become more transparent and democratic.[115] In the 1990s, this pressure was brought to a high pitch during the Seaborn panel's review of the concept for deep geological disposal. During its hearings, many participants expressed views critical of the nuclear energy industry and, in particular, Ontario Hydro and AECL. Many voiced a deep mistrust of organizations within this industry. These concerns were echoed in the Seaborn panel's findings and recommendations.[116] Based on both oral and written public submissions, the panel noted that "the chances of finding an acceptable concept and site(s) will be remote unless there is early and thorough public participation in all aspects of managing nuclear fuel wastes ... Past public participation strategies, although well intended, do not appear to have been effective because a significant portion of the public did not trust the nuclear industry and the regulatory agency."[117]

On the heels of the Seaborn panel hearings and report, elites within both NRCan and the Canadian nuclear energy industry began to express a commitment to opening up their decision-making processes to not only the broader policy community but also the broader Canadian public. The Seaborn report and the government response to it laid foundations for the Nuclear Fuel Waste Act, which required the NWMO to hold public consultations in its study of waste management and disposal options. It granted the NWMO flexibility in the design, operation, and oversight of its consultations. Going beyond the legislated requirements, the NWMO appears to have sought procedures more in line with deliberative democracy. In designing its consultation process, NWMO management and staff were likely well aware of the necessity of addressing concerns for greater transparency and openness and of establishing better relationships of trust with Canadians.[118] In light of the opposition raised by members of the public participating in the Seaborn panel hearings and in light of the panel's finding of a lack of societal acceptance for the concept of deep geological disposal, NWMO elites may have been motivated to ensure broad public participation and deliberation in their own study. As stated in its final study report on waste management options:

> The views of Canadian society in judging benefits or risks, and assessing the social implications of various approaches for long-term management, are critical to the development of a socially acceptable recommendation. Canadians expect that the best scientific and technical knowledge must be brought to bear in identifying and understanding the source and nature of risk and the ways in which safety can be assured. However, the decision as to whether safety has been assured to a sufficient degree to warrant implementation is a societal one.[119]

From this perspective, the NWMO's process can be understood as a response to a history of suspicion and mistrust on the part of environmentalists, religious organizations, and Aboriginal nations across the country and members of communities located close to nuclear facilities.

The NWMO likely designed and ran its national consultation process not only because it was legislatively required to, but also because it was necessary for strategic purposes related to advancing deep geological disposal at home and abroad. Of course, the public acceptance of any high-risk technology is important for both strategic and ethical reasons. Some policy decisions can have such high-magnitude consequences that the broader public should be made aware of them, should deliberate on them, and should accept them. This is true of nuclear waste management. Problems, however, occur when procedures for deliberation are not tied into a decision-making mechanism or are not, at least, decision oriented. They are exacerbated when the outputs of the procedures are valid and reasonable but conflict with ensuing policy decisions. The NWMO's process achieved elements of deliberative democratic procedures but, in doing so, created an expectation that its outputs would inform public policy. Instead, the policy was significantly at odds with important views consistently expressed in the process. These views related to the need to connect a public debate and discussion of nuclear's role in Canada's energy portfolio to a plan for nuclear waste management and disposal, as well as to the need for ongoing public dialogues on the siting, construction, and operation of waste management facilities. From this angle, the NWMO's consultation process can be understood as a sophisticated trope to gain public acceptance while masking the effective continuation of the status quo approach to decision making initiated with Canada's nuclear waste management program in the 1970s.

We see in this case abundant resources being funnelled into a national consultation process that ultimately may have resulted in a proposal for a nuclear waste management option that historically has been preferred by Canada's nuclear energy industry. The NWMO's proposal seems to be a re-articulation of the nuclear industry's historical policy preference.[120] One way of looking at this process and at the proposal it yielded is as a confirmation of the soundness of the concept of deep geological disposal and its development into adaptive phased management. From another vantage point, however, it looks as though the NWMO may have had a desired preference and may have sought to ensure that the consultation process resulted in advancing this preference. Despite the topic's importance, the committed and informed participants, their consistent articulation of concerns with deep geological disposal and with nuclear's role in Canada's energy policy, and the deliberative-democratic characteristics of aspects of the NWMO's national consultation process, that process arguably had little substantive impact on Canada's plan for its nuclear fuel wastes. It is ironic, moreover, that this consultation process may ultimately result in a decision-making approach involving primarily officials from the NWMO and from and around potential host jurisdictions. This process was intended to be an endeavour in public collaboration, but may result in justifying prolonged elite negotiations, although it is too early to tell and more research is needed.

This case raises basic but important questions. Indeed, why should we engage in public deliberation? Why should we seek public deliberation on public issues and in public policy? We have ethical responses to these questions. From an ethical perspective, members of a democracy should become informed and have a direct say in policies that could profoundly affect their lives. But, given the realities in which deliberative exercises in policy development and implementation are necessarily situated, these kinds of responses may fall flat. Too often, it seems that deliberation in the real world of public policy results in advancing predetermined interests and in upholding pre-existing power structures. That said, if we give up the hope of realizing greater participatory and deliberative democracy, we may effectively be granting increased decision-making power to, and legitimating the exercise of that power by, elites in corporations and governments.

Chapter Five

Embedded Policy Consultations and Nunavut's Official Languages

Nunavut emerged from a land claims agreement in the early 1990s that had been negotiated for close to twenty years. When the territory came into existence, it represented a dream of the Inuit of Canada's central and eastern Arctic to both establish a land cession treaty with the Canadian government and gain control of their political, social, and economic futures. The 1993 Nunavut Land Claims Agreement gave rise not only to a public government representing the residents of the new territory but also to several designated organizations representing Inuit beneficiaries. In terms of both political institutions and day-to-day politics, Nunavut is a hybrid, delivering and managing goods and services in ways at once similar to and distinct from other provincial and territorial governments in Canada. Indeed, the Government of Nunavut has obligations to all residents generally as well as to Inuit specifically. In principle, the territorial government, the designated Inuit organizations, and the Government of Canada work together to develop and implement policy for the territory. According to the land claims agreement, Inuit have a certain right to participate in formulating and implementing social and cultural policies, and the government is legally obligated to provide opportunities for this participation. In this context, we find a series of public consultations, embedded in policy processes, that can be understood as based on principles similar to those of deliberative democracy.[1]

I examine in this chapter processes concerning Nunavut's official languages policy between 2000 and 2012.[2] A strong impetus for the creation of the territory was the desire of its people – *Nunavummiut* – to promote and advance the Inuit language, which expresses Inuit culture and identity. As such, the Official Languages Act and Inuit Language

Protection Act, tabled in Nunavut's Legislative Assembly in 2008, were profoundly important to Inuit of the territory. While the processes involved in their formulation were inclusive and comprehensive, those for developing their implementation plans fell short of the expectations of representatives of designated Inuit organizations and other important members of this policy community. While we see language policies generally congruent with the aims of the designated Inuit organizations and supported by the broader community, we also see a narrowing in the development of plans for their realization. Inuit organizations and other stakeholders felt that their views were being excluded from, and that their interests were not being fully incorporated into, this stage of the policy process. Ultimately, we see what appears to have been an approach to policy formulation that was deliberative, but that transitioned to a more government elite–driven approach to policy implementation. An elite approach may have been necessary in the implementation stage. But, given the importance of the language policies, many expected the entire policy process to be inclusive and participatory. In the following, I outline the emergence of Nunavut, examine the development of its language policies, and highlight and explain apparent paradoxes in the processes by which they were formulated and implemented.

The Emergence of Nunavut

On 1 April 1999, Nunavut came into operation. The Nunavut Act of 1993, which laid out provisions for the establishment of the territory, emerged from a two-decade negotiation of the Nunavut Land Claims Agreement (NLCA). The Inuit Tapirisat of Canada (ITC), representing the interests of Canadian Inuit in federal policy regarding Aboriginal comprehensive land claims, proposed the idea of creating Nunavut in 1975.[3] Its proposal was for a new political entity in the Canadian central and eastern Arctic, which at the time was within the boundaries of the Northwest Territories (NWT). ITC was motivated by a desire among Inuit of the NWT, who were the demographic and cultural majority in that part of the territory, to address the historical absence of a land cession treaty with the Canadian government and to gain control over their political, social, and economic agendas.[4]

ITC's basic idea was a political entity that would "better reflect Inuit values and perspectives."[5] In 1981, ITC created the Tungavik Federation of Nunavut (TFN), which would become responsible specifically for representing Inuit in the NWT and advancing their interests in land claims negotiations with the Canadian government. From the early 1980s, the principal actors in these negotiations were the TFN, Government of the Northwest Territories, and Government of Canada. In April 1990, the Nunavut land claims agreement in principle was signed, which included an article specifically concerning the establishment of Nunavut – "our land" in Inuktitut.[6] In a May 1992 plebiscite, residents of the Northwest Territories voted to endorse the divisional boundary existing today. Those in Inuit areas voted overwhelmingly in support of the proposed boundaries, while those in the western part of the NWT were less enthusiastic. These boundaries, encompassing approximately 2 million square kilometres, extend from west of Kugluktuk to Baffin Bay and Davis Strait in the east, and south of Arviat to beyond the far reaches of Ellesmere Island in the north. This land contains twenty-five communities widely dispersed across three regions (i.e., the Qikiqtaaluk, Kivalliq, and Kitikmeot).[7] The text of the agreement was then ratified in a November 1992 vote by eligible Inuit.[8] Barry Dewar writes: "It was evident that the successful ratification vote was highly dependent on the commitment to create Nunavut."[9] Finally, on 25 May 1993, TFN and government representatives signed the Nunavut Land Claims Agreement. As Ailsa Henderson writes, with "their land claim, Inuit gained title to 350,000 square kilometers; over $1.1 billion in federal money to be transferred over a period of fourteen years; royalties from oil, gas, and mineral development on Crown land; hunting and fishing rights; and participation in land and resource management decisions through co-management boards."[10] In June 1993, Parliament enacted not only the Nunavut Land Claims Agreement Act but also the Nunavut Act.[11]

Because the land claims process was intertwined with the desire of TFN representatives for greater Inuit control of social, cultural, environmental, and economic policy, it gave rise to what can be understood as a de facto form of self-government. De jure, the Government of Nunavut is public, despite 85 per cent of the population of the territory being Inuit. As Henderson writes, Nunavut's government is "elected by voters regardless of their ethnicity and it governs for all."[12] As it has done with other territorial governments, the federal government devolved powers to Nunavut. The territory has a commissioner, which is a federally appointed position similar to that of a provincial lieutenant governor. Its legislative assembly has twenty-two elected members,[13] who in turn cast secret ballots for a premier and executive council. There are no political parties; each assembly member sits as an independent. Members make decisions, at least in principle, on a consensus basis. A public service, which includes ten departments, supports the cabinet.

Nunavut's government, while public, is bound in several important respects by the NLCA. In its preamble, the agreement states that it is based on and reflects the objectives of providing certainty and clarity of rights to ownership, land usage, and wildlife, and rights for Inuit to participate in decision making in the use, management, and conservation of land, water, and resources, as well as in "wildlife harvesting."[14] Another objective articulated in the agreement is to "encourage self-reliance and the cultural and social well-being of Inuit."[15] Specific articles of the agreement thus entail the nomination and appointment of individuals by the federal government, Nunavut government, and Inuit of Nunavut to administrative bodies such as the Nunavut Wildlife Management Board, Nunavut Planning Commission, Nunavut Impact Review Board, Nunavut Water Board, and Nunavut Surface Rights Tribunal. The agreement also specifies that the number of Inuit employed in the public service be proportional to the number of Inuit in Nunavut. The objective of article 23 is "to increase Inuit participation in government employment in the Nunavut Settlement Area to a representative level."[16] Another important example of the NLCA tying into the Government of Nunavut is the rights it entrenches in article 32 for Inuit to have opportunities to participate in developing social and cultural policies.[17]

The process of developing a land claims agreement involved the establishment of four officially designated organizations representing Inuit beneficiaries. Nunavut Tunngavik Incorporated (NTI) was established in 1993 to represent all Inuit beneficiaries in the territory. Its basic responsibility is to monitor and ensure the implementation of NLCA. By upholding the provisions of the agreement, it is involved in many aspects of life in Nunavut. While the Nunavut Trust manages the funds from the NLCA, NTI offers various services and programs to Inuit of the territory. In addition to NTI, each region of Nunavut has its own designated Inuit organization. These are the Qikiqtani Inuit Association in the Baffin/Qikiqtaaluk region, the Kitikmeot Inuit Association in the Kitikmeot, and the Kivalliq Inuit Association in the Keewatin.

When Nunavut came into existence, its population was just 27,000.[18] As of April 2013, Nunavut's population was 36,408.[19] Inuit constitute 85.4 per cent of the territory's population, followed by 13.7 per cent non-aboriginal, 0.4 per cent Metis, and 0.4 per cent First Nations.[20] Inuit share one language comprising multiple dialects including Inuktitut and Inuinnaqtun. Inuinnaqtun, which uses Roman orthography, is spoken principally in the western part of Nunavut. Inuktitut, using both the Roman alphabet and syllabics, is spoken in the eastern part of the territory. The Inuit language is a polysynthetic, agglutinative language, where words can change meaning and grammatical function by adding suffixes to roots. For example, Nunavut means "our land"; *Nunavummut* means "to Nunavut"; *Nunavummuaqtuq* means "he/she goes to Nunavut"; and *Nunavummuaqlaaqtuq* means "he/she will go to Nunavut."[21] In the 2001 Canadian census, Inuktitut (which was used to refer to the Inuit language as a whole) was the mother tongue of 70 per cent, with 26 per cent English, and 1 per cent French.[22] According to 2001 census estimates, 53 per cent of Nunavut's population used Inuktitut as their home language, 46 per cent used English, and less than 1 per cent French.[23] In 2006, Inuktitut and Inuinnaqtun was the mother tongue of 70 per cent of the population, followed by English (26%), and French (1%).[24] In 2011, the percentage of residents whose mother tongue was either Inuktitut or Inuinnaqtun dropped to 68 while the percentage for English rose to 28 and that for French remained constant.[25] The use of the Inuit language at home has also dropped over the years, to approximately 52 per cent in 2011.[26] Based on multiple Inuit language use and transmission data, the United Nations Educational, Scientific and Cultural Organization has determined several Inuit dialects to be "vulnerable" and Inuinnaqtun "definitely endangered."[27] The predominance of English in government, media, commerce, schools, and, increasingly, the home, represents a real threat to the Inuit language, culture, and identity.

Nunavut inherited the Northwest Territories' Official Languages Act. While relevant to language concerns in the NWT, the act was out of step with the linguistic and cultural aims of the Inuit of Nunavut in that it designated multiple official languages, that is, Chipewyan, Cree, Dogrib, English, French, Gwich'in, Inuktitut (including Inuvialuktun and Inuinnaqtun), and North and South Slavey. Only four of these are spoken in Nunavut: English, French, Inuktitut, and Inuinnaqtun. Moreover, the act specified only rights to use English and French in legislative, judicial, quasi-judicial, and administrative communications of the territorial government. Only these languages were authoritative in judicial rulings and required in all official government contexts. In contrast, First Nations and Inuit languages *could* be used in legislative debates and judicial proceedings, but they had no legal authority.

Furthermore, there was no requirement to provide translations in these languages. The act granted the languages commissioner and territorial court the discretion to determine whether language services would be provided in these languages. In early 2001, the members of Nunavut's Legislative Assembly initiated a public review of this language policy.

This process, which would feed into the development of Nunavut's two language acts, can be understood as realizing principles similar to those of deliberative democracy. The Government of Nunavut had an obligation to provide Inuit and representatives of designated Inuit organizations opportunities not merely to be consulted but to be participants in the creation of new language legislation for the territory as per article 32 of the NLCA. It also had obligations to the residents of the Nunavut as a whole. The territorial government thus launched a comprehensive process involving individuals and groups with a broadly understood interest or stake in the policy (e.g., Inuit elders, Inuit youth, representatives of the francophone community, and members of the business community). A defining feature of this process was the deliberative engagement of participants and policymakers.

Nunavut's Embedded Policy Consultations

Early in the planning for the new territory, the importance of public participation and deliberation towards broad societal agreements on language policy issues was clear. It was also evident that addressing key language issues concerning, for example, standardizing the Inuit language, would be very challenging. These challenges would stem from the nature of the language, which exists in multiple dialects, the relationship between language and culture, and the history of Inuit. Early territorial leaders knew that in order for a language policy to have an effect on the diminishing numbers of Inuit speakers in both the home and workplace, it would have to be accompanied by a consistent and widely accepted understanding of the language. With prescience, they understood that attempts to standardize it would be both highly emotional and political.

The Nunavut Implementation Commission (NIC) – the commission responsible for the political and institutional lead-up to the operation of Nunavut in 1999 – thus urged Nunavut Tunngavik Incorporated, the Government of the Northwest Territories, and the Government of Canada to convene a conference as a "necessary step in pulling together an adequate societal consensus on the place of language in the future of Nunavut, with particular attention to the preservation and promotion of the Inuit language."[28] The NIC called for this conference to be planned "with a view to maximizing public participation, drawing on the variety of Nunavut organizations that focus exclusively or heavily on social and cultural issues, as well as having the active sponsorship of the three parties to the Nunavut Political Accord."[29] The Nunavut Language Policy Conference was held in Iqaluit in March 1998 and was attended by sixty delegates. The conference yielded fifty recommendations, including the following:

- Before legislation or policies are adopted affecting the use of syllabics or Roman orthography in Inuktitut and Inuinnaqtun in Nunavut, round-table discussions must be held to give residents (and especially elders) an adequate opportunity to understand, discuss, and debate the issues;
- Elders must be acknowledged as "experts in the fields of language, culture and traditional knowledge," and they must be granted appropriate formal recognition in Nunavut (e.g., teaching certificates, interpreter/translator accreditation, and honorary degrees);
- A permanent language school should be established to deliver language courses in Inuktitut and Inuinnaqtun on a continual basis and defined in widely accessible, concrete terms;
- All language teaching should involve "eloquent speakers" of Inuktitut and/or Inuinnaqtun to expose students to the "proper fluent speech";
- Public servants should be encouraged to learn the language of the Nunavut community in which they serve;
- Government of Nunavut employees must be able to use Inuktitut and/or Inuinnaqtun in their place of work, which should be encouraged and guaranteed in legislation;
- A language bureau should be established in the Government of Nunavut "to ensure that the needs and rights of the public are adequately met and to ensure open, clear communication between the government and the residents of Nunavut";
- Adequate resources must be allocated immediately for the development and completion of language teaching and learning materials such as stories and dictionaries;
- Funding must be made available for the development, publication, and distribution of language materials;
- More funding must be made available for TV, radio, and print media in Inuktitut and Inuinnaqtun;

- Culture and language camps should be a priority and be established in Nunavut to enable Inuit (and others) to learn or relearn their language in real-life contexts;
- Language preservation, promotion, and use must be given "a very high priority in all areas of the new government";
- Before language legislation or policy is adopted, all implications should be carefully considered "to determine whether it is necessary and advantageous to adopt formal measures, or whether less formal methods of encouragement and support might be more effective in achieving the goal";
- There should be a "Languages Commissioner in Nunavut with strong powers to ensure that rights respecting Inuktitut and Inuinnaqtun are well-known to the public and to government employees, and that these rights are fully respected and promoted";
- If a language commission is established, it must be given the authority to explore all language issues and alternatives "without restraint in order to ensure that all matters are properly and thoroughly examined"; and
- There should be more conferences on language to address the many complex issues and widely varying opinions "that must be properly considered before decisions are made."[30]

It is important to highlight these recommendations because they were an early articulation of important substantive concerns that would be consistently rearticulated throughout the long process of policy formulation and implementation.

Two years later, in 2001, Nunavut's first legislative assembly struck a special committee of MLAs to review its inherited Official Languages Act. The main purpose of the review was to make evident both possibilities for and challenges to better promoting, protecting, and developing the use of the Inuit language while also respecting the language rights of English and French speakers. The committee wanted to build on the language conference and ensure that it had a solid understanding of existing language policies and services in the territory.[31] Likely motivated by concerns similar to those of the NIC, the Special Committee launched a number of events that could be understood as deliberative. Recognizing that "many different groups and organizations hold a key stake in" and have valuable contributions to make in addressing language issues in Nunavut, the committee initiated its consultations by broadly identifying stakeholders and inviting them to become partners in the review process.[32] Stakeholder organizations contacted by the committee and invited to partner with them in the public consultations included the following (those with an asterisk indicated a willingness to partner in the review process): L'Association des francophones du Nunavut*; Qikiqtani Regional Inuit Association*; Kitikmeot Regional Inuit Association*; Kivalliq Regional Inuit Association*; Nunavut Tunngavik Incorporated*; Nunavut Social Development Council*; Nunavut Wildlife Management Board; Nunavut Impact Review Board; Nunavut Water Board; Nunavut Surface Rights Tribunal; Nunavut Literacy Council*; Inuit Heritage Trust*; Kitikmeot Heritage Society*; Government of Canada, Indian and Northern Affairs; Government of Canada, Official Languages Law Group*; Inuit Qaujimajatuqangit Tunngaviksaliuqtiit Task Force*; Languages Commissioner of Nunavut*; Baffin Chamber of Commerce; Kitikmeot Chamber of Commerce; Nunavut Association of Municipalities; and Nunavut Arctic College*.[33]

The initial round table took place in Iqaluit in June 2001, during which the Special Committee introduced itself and the objectives of its review and consultation process.[34] The committee treated this meeting as an opportunity to hear from and discuss with stakeholders their concerns and expectations regarding language policy in the territory. Subsequent round tables took place in Iqaluit, Cambridge Bay, and Rankin Inlet in January and February 2002.[35] The intention behind these round tables was to solicit "specific suggestions for changes to the *Official Languages Act*."[36] In particular, the committee sought input on the act's substantive content, as well as wording changes, additions, and deletions. The committee also met with officials from each department to collect, review, and discuss its capacity to provide services in Nunavut's official languages, its initiatives on language policy and services, and its short- and long-term initiatives relating to language use in the territory.

From September 2002 through March 2003, the Special Committee held meetings to facilitate public participation in the review process.[37] Involving an average of thirty-five participants, these public meetings took place in the communities of Arctic Bay, Taloyoak, Chesterfield Inlet, Baker Lake, Pangnirtung, Iqaluit, Kugluktuk, Sanikiluaq, and Qikiqtarjuaq. Given time constraints, the committee was not able to visit all of Nunavut's communities, but it aimed to ensure representation from as many different language and dialect groups as possible. The communities visited thus provided broad representation from the main dialect groups of the Inuit language and the largest francophone community in Nunavut.[38] These meetings were generally held in Inuktitut or Inuinnaqtun and English; Inuktitut and Inuinnaqtun interpreters were present for all of them.[39] French interpretation was also provided for the Iqaluit meeting.[40] A number of recurring themes came up, including the following: The Inuit language should be recognized as an official language equal to French and English; the new language policy should apply to the private sector and all municipalities; all government forms should also be translated into Inuktitut and Inuinnaqtun; and government information for Inuit should be available in Inuktitut and Inuinnaqtun.[41] An additional issue repeatedly raised was the role of the educational system in promoting and developing the Inuit language. There was a strong desire among members of the public and stakeholders to see Inuktitut as the language of instruction in schools.[42] While the committee was generally pleased with the contributions made by stakeholders from across Nunavut, it recognized that "representation and input from municipal governments and the private sector were lacking."[43]

In March 2002, the Special Committee issued its interim report, which it circulated to stakeholders and the broader public for consideration. In December 2003, it released its final report, which contained recommendations for the government's new language policy. These recommendations were a development of those made in the report of the language conference several years earlier. Tending to focus specifically on changes to the Official Languages Act, they proposed, in part, that

- The *Official Languages Act* provide that it be mandatory to actively offer services in all of the official languages in all sectors designated as essential";
- The *Official Languages Act* provide that government signage in all official languages be mandatory and in all other sectors be encouraged through a combination of policy and regulation";
- The *Official Languages Act*" set out the Government of Nunavut's responsibility to ensure the promotion of official languages and to support the development and enhance the vitality of languages that are at risk;
- The "Act provide that a Minister shall be designated responsible for the implementation of the Act and that the Minister responsible be required to submit an annual report to the Legislative Assembly, ... develop a government-wide official languages implementation plan,

evaluation and accountability framework, procedures and measures for tracking demand and service delivery, formally consult with the Languages Commissioner to develop a procedure for making complaints," and "report to the Legislative Assembly";

- An "official language body with effective decision-making powers be established through the legislation ... which would have the authority to develop and approve terminology, standardize writing systems, address the appropriate use of dialects and act as a resource to the government";
- The "Minister responsible for the Act work with the Association des francophones du Nunavut at the earliest opportunity to discuss and lay the foundation for the delivery of French language services as mandated under the Act";
- The "Government's first priority in the area of language legislation should be to introduce and pass a new made-in-Nunavut Official Languages Act";
- The "Government consider including those aspects of the Languages Commissioner's proposed *Inuktitut Protection Act* that specifically protect, promote, support, and strengthen the use of Inuit languages";
- The "Act apply equally to municipal governments and the Government put in place a rigorous timetable and deadlines for the meeting of this requirement";
- The Act "designate English, French, Inuktitut, and Inuinnaqtun as the Official Languages of Nunavut";
- The "Act require that Acts of the Legislative Assembly and records, journals, and sound recordings of the Legislative Assembly be produced in Inuktitut, Inuinnaqtun, English and French and further that the government put in place a rigorous timetable and deadlines for the meeting of this requirement";
- "Inuktitut, Inuinnaqtun, English, and French have equal status in all sections of the Act that pertain to court proceedings, decisions, orders, and judgments" and the "government put in place a rigorous timetable and deadline for the meeting of this requirement"; and
- The languages commissioner ensure that the commissioner has authority on a similar level to other independent officers of the Legislative Assembly to allow for full and adequate review and inquiries.[44]

The Department of Culture, Languages, Elders, and Youth (CLEY) – now the Department of Culture and Heritage – responded to this report in May 2004 with a timeline for the new language policy, including a

feasibility study to be conducted in partnership with Nunavut Tunngavik Incorporated, a set of public consultations to be held across the
territory, and the development of the new act.[45] CLEY created a Language Legislation Steering Committee consisting of officials from NTI,
various Nunavut departments (e.g., Justice, Education, and Finance),
and the Office of the Languages Commissioner to assist the department in directing and overseeing these activities. The purpose of the
feasibility study was to "identify the financial and human resources
required to implement each of the recommendations of the Special
Committee."[46] The aim of the consultations was to focus on unresolved
issues related to language policy and, in accordance with the NLCA,
to ensure Inuit participation in developing the policy.[47] The steering
committee assisted in developing a list of stakeholders to be consulted
during, including the Nunavut Association of Municipalities, chambers
of commerce, l'Association des francophones du Nunavut, regional
Inuit associations, Government of Nunavut employees, the Nunavut
languages commissioner, Inuit Qaujimajatuqangit Katimajiit (a Government of Nunavut organization made up of non-governmental experts
in Inuit traditional knowledge, or *Inuit Qaujimajatuqangit*), and Government of Nunavut departmental representatives such as those from
the Corporate Services and Policy Divisions.[48] CLEY held round-table
meetings with these stakeholders, which provided opportunities to
exchange ideas and concerns directly.

CLEY also organized focus groups to look at the particular issues
facing different segments of Nunavut's population. These focus
groups included Kivalliq elders (July 2004, Baker Lake), speakers of
Inuinnaqtun (August 2004, Kugluktuk), Qikiqtaaluk elders (August
2004, Iqaluit), Kitikmeot elders (August 2004, Taloyoak), Inuit youth
(August 2004, Iglulik), unilingual Government of Nunavut employees
(September 2004, Iqaluit), Iqaluit chamber of commerce (November
2004, Iqaluit), francophone public servants (Fall 2004, Iqaluit), Iqaluit's
francophone community (November 2004), and deaf *Nunavummiut* and
Inuit sign-language users (July 2006, Iqaluit).[49] Similarly to the round
tables, these focus groups provided an opportunity for individuals
and groups to articulate ideas and express concerns to officials in CLEY
and members of the steering committee. Also during this time, CLEY
circulated two surveys to collect input from municipalities and the
private sector on proposals for the language legislation. Government
officials followed up on the surveys with direct discussions with mayors
and senior administrative officers of each community.[50]

On the basis of this input, CLEY and the steering committee decided to explore developing two language bills – one to amend Nunavut's inherited Official Languages Act and one to protect the Inuit language. From 2006 through 2007, CLEY held additional consultations, including meetings with educational authorities, business community members, union representatives, francophone community representatives, federal government officials, and Inuit organizations. Specific meetings included presentations to and discussion with district education authorities (February 2006, Iqaluit), the Commission scolaire d'Iqaluit (March 2006, Iqaluit), the annual general meeting of the Arctic Cooperatives Ltd (May 2006, Winnipeg), the Nunavut Teachers' Union and the Nunavut Employees' Union (August 2006), community members from Cape Dorset, Whale Cove, and Rankin Inlet (December 2006), l'Association des francophones du Nunavut and Commission scolaire francophone du Nunavut (February 2007), the Workers' Compensation Board (February 2007), and the Office of the Languages Commissioner of Canada (February 2007).[51]

CLEY and the steering committee thus continued the comprehensive public process that had been initiated by the language conference and Special Committee. By many accounts, this multifaceted process was inclusive of people and perspectives.[52] Natan Obed of NTI states: "We were part of [the] steering committee leading up to the OLA [Official Languages Act] being tabled for its first, second, and third readings; we were there throughout to support the Act as it went before parliamentary concurrence in Ottawa; we played a very meaningful role in that process."[53] As a participant in the consultation process put it, the "nice thing about this territory is that no one has ever said that, as a white guy, I shouldn't be involved. I feel like I'm invited not just to observe but to participate ... I always have a voice in conversations."[54]

Specific events were well publicized in communities, and anyone could attend. Typically, these events would take place in community halls, and participants would sit in a big circle. There would be presentations by members of the steering committee, which would be followed by questions, comments, and discussion. Committee members would proceed issue-by-issue, aiming to be comprehensive in their presentations and responses. Although these meetings were often informal, they were characterized by a kind of procedural equality. Everyone had an opportunity to express his or her views, and was encouraged to do so. There was a sense among participants that they were working towards a broad basis of agreement concerning the essentials of the territory's imminent language policy. Generally, participants found that these consultations were valuable for the discussion and resolution of many issues associated with developing the language bills.

However, some views on the process were reserved, especially those concerning the recognition of designated Inuit organizations as equal partners with the Government of Nunavut. As Obed stated:

> We are the primary consulted body, but not a partner. Partnership implies joint decision making. There is no joint decision making. There is advice grudgingly taken, and perhaps there are a few concessions along the way, largely practical or grammatical. But, in the areas of content, in say the development of the language acts or implementation plan, we don't currently have a partnership role.[55]

In a similar vein, another individual active in the consultations described feeling at times excluded from the decision-making process:

> We had concluded our ... meetings, and just before the bills were tabled at the legislative assembly, government officials ... said that these are the drafts that are going to be tabled and there are a few differences. They told us about the differences and that was quite upsetting. They had their own internal process [in which] they presented to the MLAs, who provided feedback, then they handed it to their lawyers, their justice department, and then they made changes on top of our consensus-based decisions ... We ended up supporting the legislation because we had made a lot of input into the bills and because it was one of the more positive legislative developments.[56]

A general spirit of inclusion and participation continued in the Nunavut Legislative Assembly its policy formulation processes. On 28 March 2007, the minister of CLEY tabled the Official Languages and Inuit Protection bills to allow for further public consultation and debate prior to legislative debate on the proposed acts. The tabling of these bills occurred, from a procedural perspective, earlier than normally required. CLEY circulated a public consultation paper and held round tables and public meetings, all towards the end of enabling participants from each region to review and make comments on the bills. In June 2007, the bills were formally introduced in the Legislative Assembly. The minister of CLEY also tabled the department's summary report on the consultations on the bills. Bill 6, the proposed Official Languages

Act, and Bill 7, the proposed Inuit Language Protection Act, passed their first and second readings in the Legislative Assembly on 5 and 6 June 2007, respectively. They were then referred to the responsible Standing Committee of MLAs, the Ajauqtiit, for review and consultation.

Ajauqtiit issued its own call for public submissions to the proposed legislation. On 13 July 2007, the chair of Ajauqtiit wrote directly to a wide range of political, business, and labour leaders across Nunavut, enclosing a copy of the bills and inviting formal submissions on them. Recipients included all twenty-five mayors in Nunavut, the languages commissioner of Nunavut, and the presidents of the Kivalliq Chamber of Commerce, the Baffin Regional Chamber of Commerce, NTI, l'Association des francophone du Nunavut, the Nunavut Association of Municipalities, the Nunavut Employees Union, and the Nunavut Teachers' Association.[57] The bills were also made publicly available on the Legislative Assembly website for any member of the public to review and comment. The committee sought general public feedback through announcements in *Nunatsiaq News*, *News/North*, and *Kivalliq News*. In order to allow adequate time for stakeholders to fully consider the bills, the committee provided three months for submissions to be prepared. It received formal submissions from NTI (representing the Qikiqtani, Kivalliq, and Kitikmeot Inuit Associations), the languages commissioner, Arctic Co-ops Limited, the Inuit Broadcasting Corporation, l'Association des francophones du Nunavut, la Commission scolaire francophone du Nunavut, the Access to Information and Privacy Protection Commissioner, students enrolled in the interpreter/translator program at Arctic College, and a member of the public (Madeline Redfern). It also heard directly from these participants during legislative hearings in October. Based on the submissions that Ajauqtiit received in writing and during its hearings, it presented an interim report to the Legislative Assembly in late October.

Ajauqtiit invited the minister of CLEY to appear at a hearing in early December to discuss the two bills. It publicly stated that this step was taken because of the importance and complexity of the legislation being proposed.[58] Issues that were discussed with the minister included the following: the protection of the rights of francophones; the resources and powers of the territorial languages commissioner; the language capacity of police and medical professionals; the lack of legal authority of legislative and regulatory text written in the Inuit language; the scope of Inuit language instruction for primary and secondary education; the timelines for implementation and mechanisms for policy enforcement;

and the inclusion of private business and municipalities in the scope of the policy. In his oral submission to Ajauqtiit, the minister addressed concerns raised by stakeholders about the quasi-constitutional nature of the proposed official languages bill, the desire for legally authoritative Inuit language versions of all acts, the competing priorities for available resources, the benchmarks for language changes in education, the right to work in the Inuit language in the private sector, and the roles of the minister and the languages commissioner.[59]

The Nunavut Legislative Assembly passed the new Official Languages Act on 4 June 2008 and, on 18 September, the Inuit Language Protection Act, which came into force the following day. The following year, on 1 June, the Canadian House of Commons passed the motion for concurrence with the Nunavut Legislative Assembly on the new Official Languages Act without debate. The motion for concurrence with the Nunavut Legislative Assembly was introduced in the Senate on 2 June. On 4 June, the act was referred to the Standing Senate Committee on Legal and Constitutional Affairs over concern that it would diminish Aboriginal and French language rights.[60] Several senators wanted to ensure that the rights of linguistic minorities in Nunavut were not detrimentally affected by its coming into force.[61] They wanted more information concerning the five Aboriginal languages that would lose their official status (i.e., Chipewyan, Cree, Dogrib, Gwich'in, and Slavey) and the impact of the new act on francophone and anglophone minority rights. Witnesses consulted by the Senate committee confirmed that the Aboriginal languages that would be demoted by the new act were spoken primarily in the Northwest Territories and by less than 1 per cent of the population of Nunavut. With respect to the rights of francophones, the Senate committee heard that the act represented "a new paradigm for official languages in the North given the collaborative process" and that "all parties involved demonstrated good faith and a spirit of cooperation throughout the creation of the legislation, in stark contrast to the relationship between the francophone community in the Northwest Territories and its territorial government."[62]

During the Senate's proceedings, Daniel Cuerrier, former director general of l'Association des francophones du Nunavut, stated, "We fought, we argued, but we kept on talking to each other and we finally reached an agreement, we made progress and we moved forward together. It worked so well that we made several recommendations to the steering committee charged with drafting the bill. Those recommendations ended up in the final draft ... So there was a real willingness to get it right."[63] The Senate committee also heard from Joe Attagutaaluk, former executive member of the Qikiqtani Inuit Association, who was representing NTI. Attagutaaluk also praised the consultation process:

> Inuit have the right to participate in the development of social and cultural policies of the federal and territorial governments, and in the design of social and cultural programs and services, including their method of delivery within Nunavut.
>
> The changes to Nunavut's *Official Languages Act* were developed over a period of three years through a joint steering committee of the Government of Nunavut and NTI representatives, with the Nunavut Official Languages Commissioner as a special adviser. At the end of a lengthy process that involved consultation with individuals and groups with interest in language throughout Nunavut, including working closely with the Association des francophones du Nunavut and the commission scolaire francophone du Nunavut, the new *Official Languages Act* was passed on June 4, 2008. It was a day of celebration. As a result, representatives of Nunavut are strongly in support of the new act.[64]

On 11 June 2009, the Senate committee recommended that the Senate adopt concurrence of the Official Languages Act. Although including various stipulations to ensure the protection of minority francophone and minority Aboriginal languages in the territory, the Senate committee was clearly convinced that Nunavut's consultation process on its language policies was inclusive and collaborative. It described the collaborative efforts between stakeholders and the Government of Nunavut as "remarkable" and "a veritable model for language relations in Canada."[65]

However, it is important to point out that key perspectives were significantly qualified. Although many, including Attagutaaluk, praised the consultation process, a consistent underlying message from designated Inuit organizations was that they actively participated in the process but were neither fully included nor understood to be equals with officials of the Government of Nunavut.

The preamble to Nunavut's Official Languages Act states that the commissioner and the Legislative Assembly of Nunavut were determined "to advocate for and to achieve the national recognition and constitutional entrenchment of the Inuit language as a founding and official language of Canada within Nunavut."[66] As Senator Serge Joyal states in the minutes from the Senate committee hearings, this "comes close to voting a constitutional resolution by entrenching the Inuit language in the Constitution of Canada as a founding and official language of Canada within Nunavut."[67] Substantively, the act expands the circumstances in which judicial proceedings and decisions must be translated into the Inuit language and allows for the Inuit translation of legal decisions and legislated acts to be equally authoritative. Any person may rightfully ask for translation, which must be provided for all matters of interest to the public, a language community, or a participant in the proceedings. The act also expands the opportunities for officials and the public to use the Inuit language in judicial proceedings, as well as the circumstances in which government offices must provide services in Inuit by clarifying and broadening the definition of "significant demand." The act also establishes a minister responsible for promoting and advocating for the official languages and for tabling an annual report on the status of the Inuit language in the Legislative Assembly. The government may also order a service to be made available in one or more official languages in light of special concern about language loss or assimilation.

The Inuit Language Protection Act mandates Inuit language instruction to produce secondary school graduates who are fully proficient in the Inuit language, both in spoken and written forms.[68] It mandates evidence-based curriculum development with evaluation and competency measures for kindergarten through grade 3 by 1 July 2009 and grades 4 through 12 by 1 July 2019. The act also contains measures for early childhood education. Moreover, it protects the rights of Inuit language speakers to work in their language in territorial institutions, including Government of Nunavut departments, judicial and quasi-judicial bodies, and public agencies.[69] It requires all bodies, including private entities, to display public signs and advertising in Inuit with visibility commensurate with English and French. In addition, it requires rescue, health, hospitality, utility, basic household, and other services deemed essential or important by the government to be delivered in Inuit. Finally, it creates the Inuit Uqausinginnik Taiguusiliuqtiit (Inuit Language Authority), which is responsible for expanding the "knowledge and expertise available with respect to the Inuit Language" and for making "decisions about Inuit Language use, development and standardization."[70]

Although some participants in the long process of developing the language policies felt that they did not fully embody their aspirations, there was a widespread sentiment that the policies represented a major achievement in the protection and promotion of the Inuit language and culture. While there was concern about the status of the language authority, the time frame for educational requirements, and the logistics of the delivery of services and goods in the Inuit language, participants in the process whom I interviewed were satisfied with the new policies and the processes that produced them. They felt that acceptable compromises were made. For example, with reference to the language authority, an active participant in the consultation process stated the following: "Our position was that it needed to be independent. All communities, minus one, agreed that it needed to be an independent body. ... Right now, it's within the GN [Government of Nunavut] but three years after passing legislation, it has the option of becoming an independent body. It was a compromise of the GN to help start up the body."[71]

As with the other cases in this book, we see impressive procedures that were designed to facilitate participatory deliberation. Generally, the procedures for policy formulation were inclusive, based on principles of equality, supportive of an exchange of perspectives, and oriented towards an agreement. These procedures were both embedded in the process of developing the territory's language policies and integral in the making of these policies. They appeared to be based on a genuine concern to involve Inuit and non-Inuit residents. In this case, we see another concrete example of how principles related to deliberative democracy were realized, more or less, in the practice of public policy.

Implementation and the Passage of Time

However, in the implementation of these policies, there appears to have been a shift away from participatory and deliberative procedures and toward a more closed-doors approach. This shift was characterized by fewer opportunities for stakeholders and members of the public to be involved in decision making.[72] For example, CLEY held public consultations as it developed a plan for implementation, but the steering committee was not as involved as some of its members would have liked. As Obed stated in the spring of 2011:

NTI has not been involved in a comprehensive way in the development of the regulations for the OLA or ILPA ... We were part of the Steering Committee leading up to the OLA being tabled for its first, second, and third readings. We were there throughout to support the Act as it went before parliamentary concurrence in Ottawa. We played a very meaning-ful role in that process. It does feel really disheartening that we wouldn't be involved in the implementation of OLA or ILPA, although we have been involved sporadically.[73]

In a similar vein, another individual stated the following in March 2011:

We demanded ... that the [Steering] Committee should keep going and meet on a regular basis to develop the regulations for the legislation, and also have a hand in the implementation phase. This hasn't really happened. They have included us in their Language Symposium and in their recent Standardization Symposium, but we're not being included to the extent that we would like to be.[74]

This stage was also characterized by long delays in announcing the implementation plans and, more seriously, in carrying out those plans. A number of participants in the consultation process leading to the development of the bills expressed frustration with the slow progress of implementation. As the above individual put it, the "benchmarks aren't being met, and those comments from the Government of Nuna-vut that it'll take time – and that seems to be the government's favourite line when it comes to languages – but the thing is that the Inuit Lan-guage doesn't have time."[75] As another noted, people were very excited about the language legislations, and now they are waiting; people are wondering what to do from here.[76] As Cuerrier stated, "I am very much disappointed, and a little bit frustrated. It has been delayed and then again delayed, and there are all types of excuses made up for not imple-menting these acts. I think these are extremely important and as more time passes, the language is being lost."[77] In a statement released jointly by the Office of the Languages Commissioner, the Qikiqtani Inuit Asso-ciation, and Nunavut Tunngavik Inc., these sentiments were articulated in strong terms. As then acting president of NTI James Eetoolook states, it "is very worrying that the very Minister who had such a large part in passing OLA and ILPA only two short years ago is now failing to meet the provisions set out in the legislation he himself championed."[78]

Why is it that Nunavut's consultation process embedded in its for-mulation of language policies was deliberative and resulted in robust policies, but then transitioned to a more closed-doors approach to developing implementation plans? What accounts for the strengths of these processes? What accounts for their weaknesses? What questions do these limitations raise about the prospects of deliberative democracy within policy processes? Again, these contradictions can be explained by contextual factors. Thus, on the one hand, participants were very motivated given the important of the topic. Language is a principal form of cultural expression; it enables culture to survive and develop. Preserving, protecting, and promoting their language has long been a concern of Inuit and was a central objective of the land claims agreement and the formation of Nunavut as a territory. This has been consistent theme and has been embodied in virtually every policy statement concerning Inuit language and culture. Furthermore, there has been a strong recognition of the necessity to act now in order to save the language. As a participant put it, she gets "a panicky feeling," wondering if Inuit are going to be able to do it.[79] Elders are dying and they carry so much of the culture and language.[80]

With the widely shared recognition of the importance of addressing language issues in a timely manner, there was a societal expectation – not just among Inuit – that there would be opportunities for public participation. Basic principles of the Inuit approach to collective life and collective decision making, which appear broadly accepted if not ingrained in the lives of *Nunavummiut*, include the importance of working together. According to *Inuit Qaujimajatuqangit*, given the harsh climate of the Arctic, survival is only possible if people work together and pass on knowledge and skills. Big laws or *maligait* include "working for the common good," "respecting all living things," "maintaining harmony and balance," and "continually planning and preparing for the future."[81] Other principles speak to the concepts of serving, consensus decision making, skills and knowledge acquisition, collaborative relationships, environmental stewardship, and resourceful problem solving. Inuit believe that "when a person lives in obedience to these laws and principles, there is balance and harmony."[82] Living by these principles is foundational for Inuit; collective deliberation and discussion is fundamental for Inuit.

In addition to this societal pressure placed on the Government of Nunavut to engage in meaningful public deliberation, there were certain legal requirements to take a participatory approach to developing these policies. Inuit autonomy in social and cultural policies and programs was one of the primary drivers of the movement towards Nunavut's creation. Article 32.1.1 of the Nunavut Land Claims Agreement states the following: "Without limiting any rights of Inuit or any obligations of Government, outside of the Agreement, Inuit have the right as set out in this Article to participate in the development of social and cultural policies, and in the design of social and cultural programs and services, including their method of delivery, within the Nunavut Settlement Area."[83] Section 32.2.1 expresses a corresponding requirement on the part of the Government of Nunavut concerning Inuit participation in policy processes. It states:

> Government obligations under Section 32.1.1 shall be fulfilled by Government: (a) providing Inuit with an opportunity to participate in the development of social and cultural policies, and in the design of social and cultural programs and services, including their method of delivery, in the Nunavut Settlement Area; and (b) endeavouring to reflect Inuit goals and objectives where it puts in place such social and cultural policies, programs and services in the Nunavut Settlement Area.[84]

While this appears to represent a legal obligation to engage Inuit in developing social and cultural policies and programs for Nunavut, section 32 is subject to different and competing interpretations. As Kate Darling states, "Unfortunately, as compared with other parts of the NLCA, this one is conspicuous in its vagueness."[85] She goes on, stating that part of the explanation for the ambiguity is that the article deals "directly and intimately with government programming" and that some "involved in the land claim negotiations have explained that the federal government took the position that it could not preconceive government programming in a land claim agreement."[86] Some may have felt that this article represented a compromise in the area of social development in exchange for "greater protections in other areas" of the agreement.[87] In any case, there are diverse interpretations of this article, with the designated Inuit organizations understanding it in terms of direct and actual participation in policy development and implementation and civil servants understanding it in terms of offering opportunities to Inuit to participate in policy processes. The expressions of rights and obligations in the NLCA, as well as the cultural and societal pressures, likely contribute to explaining the comprehensive consultations that were embedded in the development of Nunavut's language policies. However, differing understandings of article 32 may have contributed to narrowing this process at the implementation stage.

Moreover, given the magnitude of the task of implementing these policies, elite motivation may have waned. As Cuerrier stated, "I'm convinced that there's no real commitment to enforce or implement the acts ... My hope was that through consensus, through good will, things would move forward. This is not happening so far."[88] As another individual close to language issues and policy in Nunavut put it: "There is resistance from people within the public sector [and] civil service ... You might have willingness and compliance at the front office, [and] at the storefront offices, but if ... there are pockets that aren't complying and nothing coming from above, then it is pretty hard."[89] What is certain is that politicians, bureaucrats, business people, and the people of Nunavut face enormous tasks in the implementation of these policies. Standardizing the Inuit language for educational and legal purposes is exceedingly difficult given the different dialects, regional idioms, and writing systems.[90] The difficulties will be both technical and emotional. As stated by the Special Committee back in 2003, "Dialect is an important aspect of identity, a link to Inuit culture and history and a source of pride."[91] Again, language, including dialects, constitutes a fundamental dimension of who people are as individuals and community members. Moreover, "the variations in pronunciation, grammatical usage and vocabulary across the dialects of Inuit languages pose significant challenges to Nunavut-wide policies and practices that relate specifically to the use of language."[92]

There will also be enormous obstacles related to human and economic resources. In order for these acts to be implemented, there will need to be extensive language training for the public and private sectors.[93] A number of participants expressed concern about the insufficient number of teachers and translators who are fluent in the Inuit language.[94] As the Senate committee stated:

> Sufficient funding must be available to create the infrastructure and support the initiatives necessary to implement the provisions of the Act, and to realize its stated objectives. Indeed, insufficient funding could well have the opposite effect, and could be detrimental to the cultural cohesion of Nunavut and create a climate of mistrust. In concurring with the passage of this Act, Parliament is expressing a commitment to ensuring that the objectives of the Act can be achieved. We were advised by witnesses that the Government of Canada provides financial support to francophones in Nunavut in the amount of approximately $4,000 per 1 individual annually; funding to support Inuit language initiatives pales in comparison, reaching $44 per Inuit.[95]

This raises questions concerning who should provide these resources. Nunavut has been seeking cultural and economic autonomy and independence, but is still financially dependent on Ottawa. Its geographic location, distances between communities, and harsh climate contribute to exorbitantly high costs of living. In addition to tension between the Governments of Nunavut and Canada, there is tension between the Government of Nunavut and the Inuit organizations. In the Nunavut Land Claims Agreement, the designated Inuit organizations received $1 billion Canadian as well as royalties. Some within the Government of Nunavut may feel that more of these funds should be allocated to language programs. Differences in points of view concerning financial responsibility may be contributing to the slow pace of implementation plans. In addition, while implementing these language policies is critical for the cultural survival of Inuit of Nunavut, there are many other pressing issues facing *Nunavummiut*. Resources are stretched. As a participant put it:

> There is so much immediate need. The social issues are still here. The housing issues are still here. The drop-out rates are too high. The diet issues are terrible. All these things need to change ... I don't think that people are being misled, it's just that there's so much to deal with ... It's hard to be optimistic when things have dragged on for so long, especially since it's so important. This should be the first priority for the government, but it doesn't seem to be.[96]

Indeed, many are concerned. As Obed put it:

> I'm worried that we'll continually talk about the issue in very general and introductory ways when in fact we have all the evidence we need to act. We know what people want. People want Inuit instruction in schools; they want the government to function in Inuktitut; from the federal government, they want equal funding in relation to French as far as the promotion of language in the territory; they want their society to function in the Inuit language. It is very simple when you put it in those terms. People have been saying it for years, but you still get this hand wringing from the people in power: "... It's going to cost a lot of money, we don't have the same resources." There is always an excuse.[97]

In the October 2012, the Government of Nunavut released its implementation plan for the territory's language policies. In developing the final version of this plan between the spring of 2011 and fall of 2012, the Government of Nunavut consulted with NTI. According to the plan, the Department of Culture and Heritage "established a meaningful collaboration with NTI by creating a joint steering committee, under the guidance of the languages commissioner, to develop this plan for the effective implementation of language obligations pursuant to" both the Official Languages Act and Inuit Language Protection Act.[98] Perhaps this is a signal that decision-making power in this area is shifting toward more sustained collaboration between the government and Inuit organizations.

As impressive as the process of policy formulation was, it had limitations. Representatives of designated Inuit organizations and members of the Nunavut public were granted access to portals of consultation and participation, and they made meaningful contributions to developing language policies for the territory. However, in the time lapsing between 2008 and 2012, the process of developing implementation plans seemed to become opaque. While critical time lapsed, many who were involved in the consultations contributing to the development of the policies were largely left out of the planning for their implementation. They remained on the outside of this important stage of the process until 2011, which must have been very frustrating. Over the course of more than thirteen years, the use of the Inuit language in and outside the home has diminished. This is profoundly unfortunate, and it could take decades to revitalize this language.

Chapter Six

Contextual Complexity and the Importance of Deliberative Democracy

The basic aim of this volume has been to examine deliberative democratic procedures to understand their implications for public policy. Again, my specific objectives have been to study cases of Canadian policy that seemed most likely to be successful in approximating the deliberative ideal; to evaluate these cases in terms of criteria of deliberative democracy; to account for their strengths and weaknesses by examining contextual factors; and to highlight structural conditions and design features for policy processes that are participatory, deliberative, and empowered. Digging into these cases, I found that a narrow focus on procedures fails to tell the whole story. Examining the outputs and outcomes of these procedures, as well as the contexts in which they are situated, reveals troubling nuances that include barriers to greater empowerment, legitimacy, and justice. In this conclusion, I want not only to summarize these findings but also to highlight possibilities for increasing democratization in the domain of governance. Despite the limitations found in each case, achieving deliberative democratic systems remains a worthy goal. In establishing the normative basis for collective norms and decisions, most of us would agree, the equal consideration of relevant interests is better than catering to specific interests, reasoned persuasion is better than coercion, and knowledge is better than ignorance. It is therefore important to bring into focus the positives of these cases for deliberative democratic theory and practice.

All four cases in this volume are characterized by procedures based on principles of, or similar to, deliberative democracy. In many ways, they appeared to be textbook examples in timely and important policy areas. In each, there were genuine efforts on the part of elites to realize principles of inclusion, equality, information, and reason toward reaching a broad agreement or identifying a shared interest. Elites appeared to express a concern, at a minimum, to involve a broad range of participants in their decision-making processes and, at a maximum, to have them make policy decisions. Participants were highly motivated and yielded informed and reasonable policy positions that transcended their own particular interests. They seemed to experience meaningful moments of collective deliberation. Moreover, the procedures appeared to be sustained or institutionalized, thus suggesting a shift in policy processes away from elite models and toward participatory and empowered approaches. When evaluating these procedures, we see that some aspects were better than others in realizing deliberative democratic criteria, but on the whole they all more or less fulfilled them. From this angle, the cases were success stories. However, from another viewpoint, we see that their impact on policy and on the distribution of power was limited.

Indeed, a detailed examination of the broader contexts in which these cases were situated reveals fundamental limitations. The procedures appeared deliberative, but when taking into consideration the impact of their outputs on policy decisions, we see that they were curtailed. The procedures seemed empowering of participants during deliberation, but when stepping back to consider their longer-term outcomes for existing decision-making power relations, we see that they were ultimately non-empowering. Arguably, these procedures represented a certain truth, which is that they operationalized principles of deliberative democracy. This truth, however, was complicated. In each case, we see contradictions that have implications for the prospects of realizing not only deliberative democratic procedures but also a broader system of deliberative governance.

The TCHC's Tenant Participant System facilitated certain forms of democratic deliberation among residents and staff. The outputs of its procedures were well informed and well reasoned. Yet their scope was very circumscribed. The procedural and institutional structure of the budgeting process was highly localized and compartmentalized. City-wide deliberations took place only once a year during the 1.8 Day. There was no city-wide network through which residents could communicate, organize, and empower themselves relative to the TCHC's management structure. Arguably, in this context, the TCHC's participatory budgeting served merely to transfer from management to residents the burdens of identifying priorities and making plans for repairs to dilapidated buildings and their grounds. Perhaps more cynically, it may have functioned as a foil to deflect questions away from the activities of some staff and management and away from an ethos of dubious practices.

Similarly, NSPI's Deliberative Polling was characterized by contradictions. On the one hand, it was a sophisticated participant engagement process. Here, again, participants came to very sound positions on demand- and supply-side energy options. On the other hand, the connection between the polls and NSPI's energy conservation programs was highly filtered. The utility's 2005 submission to the UARB seemed recalcitrant in its proposed conservation programs. In response to a perceived or real conflict of interest, and in response to its own consultation process, the Government of Nova Scotia would eventually transfer responsibility for conservation to an independent body, Conserve Nova Scotia. It is worth noting reports that, because of the work of Conserve Nova Scotia, the province is now at Canada's forefront in energy conservation.[1] Arguably, NSPI and its Customer Energy Forums played a much more limited role in this achievement. The polls seemed to have had even less direct impact on the utility's renewable energy plans. Instead, the utility seemed to be responding much more directly to provincial standards and requirements for renewable energy. While the polls were good optics and may have served an important public relations function, they were limited.

With respect to the NWMO's national consultation process, we also see an ambiguity in its impact on policy. The NWMO's final report speaks to the importance of a broad public discussion and debate on the topic of nuclear energy in Canada, yet it did not explicitly incorporate this perspective into its recommendation to the federal government. Public consultation on energy policy may have been beyond the official remit of the NWMO, but participants in this process consistently articulated concerns about the role of nuclear energy in Canada's portfolio and about the size of the country's growing stockpile of nuclear waste. In their view, the amount of existing and projected waste contributes to determining the nature of the problem and range of management options by which to address it. Even more controversially, it may be that adaptive phased management is not substantively different from the nuclear energy industry's long-established preference for deep geological disposal – a preference that does not appear to have been significantly modified by the NWMO's consultations. In addition, while it is too early to tell for certain, we may see a return to a more closed-door, elite-driven process as the NWMO moves forward in its negotiations with officials from and around prospective host municipalities concerning the long-term waste management and disposal facility. Although the principle of informed community willingness is paramount, how it is defined is somewhat opaque and how it will be expressed remains to be seen.

In the final case study of this volume, while embedded policy deliberations on Nunavut's official languages directly influenced the formulation of two very important acts, they were narrowed in the implementation stage of these policies. Members of designated Inuit organizations, as well as of the community more broadly, had been seeking inclusion in the development of an implementation plan. It was not until towards the end of the process of developing this plan that NTI was brought back into the discussion. This narrowing may have been due to a lack of capacity within the Government of Nunavut, especially in light of the many social and economic issues that the territory must address. In any case, the policy process has not yet yielded the decisive measures that may be necessary to ensure the survival of the Inuit language. The process, initiated before Nunavut came into operation, lasted over a decade. The Inuit Language Protection Act and Official Languages Act were passed in the Nunavut legislature in 2008. Their implementation plan was not tabled until 2012. Critical time was lost.

All of these cases suffered from two limitations. The first involves the characteristics of the procedures and significance of their outputs. Focusing on the procedures, we see that they met requirements of deliberative democratic principles. Taking a broader perspective to capture their policy context, however, we see that the significance of outputs for policy was limited. Procedures and their outputs were connected to subsequent policies either in ways that were very circumscribed or in ways that were filtered through the interests of the host entity. The second kind of limitation involves the more long-range outcomes of the procedures. The deliberative democratic procedures may have been empowering when participants were exchanging reasons, discussing issues, and reaching conclusions, and they may have appeared empowering in terms of representing institutionalized opportunities to transfer exclusive decision-making power away from traditional elites and toward affected publics. They were, however, ultimately non-empowering in terms of outcomes that did not more systemically challenge the status quo approach to policy formulation and implementation. In these cases, we see how exercises in deliberative democracy can serve to uphold pre-existing power structures and elitist approaches to policy, and thus thwart deliberative democracy's rich ethical ends. These cases highlight the institutional possibilities for deliberative democracy, but they also cast light on context-specific factors that may complicate these possibilities.

These factors included the framing of the topic of deliberation, general characteristics of participants in deliberation, elite commitment to deliberative procedures, public pressure for increased consultation, participation, and deliberation, policy requirements for public consultation and participation, and predominant economic and strategic interests, aims, and constraints. Strengths resulted from a genuine understanding held by both elites and participants that the particular topic of deliberation was very important. Both elites and participants were committed to establishing and partaking in procedures that would facilitate collective deliberation on these topics. Elites were responding to a history of public pressure to open up and democratize their policy processes. They were also responding to policy requirements for public consultation or participation. Nonetheless, entrenched material interests and dominant forms of decision making appear to have persisted, and elite commitment waned against this backdrop.

My analysis suggests that contextual forces impeded a more deliberative democratic shift in decision making. In each case, there appears to have been an ethos of hierarchical decision making that prevented a transformation of relations between elites and their affected public. Social housing in Toronto has historically been managed in terms of a landlord-tenant model; energy policy in Nova Scotia has always been driven by the provincial government in consultation with the province's primary utility; nuclear energy and nuclear waste management have, since the 1960s to the 1990s, been the policy domains of exclusively expert, industry, and government elites; and, before the existence of Nunavut and article 32 of the NLCA, Inuit did not have explicit rights to participate in decision making concerning their social

Table 4 Salient contextual factors

Contributors to robust deliberative democratic procedures	Contributors to limited outputs/outcomes
• Important topic • Motivated participants • Committed elites • Public pressure • Policy requirement	• Economic and strategic interests and aims • Ethos of and habituation to hierarchical decision-making processes

and cultural policies. Dominant actors in these policy areas may have been too habituated to functioning within the established decision-making approaches to fully comprehend the normative implications of deliberative democratic approaches and the importance of democratic empowerment.

My findings may contribute to the widespread scepticism directed towards deliberative democracy. The substance of this scepticism is that politics and policy will continue to be characterized by a primacy of power, a dominance of economic interests, and entrenched elite decision making. However, more positive conclusions can and should be drawn. As we've seen, deliberative democratic procedures can and are being realized in areas of public policy. Histories of public pressure can give rise to policy requirements for and elite commitment to such procedures. These procedures, and participants in them, can yield sound outputs based on information and reason. Participants can be motivated to learn about complex issues, exchange reasons, transcend their individual interests, and articulate their substantive preferences to policymakers. Contrary to concerns about the soundness and effectiveness of outputs of deliberative procedures, these cases consistently suggest that participants are very capable of making reasonable decisions appropriate to specific policies. Participants take their roles seriously and want to contribute to making good policy.

Inspired by Carole Pateman, I believe that deliberative democratic procedures need to be "integrated into the overall system of representative government" and "become part of the regular political cycle in the life of a community."[2] And with Joshua Cohen and Archon Fung, I believe we need more opportunities for participatory deliberation that has a direct impact on public policy.[3] What, then, are the concrete "takeaways" from these cases for seeking to realize greater justice, legitimacy, and empowerment in policy and policy processes?

From the cases in this volume, we can draw specific design features by which to achieve these ends. Participatory budgeting, with self-selected participants, is arguably the most inclusive of individuals. As it exists in both Porto Alegre and, to a lesser extent, the TCHC, it is also the most demanding in terms of participant involvement. Cycles take place all year round; they are not limited to an expressly finite number of years. Extended beyond budgetary issues to include areas of social, economic, and environmental policy, this form of participation would likely be far too burdensome on individuals. Thus, while very inclusive, it needs to be confined to a limited number of policy areas.

Deliberative Polls and other mini-publics involving a statistically representative sample of a population usually entail a much shorter commitment of time and energy. Deliberative Polls typically take place over a couple of days. The British Columbia and Ontario Citizens' Assemblies took place over several consecutive weekends.[4] These forums are well designed for collective, informed deliberation on specific topics. If such forums include provisions for the wide dissemination of information concerning expert perspectives, deliberative proceedings, and their outputs, as well as for a referendum on the policy issue, their high-quality deliberations could be coupled with broader engagement and participation. These are the aspirations of the Oregon Citizen Initiative Review Process, now in its fifth year.[5] This review process involves a week-long deliberation among a representative panel of citizens on an initiative scheduled for a wider public vote. These citizens engage with each other on the initiative, interact with advocates and experts, and develop both pro and con position statements. The statements are then sent out to every eligible voter, who can use them to inform his or her referendum vote. Ideally, these review processes stimulate broader public thought, discussion, and action on important initiatives and have a direct impact on public policies.

We can also draw from the ways in which the NWMO ensured that participants in its consultation process had access to a wide range of information concerning the technical, social, and environmental dimensions of nuclear waste management. There were many impressive features of the NWMO's consultation process, but the standout is its sharing of information. The organization's website has consistently offered a wealth of information, with links to its own reports, as well as consultation, expert, and critics' reports. While primarily in English, this information is widely available to most people in Canada and many worldwide. Many who wish to become well informed on issues related to nuclear waste management can begin by accessing this comprehensive source information. The archive on its website is an important contribution to public knowledge and debate concerning nuclear energy and nuclear waste management.

Finally, we can draw from the case of Nunavut's official languages to understand how deliberative procedures can be embedded in policy processes. Especially with respect to policy formulation, the participatory involvement of *Nunavummiut* seemed routinized. During this stage, it appeared to be a given that meaningful and participatory deliberations would take place and that they would have a direct influence on the ensuing policies. There seemed to be an understanding among elites and participants in the process that the deliberations would be empowered and would be a direct contribution to a highly important aspect of Inuit culture and life in Nunavut. In this case, we see a glimpse of how deliberative procedures could be entrenched in policy formulation and, perhaps, in additional policy stages.

What about the features of these cases that thwarted empowerment? What about the propensity of elites to host deliberative events but not to empower them? An institutional response may lie in policy requirements. In the same way that policy requirements contributed to the realization of these events, they could also serve in ensuring that policymakers are bound by their outputs. We see strong prescriptive language concerning public participation in the TCHC and Nunavut cases. Looking back to the history of nuclear waste management policy, we also see strong recommendations for public participation in the recommendations to the federal government in the Canadian Environmental Assessment Agency's report, which preceded the Nuclear Fuel Waste Act.[6] This kind of language, expressed as a requirement for public participation, could result in tying deliberative procedures more directly to policy processes. It could effectively help to shift decision-making power onto a more horizontal plane. It could result in a transformation of state institutions, as Frank Fischer writes, "in ways that lead to the restructuring of the administrative agencies responsible for dealing with problems"[7] so they are democratically empowered.

The participatory and deliberative procedures that we've seen in these policy areas are fundamentally different from existing approaches to formulating and implementing policy. If empowered, they could present both a direct challenge and a complement to existing models. Both contributions would be salutary by providing channels through which citizens are able to voice concerns about existing policies and make concrete contributions to future policies. However, transitioning towards such a governance approach, even within certain policy areas (as opposed to within all policy areas), is not merely an institutional challenge. Perhaps even more difficult is reforming the dominant cultures in governments and corporations that are currently geared towards a concentration of decision-making power in elite hands.

Ultimately, contextual factors matter in mediating the design, operation, and significance of deliberative democratic procedures. Those of us interested in achieving greater opportunities for deliberative democracy need to be attentive to the factors that can either facilitate or thwart this end. It is important not to lose sight of individual instantiations of deliberative democracy, especially where these appear institution-alized. They can provide us with enormous insight into what works and what does not as a contribution to larger deliberative systems. Studying specific procedures can provide assurances that the apparent deliberative qualities of the whole are not masking its non-deliberative elements. In particular, we must be attentive to factors that give rise to deliberative democratic procedures as public consultations "dressed up." This might be a trite way of putting it, but the implications are serious. They bear upon how we are governed and, more crucially, how we govern ourselves. Harking back to an admittedly romantic view of Ancient Athens, there are consequences for ourselves as well as our political communities. Do we want to be more fully engaged as human beings, community members, and citizens? Do we want to have an active, direct, and meaningful voice in our governance? Do we want to be responsible, dialogical knowledge seekers who aim to govern ourselves on the basis of publicly discussed and debated reasons and mutually acceptable resolutions? Or are we content as passive recipients of policies imposed on us by those with political and corporate power? Are we content with mere illusions of democracy?

Interpretive Case-Study Research, Its Challenges and Rewards

When I initially embarked on this project, I thought that a volume looking at case studies of deliberative democratic procedures would be straightforward. I had had experience researching, analysing, and writing about deliberative democracy and the case of nuclear waste management in Canada.[1] I believed I could apply the basic methodology that I had developed to other cases of Canadian policy and thought I could execute this project in a matter of months, a year, tops. Several years later, I've finally managed to produce this volume. Over this lengthy process, I've learned a great deal about not only the substance of these cases but also about the processes of qualitative and interpretive research, as well as the importance of doing this kind of research. While even a close analysis of any case results in mere snapshots of a policy or set of policies, it can provide great insight into the nuances of important issues – insight not available to those conducting less context-focused research. In addition to yielding detailed information and knowledge about particular issues, case studies play a larger epistemological role. They enable us to comprehend more fully the findings, conclusions, and implications of all humanistic and social scientific research. They are key to all research in the humanities and social sciences and foundational in understanding the individual and collective endeavours of humans.

The cases I've examined in this volume are rich in detail, and I've only scratched at their surfaces. Similarly to most other cases of policy, they are intricate stories about people, how they express their concerns, values, and interests, how they negotiate norms and procedures, and how they understand and respond to decisions that ultimately become public policy, all the while embedded within a broader social, political, and institutional context. Policy cases are complex and engaging in case studies is a complex activity. To do it well involves carefully examining a wide range of materials, including policy documents, official reports, hearing submissions and transcripts, press releases, and media reports, all of which may date back to earlier decades. It also involves first-person interviews with actors who represent or reflect the various views in given policy contexts. This entails finding relevant people to interview, contacting them to break the ice, making arrangements with them to meet and talk, and travelling to sometimes remote locations to conduct these meetings.

The intention of the researcher engaging in this process is to learn about the details of the case from the points of view of insiders within the case. The researcher seeks to understand what events related to a policy mean to those directly involved. The researcher, ideally, seeks out these meanings from a broad range of individuals involved in the policy area or affected by the policy. The overarching challenge is that she is often an outsider, having a presence within the policy area for essentially mere moments. Generally speaking, in the initial research phase of her project, she is a non-expert in the substance of the particular case; she doesn't derive her livelihood from working day-to-day in the area; she doesn't have a vested economic, cultural, or personal interest at stake in the policy; and she doesn't necessarily know how to navigate the personalities involved. She is an outsider as much in the area of social housing policy in Toronto as she is in language policy in Nunavut. Of course, this outsider status is important in that it ensures some distance from the research topic, as well as from the research "subjects" and issues that arise among them. The distance is important not only to attain a reasonable level of impartiality, but also to see the larger trends and bigger pictures that emerge from people's stories. But researchers must bridge this distance in order to interpret those stories and understand the case. Those who engage in qualitative and interpretative policy research thus face significant challenges.

Some of these obstacles can be addressed in a fairly straightforward manner. It is important for researchers to be as comprehensive as possible in the initial collection, reading, and analysis of relevant materials to understand basic chronologies of events and episodes in the policy area and to generate a template of working hypotheses and interview questions. It is also important to seek out prospective interviewees who collectively constitute a balanced and wide range of interests, perspectives, and epistemologies at play within a policy area. It is critical that researchers interview individuals who can provide detailed and reasoned accounts of the policy area, their interests in it or perspectives on it, and how conflicts might be resolved. But it is also critical that they reach out to those who may be marginally positioned vis-à-vis the policy, who may be insider-outsiders. Researchers must be prepared to invest plenty of time in their case studies and the people who give life and meaning to them.

Once a reasonably broad set of interviewees is lined up, the researcher then needs to formulate and pose questions in a way that will encourage candid and informative responses. Of course, an ethics protocol for communicating with interviewees must be in place. As I'm learning in new research into sex work governance,[2] the protocol needs to include a mechanism for providing consent in spoken as opposed to written format by interviewees who for important reasons may be reluctant to engage with researchers. My advice to anyone conducting semi-structured interviews is to be humble and respectful and to listen while not being afraid to push for detail and clarity. The researcher has only a few hours (at the most) of face-to-face time with each insider she interviews, and needs to make the most of this time while respecting the individual and his or her story. All of this requires a great deal of care and sensitivity to the people and their stories that constitute the life of a policy.

A policy is not just a set of written documents feeding into a policy cycle, nor just a collection of conventions and rules that govern the stages of the policy process. Beyond formal characteristics, a policy is formed from multiple and diverse meanings assigned to it or created by many individual human beings involved in particular and overlapping policy areas. To understand the policy, researchers must endeavour to understand these meanings as they are embedded in and emerge from specific contexts. Meanings shift, which causes additional research challenges. While researchers must try to ensure that their analyses are timely and up-to-date, we will only ever capture moments of a policy. Our findings are always contingent. Despite these limitations, this kind of research is fundamental because only it can provide a carefully detailed look into the day-to-day realities of a policy, those who contribute to it, and those affected by it.

The work that I've presented here comprises a relatively coherent set of snapshots of policies, their processes, and their contexts that have been in motion for decades. The lives of these policies will likely continue for decades. They warrant much greater study than a single researcher could ever achieve. I hope that others will be inspired and intrigued by these cases and further this type of context-intensive research.

Notes

1. The Hope for and Illusion of Deliberative Democracy

1 I employ "citizen" in this volume in the same way as Archon Fung, who writes, "[By] *citizen*, I do not mean to indicate individuals who possess the legal status of formal citizenship but rather individuals who possess the political standing to exercise voice or give consent over public decisions that oblige or affect them." See Archon Fung, "Varieties of Participation in Complex Governance," *Public Administration Review* 66 (Dec. 2006): 74.

2 Deliberative Polling® is a registered trademark of James S. Fishkin. Any fees from the trademark are used to support research at the Center for Deliberative Democracy.

3 There are multiple Canadian cases representing excellent examples of participatory and deliberative democratic procedures. These include the royal commission, led by Thomas Berger, to consider the social and economic impact in the Canadian north of a proposed pipeline through the Mackenzie Valley and the royal commission, led by Roy Romanow, to examine the future of health care in Canada. See Minister of Supply and Services, *Northern Frontier, Northern Homeland*, Report of the Mackenzie Valley Pipeline Inquiry 1 (Ottawa, 1977) and Privy Council, Commission on the Future of Health Care in Canada, *Building on Values: The Future of Health Care in Canada*, Final report (Ottawa, 2002). More recently, Canada has held citizens' assemblies on electoral reform in British Columbia and Ontario. See Amy Lang, "But Is It for Real? The British Columbia Citizens' Assembly as a Model of State-Sponsored Citizen Empowerment," *Politics and Society* 35, no. 1 (2007): 35–70, and Mark E. Warren and Hilary Pearse, eds, *Designing Deliberative Democracy: The British Columbia Citizens' Assembly* (Cambridge: Cambridge University Press, 2008).

4 Maarten Hajer and Sven Kesselring, "Democracy in the Risk Society? Learning from the New Politics of Mobility in Munich," *Environmental Politics* 8, no. 3 (1999): 5.

5 John Parkinson, *Deliberating in the Real World: Problems of Legitimacy in Deliberative Democracy* (Oxford: Oxford University Press, 2006), 8.

6 Mark Warren, "Governance-Driven Democratization," *Critical Policy Studies* 3, no. 1 (2009): 3–13.

7 John Dryzek, "Democratization as Deliberative Capacity Building," *Comparative Political Studies* 42, no. 11 (2009): 1379–402. See also Carole Pateman, "APSA Presidential Address: Participatory Democracy Revisited," *Perspectives on Politics* 10, no. 1 (2012): 7–19. In addition, see Seyla Benhabib, ed., *Democracy and Difference: Contesting the Boundaries of the Political* (Princeton, NJ: Princeton University Press, 1996); James Bohman and William Rehg, eds, *Deliberative Democracy: Essays on Reason and Politics* (Cambridge, MA: MIT Press, 1997); Simone Chambers, *Reasonable Democracy: Jürgen Habermas and the Politics of Discourse* (Ithaca, NY: Cornell University Press, 1996); Joshua Cohen, "Deliberation and Democratic Legitimacy," in *Deliberative Democracy: Essays on Reason and Politics*, ed. James Bohman and William Rehg (Cambridge, MA: MIT Press, 1997), 67–91; Joshua Cohen, "Procedure and Substance in Deliberative Democracy," in *Democracy and Difference: Contesting the Boundaries of the Political*, ed. Seyla Benhabib (Princeton, NJ: Princeton University Press, 1996), 95–119; Samuel Freeman, "Deliberative Democracy: A Sympathetic Comment," *Philosophy and Public Affairs* 29, no. 4 (2000): 371–418; Amy Gutmann and Dennis Thompson, *Democracy and Disagreement: Why Moral Conflict Cannot Be Avoided in Politics, and What Should Be Done about It* (Cambridge, MA: Harvard University Press, 1996); Amy Gutmann and Dennis Thompson, "Why Deliberative Democracy Is Different," *Social Philosophy and Policy* 17, no.1 (2000): 161–80; Jürgen Habermas, *Moral Consciousness and Communicative Action* (Cambridge, MA: Polity Press, 1995); Stephen Macedo, ed., *Deliberative Politics: Essays on Democracy and Disagreement* (New York: Oxford University Press, 1999); and John Parkinson and Jane Mansbridge, eds, *Deliberative Systems: Deliberative Democracy at the Large Scale* (Cambridge: Cambridge University Press, 2012).

8 The study of deliberative democratic principles is an expanding field. Contemporary studies have benefited from a wide range of empirical examples. See, for example, Michael X. Delli Carpini et al., "Public Deliberation, Discursive Participation, and Citizen Engagement: A Review of the Empirical Literature," *Annual Review of Political Science* 7 (2004): 315–44; Archon Fung, "Survey Article. Recipes for Public Spheres: Eight Institutional Design Choices and Their Consequences," *Journal of Political Philosophy* 11, no. 3 (2003): 338–67;

Parkinson, *Deliberating in the Real World*; Jürg Steiner, *The Foundations of Deliberative Democracy: Empirical Findings and Normative Implications* (Cambridge: Cambridge University Press, 2012); Dennis F. Thompson, "Deliberative Democratic Theory and Empirical Political Science," *Annual Review of Political Science* 11 (2008): 497–520; and Warren and Pearse, eds, *Designing Deliberative Democracy*.

9 Of course, we can and *should* also celebrate this era for its intellectual, cultural, artistic, and architectural accomplishments.

10 Robert Garland, *Daily Life of the Ancient Greeks* (Indianapolis, IN: Hackett Publishing, 2008), 13.

11 John Stuart Mill, "Representative Government," in *On Liberty and Other Essays*, ed. John Gray (Oxford: Oxford University Press, 1991), 244.

12 Ibid., 256.

13 Joshua Cohen and Archon Fung, "The Radical Democracy Project," *Délibération et Action Publique* (2004): 23–34.

14 Ibid., 29.

15 Cohen, "Procedure and Substance," 99.

16 Ibid.

17 Ibid.

18 Gutmann and Thompson, *Democracy and Disagreement*.

19 Ibid., 40.

20 Ibid.

21 Seyla Benhabib, "Toward a Deliberative Model of Democratic Legitimacy," in *Democracy and Difference: Contesting the Boundaries of the Political*, ed. S. Benhabib (Princeton, NJ: Princeton University Press, 1996), 67–94.

22 Ibid., 73–4; emphasis in original.

23 Jane Mansbridge, James Bohman, Simone Chambers, Thomas Christiano, Archon Fung, John Parkinson, Dennis Thompson, and Mark Warren, "A Systematic Approach to Deliberative Democracy," in *Deliberative Systems: Deliberative Democracy at the Large Scale*, ed. Parkinson and Mansbridge, 2.

24 Ibid.; emphasis in original.

25 Ibid.

26 See William Smith on the debate within theories of deliberative democracy regarding who should, in principle, be included. See "Democracy, Deliberation, and Disobedience," *Res Publica* 10, no. 4 (2004): 353–77.

27 See Iris Marion Young, "Justice, Inclusion, and Deliberative Democracy," in *Deliberative Politics: Essays on Democracy and Disagreement*, ed. S. Macedo (New York: Oxford University Press, 1999), 151–8.

28 James Bohman, "Deliberative Democracy and Effective Social Freedom: Capabilities, Resources, and Opportunities," in *Deliberative Democracy: Essays*

on Reason and Politics, ed. James Bohman and William Rehg (Cambridge, MA: MIT Press, 1997), 324.

29 Ibid., 325.

30 Cohen, "Procedure and Substance," 106.

31 Gutmann and Thompson, *Democracy and Disagreement*, 53.

32 Jane Mansbridge, James Bohman, Simone Chambers, David Estlund, Andreas Føllesdal, Archon Fung, Cristina Lafont, Bernard Manin, and José Luis Martí, "The Place of Self-Interest and the Role of Power in Deliberative Democracy," *Journal of Political Philosophy* 18, no. 1 (2010): 67.

33 Gutmann and Thompson, *Democracy and Disagreement*, 53.

34 John S. Dryzek, "Deliberative Democracy in Divided Societies: Alternatives to Agonism and Analgesia," *Political Theory* 33, no. 2 (2005): 218–42.

35 Christian F. Rostbøll, "Emancipation or Accommodation?: Habermasian vs. Rawlsian Deliberative Democracy," *Philosophy and Social Criticism* 34, no. 7 (2008): 707–36.

36 John S. Dryzek and Simon Niemeyer, "Reconciling Pluralism and Consensus as Political Ideals," *American Journal of Political Science* 50, no. 3 (2006): 634. John Elster, for example, sees consensus as the ideal for public agreement. See Elster, "The Market and the Forum: Three Varieties of Political Theory," in *Foundations of Social Choice Theory*, ed. Jon Elster and Aanund Hylland (Cambridge, MA: Cambridge University Press, 1986), 103–32.

37 Dryzek rightfully notes that the "ideal of consensus has long been rejected by most deliberative democrats, even those sympathetic to the Habermasian tradition where consensus once played a central role in the counterfactual standard of the ideal speech situation." See John S. Dryzek, "Legitimacy and Economy in Deliberative Democracy," *Political Theory* 29, no. 5 (2001): 661.

38 Gutmann and Thompson, *Democracy and Disagreement*, 93–4.

39 James Bohman, *Public Deliberation: Pluralism, Complexity and Democracy* (Cambridge, MA: MIT Press, 1996).

40 Ibid., 100; emphasis in original.

41 Jorge Valadez, *Deliberative Democracy: Political Legitimacy, and Self-Determination Societies* (Boulder, CO: Westview Press, 2001).

42 Cass Sunstein, "Deliberation, Democracy, Disagreement," in *Justice and Democracy: Cross-Cultural Perspectives*, ed. Ron Bontekoe and Marietta Stepaniants (Honolulu: University of Hawaii Press, 1997), 96.

43 Simon Niemeyer and John S. Dryzek, "The Ends of Deliberation: Meta-consensus and Inter-subjective Rationality as Ideal Outcomes," *Swiss Political Science Review* 13, no. 4 (2007): 497–526.

44 Ibid., 500.

45 Ibid.

46 James Fishkin, "Deliberative Polling: Toward a Better-Informed Democracy," 2004. http://cdd.stanford.edu/polls/docs/summary/.

47 For examples, see Benhabib, *Democracy and Difference*; Bohman, *Public Deliberation*; Chambers, *Reasonable Democracy*; Cohen, "Procedure and Substance" and "Deliberation and Democratic Legitimacy"; John S. Dryzek, *Discursive Democracy: Politics, Policy and Political Science* (Cambridge: Cambridge University Press, 1990) and *Deliberative Democracy and Beyond: Liberals, Critics, Contestations* (New York: Oxford University Press, 2000); Freeman, "Deliberative Democracy"; Fung, "Varieties of Participation in Complex Governance"; Gutmann and Thompson, *Democracy and Disagreement*, "Why Deliberative Democracy Is Different," and *Why Deliberative Democracy?* (Princeton: Princeton University Press, 2004); Parkinson, *Deliberating in the Real World*; Valadez, *Deliberative Democracy*; Warren, "Governance-Driven Democratization"; Melissa S. Williams, "The Uneasy Alliance of Group Representation and Inclusion, and Deliberative Democracy," in *Citizenship in Diverse Societies*, ed. Will Kymlicka and Wayne Norman (Oxford: Oxford University Press, 2000), 124–52; and Young, "Justice, Inclusion, and Deliberative Democracy."

48 See Andrew Knops, "Delivering Deliberation's Emancipatory Potential," *Political Theory* 34, no. 5 (2006): 594–623.

49 Archon Fung, "Deliberative Democracy, Chicago Style: Grass-roots Governance in Policing and Public Education," in *Deepening Democracy: Institutional Innovations in Empowered Participatory Government*, ed. Archon Fung and Erik Olin Wright (London: Verso, 2003), 118–19.

50 Stephen Elstub, "Weber's Dilemma and a Dualist Model of Deliberative and Associational Democracy," *Contemporary Political Theory* 7, no. 2 (2008): 170.

51 Jason Barabas, "How Deliberation Affects Policy Opinions," *American Political Science Review* 98, no. 4 (2004): 687–701.

52 Ibid., 699.

53 Ibid.

54 Robert E. Goodin and John S. Dryzek, "Deliberative Impacts: The Macro-Political Uptake of Mini-Publics," *Politics and Society* 34, no. 2 (2006): 219–44.

55 Elstub, "Weber's Dilemma," 169–70.

56 Ibid., 179.

57 Henrik Wagenaar, "Democracy and Prostitution: Deliberating the Legalization of Brothels in the Netherlands," *Administration and Society* 38, no. 2 (2006): 198–235.

58 John Gastil and Katherine Knobloch, *Evaluation Report to the Oregon State Legislature on the 2010 Oregon Citizens' Initiative Review* (Seattle: University of Washington, 2010) and Katherine Knobloch, John Gastil, Robert Richards,

and Traci Feller, *Evaluation Report on the 2012 Citizens' Initiative Reviews for the Oregon CIR Commission* (State College: Pennsylvania State University, 2013).

59 John Gastil, Robert Richards, and Katherine Knobloch, "Vicarious Deliberation: How the Oregon Citizens' Initiative Review Influenced Deliberation in Mass Elections," *International Journal of Communication* 8 (2014): 62–89.

60 Vibeke Normann Andersen and Kasper M. Hansen, "How Deliberation Makes Better Citizens: The Danish Deliberative Poll on the Euro," *European Journal of Political Research* 46, no. 4 (2007): 531–56.

61 Ibid., 553. See Mansbridge, Bohman, Chambers, Estlund et al., "The Place of Self-Interest and the Role of Power in Deliberative Democracy."

62 Carolyn Hendriks, "When the Forum Meets Interest Politics: Strategic Uses of Public Deliberation," *Politics and Society* 34, no. 4 (2006): 573.

63 Ibid., 593.

64 Paul J. Maginn, "Deliberative Democracy or Discursively Biased? Perth's Dialogue with the City Initiative," *Space and Polity* 11, no. 3 (2007): 331–52.

65 Yannis Papadopoulos and Philippe Warin, "Are Innovative, Participatory, and Deliberative Procedures in Policy Making Democratic and Effective?" *European Journal of Political Research* 46, no. 4 (2007): 449–50 and 459.

66 Ibid., 459.

67 Archon Fung and Erik Olin Wright, "Thinking about Empowered Par-ticipatory Governance," in *Deepening Democracy: Institutional Innovations in Empowered Participatory Government*, ed. Archon Fung and Erik Olin Wright (London: Verso, 2003), 23.

68 Andrea Cornwall, "Deliberating Democracy: Scenes from a Brazilian Municipal Health Council," *Politics and Society* 36, no. 4 (2008): 508–31.

69 Ibid., 525.

70 Leonardo Avritzer, "New Public Spheres in Brazil: Local Democracy and Deliberative Politics," *International Journal of Urban and Regional Research* 30, no. 3 (2006): 623–37.

71 Ibid., 623.

72 Ibid.

73 Celina Sousa, "Local Democratization in Brazil: Strengths and Dilemmas of Deliberative Democracy," *Development* 50, no. 1 (2007): 90–5.

74 Ibid., 93.

75 See Hendrik Wagenaar, *Meaning in Action: Interpretation and Dialogue in Policy Analysis* (Armonk, NY: M.E. Sharpe, 2011).

2. Participatory Budgeting and the Toronto Community Housing Corporation

1 I prefer the term resident to tenant. Tenant, as a term, suggests a holding of property for a limited period of time. While TCHC residents are renters, and the TCHC is the landlord, they also form communities among themselves, some of which are more long term and stable than "tenant" suggests. "Resident" better captures this idea of community. I use "tenant" when referring directly to the TCHC's Tenant Participation System.

2 See "TCHC Citizen Board Members Resign En Masse: Spending Shows 'Blatant Disregard': Auditor General," *CBC News*, 3 March 2011, http://www.cbc.ca/news/canada/toronto/tchc-citizen-board-members-resign-en-masse-1.1006242, accessed 5 December 2014; "City Hall Dissolves TCHC Board, Replaces It with One Director," *National Post*, 10 March 2011, http://news.nationalpost.com/2011/03/10/ford-urges-fresh-start-at-tchc/, accessed 5 December 2014; and *Globe and Mail*, "'One Man Board' Oust TCHC CEO," 17 March 2011, http://www.theglobeandmail.com/news/toronto/one-man-board-ousts-tchc-ceo/article573016/, accessed 5 December 2014.

3 Auditor General's Office, City of Toronto, *Toronto Community Housing Corporation Controls over Employee Expenses Are Ineffective. Appendix 1* (Toronto, 7 December 2010), 2.

4 Auditor General's Office, City of Toronto, *Toronto Community Housing Corporation Procurement Policies and Procedures Are Not Being Followed* (Toronto, 7 December 2010).

5 Auditor General's Office, City of Toronto, *Review of Controls over Procurement and Payment Functions at TCHC Subsidiary: Housing Services Inc.* (Toronto, 9 December 2011).

6 Participatory Budgeting (PB), Toronto Community Housing, http://www.torontohousing.ca/pb, accessed 15 August 2013, 2.

7 Participatory Budgeting (PB), Toronto Community Housing, http://www.torontohousing.ca/pb, accessed 15 August 2013.

8 The 2001/2 allocation to tenant participation was $18 million. Subsequent allocations were $9 million a year (1.8 for distribution by the Inter-CHU and 7.2 for distribution within CHUs). See TCHC, *Community Management Plan 2006, 2007, 2008* (Toronto, 2005), 44.

9 Former TCHC board member, interview with author, Toronto, 13 August 2007.

10 TCHC, "Participatory Planning and Budgeting – Our Own Story," Lifelong Citizenship Learning, Participatory Democracy, and Social Change

Conference (Toronto: Ontario Institute for Studies in Education, University of Toronto, 15–17 May 2003).

11 Andreas Novy and Bernhard Leubolt, "Participatory Budgeting in Porto Alegre: Social Innovation and the Dialectical Relationship of State and Civil Society," *Urban Studies* 42, no. 11 (2005): 2026.

12 Ibid.

13 Ibid.

14 Graham Smith, *Democratic Innovations: Designing Institutions for Citizen Participation* (New York: Cambridge University Press, 2009), 35.

15 Novy and Leubolt, "Participatory Budgeting in Porto Alegre," 2028.

16 Ibid.

17 See Tarso Genro and Ubiritan de Souza, *Orçamento Participativo: A experiência de Porto Alegre* (São Paulo: Fundação PerseuAbramo, 1997) and L. Fedozzi, *Orçamento Participativo: Reflexões sobre a experiência de Porto Alegre*, 3rd ed. (Porto Alegre: Tomo Editorial, 2001), cited in Novy and Leubolt, "Participatory Budgeting in Porto Alegre," 2027.

18 Pateman, "Participatory Democracy Revisited," 12.

19 Yves Cabannes, *72 Frequently Asked Questions about Participatory Budgeting: Global Campaign on Urban Governance* (Quito: United Nations Human Settlements Programme, 2004), 40.

20 Ibid.

21 For a more detailed accounted, see Rebecca Neaera Abers, "Learning Democratic Practice: Distributing Government Resources through Popular Participation in Porto Alegre, Brazil," in *Cities for Citizens*, ed. Mike Douglass and John Friedmann (Chichester and New York: Wiley, 1998), 39–65; Rebecca Neaera Abers, *Inventing Local Democracy: Grassroots Politics in Brazil* (Boulder, CO, and London: Lynne Rienner, 2000); Gianpaolo Baiochi, "Participation, Activism and Politics: The Porto Alegre Experiment," in *Deepening Democracy: Institutional Innovations in Empowered Participatory Governance*, ed. Archon Fung and Erik Olin Wright (London: Verso, 2003) 45–76. See also Cabannes, *72 Frequently Asked Questions about Participatory Budgeting*; Cabannes, "Participatory Budgeting: A Significant Contribution to Participatory Democracy," *Environment and Urbanization* 16, no. 1 (2004): 27–46; Harvard University Center for Urban Development Studies, *Assessment of Participatory Budgeting in Brazil* (Washington, DC: Inter-American Development Bank, 2003); and Pateman, "Participatory Democracy Revisited."

22 Boaventura de Sousa Santos, "Participatory Budgeting in Porto Alegre: Towards a Redistributive Democracy," *Politics and Society* 26, no. 4 (1998): 468–9; Smith, *Democratic Innovations*; and Cabannes, *72 Frequently Asked*

Questions. See also http://lproweb.procempa.com.br/pmpa/prefpoa/op/ usu_doc/ciclo_op_2013_detalhado.pdf, accessed 15 August 2013.

23 Smith, *Democratic Innovations*, 36–7.
24 Ibid., 37.
25 Santos, "Participatory Budgeting," 473. See also http://lproweb.procempa. com.br/pmpa/prefpoa/op/usu_doc/ciclo_op_2013_detalhado.pdf.
26 See Smith, *Democratic Innovations*, 37.
27 Novy and Leubolt, "Participatory Budgeting in Porto Alegre," 2027.
28 Cabannes, *72 Frequently Asked Questions about Participatory Budgeting*, 20.
29 Ibid., 21.
30 Brian Wampler, "A Guide to Participatory Budgeting," in *Participatory Budgeting*, Public Sector Governance and Accountability Series, ed. Anwar Shaw (Washington, DC: International Bank for Reconstruction and Development /The World Bank 2007), 22–3.
31 Smith, *Democratic Innovations*, 34.
32 Ibid.
33 TCHC, *Annual Report 2012* (Toronto, May 2013), 2.
34 Ibid.
35 According to the TCHC, the corporation "has an annual budget of about $600 million, $6 billion in assets, an investment portfolio of over $150 million, and 10 property development projects underway," which represents "$1 billion of new construction"; see http://www.torontohousing.ca/ general_counsel_tchc, accessed 15 August 2013.
36 TCHC, *Annual Report 2012*, 17–18.
37 See http://www.toronto.ca/abcc/obca-community-housing.htm, accessed 15 August 2013.
38 See "2011 Organizational Structure," http://www.torontohousing.ca/ webfm_send/7371/1, accessed 15 August 2013.
39 See http://www.torontohousing.ca/our_housing, accessed 30 November 2014.
40 Former TCHC board member, interview and Penny Milton (former TCHC board member), interview with author, Toronto, 14 May 2008.
41 Ibid.
42 TCHC, *2009 Annual Review: Tenants First—Collaboration, Cooperation, Community* (Toronto, 2009), 5.
43 Josh Lerner and Estair Van Wagner, "Participatory Budgeting in Canada: Democratic Innovations in Strategic Spaces," unedited chapter in *Progressive Cities*, ed. Daniel Chavez and Einaar Braathen, (Norwegian Institute for Urban and Regional Research, 2006), http://www.tni.org/archives/ newpol-docs_pbcanada.

44 TCHC, *Community Based Business Planning in Toronto Community Housing* (Toronto, 2003).

45 Ibid.

46 TCHC, *Community Management Plan 2006, 2007, 2008*, 44.

47 TCHC, *A Guide to Toronto Community Housing Tenant Elections: Tenant Participation – Shaping Our Future Together* (undated), 3.

48 Ibid.

49 Martha McGuire, *The Toronto Community Housing Corporation Tenant Participation System: Final Evaluation Report* (Toronto: TCHC, 2006), 17–18.

50 http://www.torontohousing.ca/news/20090623/tenant_elections_2009_ tenants_vote_shape_their_future, accessed 3 September 2013.

51 Penny Milton, interview, Toronto, 13 August 2007.

52 Gail Johnson (former community health consultant, TCHC), interview with author, Toronto, 13 August 2007.

53 Ken Thompson (former manager of community health, TCHC), interview with author, Toronto, 13 August 2007.

54 Derek Ballantyne (former CEO, TCHC), interview with author, Toronto, 14 August 2007; former TCHC board member, interview; CHU manager no. 1, interview with author, Toronto, 13 August 2007; Gail Johnson, interview, 13 August 2007; Ken Thompson, interview.

55 McGuire, *The Toronto Community Housing Corporation Tenant Participation System*, 17–18.

56 City of Toronto, "Results of Tenant Election to Toronto Community Housing Corporation Board of Directors" (8 November 2007), 2.

57 In 2009, subsequent to the reorganization of the CHUs into operating units, there were changes to the participation system, including having multiple Allocation Days. See Josh Lerner, *Participatory Budgeting at Toronto Community Housing: Findings and Recommendations from Participatory Research with Tenants and Staff*, Evaluation report (Toronto, 2009), 6.

58 TCHC, "Youth Tenant Elections – Update" (17 June 2010), 1.

59 Lerner and Van Wagner, "Participatory Budgeting in Canada."

60 Gail Johnson, interview, 13 August 2007, and CHU manager no. 1, interview, 13 August 2007.

61 Former TCHC board member, interview, and Gail Johnson, interview, 13 August 2007.

62 McGuire, *Toronto Community Housing Corporation Tenant Participation System*, 10.

63 Lerner, *Participatory Budgeting at Toronto Community Housing*, 3.

64 McGuire, *Toronto Community Housing Corporation Tenant Participation System*, 13–14. This concern also surfaced in the 2009 evaluation. See Lerner, *Participatory Budgeting at Toronto Community Housing*, 14.

65 Gail Johnson, interview, 13 August 2007.
66 McGuire, *Toronto Community Housing Corporation Tenant Participation System*, 12.
67 Lerner, *Participatory Budgeting at Toronto Community Housing*, 20.
68 Ibid., 13–14.
69 Ibid., 19.
70 McGuire, *Toronto Community Housing Corporation Tenant Participation System*, 12.
71 Lerner, *Participatory Budgeting at Toronto Community Housing*, 14–21.
72 Ibid., 8.
73 Lerner and Van Wagner, "Participatory Budgeting in Canada."
74 Ibid.
75 TCHC resident no. 1, interview with author, Toronto, 13 August 2007.
76 Former TCHC board member, interview.
77 TCHC tenant representative no. 3, interview with author, Toronto, 25 June 2008.
78 McGuire, *The Toronto Community Housing Corporation Tenant Participation System*, 9.
79 "Participatory Budgeting – Working Together, Making a Difference." http://www.torontohousing.ca/participatory_budgeting, accessed 4 August 2013.
80 McGuire, *The Toronto Community Housing Corporation Tenant Participation System*, 9.
81 Lerner, *Participatory Budgeting at Toronto Community Housing*, 9 and 19.
82 Ibid., 9.
83 Ibid., 19.
84 City of Toronto, "Infrastructure Ontario Refinancing of Toronto Community Housing Mortgages" (Toronto, 6 March 2013), 6.
85 TCHC employee, interview with author, Toronto, 25 June 2008.
86 City of Toronto, "Infrastructure Ontario Refinancing."
87 McGuire, *Toronto Community Housing Corporation Tenant Participation System*, 9.
88 Ibid.
89 Lerner, *Participatory Budgeting at Toronto Community Housing*, 19.
90 Ibid., 21.
91 TCHC resident no. 2, interview with author, Toronto, 25 June 2008; TCHC tenant representative no. 3, interview; and TCHC tenant representative no. 4, interview with author, Toronto, 25 June 2008.
92 TCHC resident no. 2, interview.
93 Derek Ballantyne, interview.
94 Ibid.
95 Penny Milton, interview, Toronto, 14 May 2008.

96 See for example, CHU manager no. 4, interview with author, Toronto, 16 May 2008; CHU manager no. 5, interview with author, Toronto, 16 May 2008; and Gail Johnson, interview, 16 May 2008.

97 CHU manager no. 1, interview, 14 May 2008.

98 TCHC resident no. 1, interview; TCHC tenant representative no. 1, interview with author, Toronto, 18 June 2008; and TCHC tenant representative no. 2, interview with author, Toronto, 24 June 2008.

99 Lerner and Van Wagner, "Participatory Budgeting in Canada."

100 TCHC employee, interview, and TCHC management employee, interview with author, Toronto, 15 May 2008.

101 TCHC management employee, interview.

102 Derek Ballantyne, interview.

103 City of Toronto to the Toronto Community Housing Corporation, *Shareholder Direction: Joint Policy and Finance / Community Services Report 1(1) as Amended* (2001), 11.

104 Lerner and Van Wagner, "Participatory Budgeting in Canada."

105 Ibid.

106 TCHC management employee, interview; TCHC resident no. 2, interview; and TCHC tenant representative no. 3, interview.

107 CHU manager no. 4, interview.

108 CHU manager no. 1, interview, 14 May 2008.

109 Auditor General's Office, *Toronto Community Housing Corporation Controls over Employee Expenses Are Ineffective*, 2.

110 Ibid.

111 Ibid.

112 Ibid.

113 Ibid., 9.

114 Auditor General's Office, *Toronto Community Housing Corporation Procurement Policies and Procedures* and *Review of Controls over Procurement and Payment Functions*.

115 Auditor General's Office, *Procurement Policies and Procedures*, 4.

116 TCHC resident no. 4, interview with author, Toronto, 25 June 2008.

3. Deliberative Polling and Nova Scotia Power Incorporated

1 See NSPI, *Nova Scotia Power Customer Energy Forum* (Halifax, 2004); Will Guild, Ron Lehr, and Dennis Thomas, "Nova Scotia Power Customer Energy Forum: Summary of Results" (The Public Decision Partnership, 2004); NSPI, *Customer Energy Forum 2005* (Halifax, 2005); and NSPI, *Customer Energy Forum 2009* (Halifax, 2009).

2 NSPI, *Customer Energy Forum 2009*, 2.

3 NSPI, "How We Make Electricity," https://www.nspower.ca/en/home/ about-us/how-we-make-electricity/thermal-electricity/default-aspx, accessed 12 July 2012.

4 "Special Report: A Report on Canada's Largest Greenhouse Gas Polluters in 2006," *Corporate Knights: Investment Issue* (Winter 2008): 21.

5 Nova Scotia Department of Energy, *Toward a Greener Future: Nova Scotia's 2009 Energy Strategy* (Halifax, 2009), 8.

6 NSPI's current electricity generating portfolio is the following: Coal 59%; Natural Gas 21%, Renewables (wind, hydro, tidal, and biomass) 18%; and other (imported power and oil) 2%. See https://www.nspower.ca/ en/home/about-us/how-we-make-electricity/default.aspx, accessed 19 November 2014.

7 Efficiency Nova Scotia, *Be the Change: Using Energy Better Annual Report* (Dartmouth, 2012), 6.

8 Guild, Lehr, and Thomas, "Nova Scotia Power Customer Energy Forum," 9.

9 See NSPI, *Customer Energy Forum 2005*; NSPI, "Nova Scotia Power Acts on Customer Advice," press release (Halifax, 28 June 2005); and NSPI, *Customer Energy Forum 2009*.

10 James Fishkin, interviewed by Masahiro Tsuruoka, "Interview with James Fishkin: Deliberative Polling Should Be Used in Key Policy Issues Like Energy," *Asahi Shimbun: The Electric Daily News*, 24 February 2012.

11 Ibid.

12 James Fishkin and Cynthia Farrar, "Deliberative Polling: From Experiment to Community Resource," in *The Deliberative Democracy Handbook: Strategies for Effective Civic Engagement in the 21st Century*, ed. John Gastil and Peter Levine (San Francisco: Jossey-Bass, 2005), 68–79.

13 Ibid., 71.

14 Ibid., 75.

15 Ibid., 74.

16 Ibid.

17 Ibid.

18 Ibid.

19 Ibid., 74–5.

20 Ibid., 72.

21 Ibid.

22 Ibid.

23 Ibid., 76.

24 Ibid.

25 Ibid.
26 Ron Lehr, Will Guild, Dennis Thomas, and Blair Swezey, "Listening to Customers: How Deliberative Polling Helped Build 1,000 MW of New Renewable Energy Projects in Texas" (Golden, CO: National Renewable Energy Laboratory, June 2003), 1.
27 Ibid.
28 Ibid.
29 Ibid.
30 Ibid.
31 NSPI, "Return on Equity (ROE)," http://www.nspower.ca/en/home/aboutnspower/operations/roe.aspx, accessed 11 September 2013.
32 Desiree Finhert, "Nova Scotia Power to Pay Customers Back out of Extra Profits," 21 July 2011, http://www.news957.com/2011/07/21/nova-scotia-power-to-pay-customers-back-out-of-extra-profits/, accessed 11 September 2013.
33 https://www.nspower.ca/en/home/about-us/who-we-are/default.aspx, accessed 23 November 2014.
34 Ibid.
35 NSPI employee no. 2, interview with author, Halifax, 21 May 2008, and NSPI employee no. 3, interview with author, Halifax, 22 May 2008.
36 Guild et al., "Nova Scotia Power Customer Energy Forum," 4.
37 Ibid., 9.
38 NSPI, *Nova Scotia Power Customer Energy Forum*, 4.
39 Ibid., 6.
40 Ibid., 5.
41 "Nova Scotians Discuss Future Energy Alternatives," The Center for Deliberative Democracy, Stanford University, 19 November 2004, http://cdd.stanford.edu/polls/energy/2004/ns-discuss-energy.html.
42 Guild et al., "Nova Scotia Power Customer Energy Forum," 9.
43 Ibid., 10.
44 Nova Scotia Department of Finance, Economics and Statistical Division, *Nova Scotia Statistical Review 2004* (Halifax, 2004), xiii. In 2013, the population was estimated to be 945,015. See Nova Scotia Finance and Treasury Board, "Nova Scotia Population Estimates as of April 1, 2013," http://www.gov.ns.ca/finance/statistics/archive_news.asp?id=8736&ym=3.
45 Guild et al., "Nova Scotia Power Customer Energy Forum," 8.
46 Ibid.
47 Ibid., 4.
48 Ibid.
49 See NSPI, *Nova Scotia Power Customer Energy Forum*, 58.

50 Megan Leslie (former Community Legal Worker, Dalhousie Legal Aid), telephone interview with author, Halifax, 20 August 2007.
51 Conserve Nova Scotia employee, interview with author, Halifax, 12 June 2007 and Judith Lipp (consultant on energy issues), interview with author, Toronto, 17 June 2007.
52 Guild et al., "Nova Scotia Power Customer Energy Forum: Summary of Results," 59.
53 NSPI, "NSPI Customer Energy Forum Expert Panels," internal document (Halifax, 26 Oct. 2004).
54 Customer Energy Forum moderator, interview with author, Halifax, 13 June 2007.
55 Ibid. and Judith Lipp, interview, 17 June 2007.
56 Guild et al., "Nova Scotia Power Customer Energy Forum," 58.
57 Ibid.
58 Bruce Cameron (Nova Scotia Department of Energy), interview with author, Halifax, 11 June 2007.
59 Ibid.
60 Customer Energy Forum moderator, interview, and NSPI employee no. 1, interview with author, Halifax, 11 June 2007.
61 NSPI employee no. 1, interview.
62 Guild et al., "Nova Scotia Power Customer Energy Forum," 13.
63 Ibid.
64 Ibid., 14.
65 Ibid., 5.
66 Ibid.
67 Ibid., 44.
68 Ibid., 7.
69 Guild et al., "Nova Scotia Power Customer Energy Forum."
70 NSPI, "Nova Scotia Power Acts on Customer Advice, Proposes $5 Million More for Conservation," 28 June 2005, http://www.emera.com/en/home/mediacentre/archivedpr/2005/novascotiapower5million.aspx.
71 Brendan Haley (former Ecology Action Centre energy coordinator), interview with author, Halifax, 12 June 2007, and Nova Scotia Utility and Review Board, "Application by Nova Scotia Power Incorporated for approval of certain revisions to its rates, charges, and regulations" (Nova Scotia, 2006).
72 Ibid., 36.
73 NSPI, "Nova Scotia Power Proposes Conservation and Energy Efficiency Plan," news release (Halifax, 31 January 2008).
74 Ibid.

75 NSPI, "Conservation and Energy Efficiency Programs to Go Forward," news release (21 April 2008).
76 Nova Scotia Department of Energy, *Renewable Electricity Plan: A Path to Good Jobs, Stable Prices, and a Cleaner Environment* (Halifax, April 2010), 7.
77 Nova Scotia, *Seizing the Opportunity: Nova Scotia's Energy Strategy*, vol. 1 (Halifax, 2001).
78 Ibid., 28.
79 Ibid., 29.
80 Nova Scotia Department of Energy, *Renewable Electricity Plan*, 6.
81 Nova Scotia Department of Energy, *Renewable Energy Standard*, NS Reg. 35/2007 (Halifax, 2007), 4(1). Amended in 2013.
82 Ibid., s. 5(2)(b).
83 Nova Scotia Department of Energy, *Renewable Electricity Plan*, 2.
84 Nova Scotia Department of Energy, *Renewable Energy Standard*, NS Reg. 155/2010 (Halifax, 2010).
85 NSPI, "New Wind Power for Nova Scotia," news release (Halifax, 19 November 2007).
86 NSPI, "Backgrounder on Key Renewable Milestones" (Halifax, 2009).
87 Nova Scotia, Environmental Goals and Sustainability Prosperity Act (Halifax, 2007). See also Nova Scotia, *Renewable Energy Standard Regulations*, NS Reg. 35 (Halifax, 2007).
88 NSPI employee no. 2, interview.
89 Brendan Haley, interview, 22 May 2008, and Judith Lipp, interview, 16 May 2008.
90 Department of Energy employee, interview with author, Halifax, 22 May 2008.
91 NSPI employee no. 3, interview.
92 The 2004 Deliberative Poll cost approximately $258,000. See NSPI, "Deliberative Polling Budget Estimates," internal document (Halifax, 6 May 2004).
93 NSPI employee no. 1, interview.
94 NSPI employee no. 3, interview.
95 Conserve Nova Scotia employee, interview; Nova Scotia Department of Energy employee, interview; NSPI employee no. 1, interview; NSPI employee no. 2, interview; and NSPI employee no. 3, interview.
96 Department of Energy employee, interview, and Judith Lipp, interview, 16 May 2008.
97 NSPI employee no. 3, interview.
98 Interview, 22 May 2008.
99 NSPI employee no. 3, interview; Brendan Haley, 22 May 2008; and Judith Lipp, interview, 16 May 2008.

100 Nova Scotia Department of Energy employee, interview.
101 NSPI employee no. 2, interview.
102 Brendan Haley (former Ecology Action Centre energy coordinator), interview, 12 June 2007; Judith Lipp, interview, 17 June 2007; and Megan Leslie, interview.
103 Brendan Haley, interview, 12 June 2007; Judith Lipp, interview, 17 June 2007; and Nova Scotia commentator, interview with author, Halifax, 30 July 2007.
104 Nova Scotia commentator, interview.
105 Ibid.
106 "Deliberative Opinion Poll Conducted on Future Energy Choices," *Denki Shimbun* (The Electric Daily News), 7 August 2012.
107 "Editorial: 'Deliberative Polling' Is a Good 1st Step," *Asahi Shimbun* (The Electric Daily News), 8 August 2012.

4. National Consultations and the Nuclear Waste Management Organization

1 This chapter is a development of previous work published in Genevieve Fuji Johnson, *Deliberative Democracy for the Future: The Case of Nuclear Waste Management Policy in Canada* (Toronto: University of Toronto Press, 2008).
2 In 2004, the Government of New Brunswick assigned responsibility for the province's nuclear generating assets to a new subsidiary corporation, NB Power Nuclear.
3 NWMO, *Choosing a Way Forward: The Future Management of Canada's Used Nuclear Fuel. Final Study Report* (Toronto: NWMO, 2005), 4.
4 Ibid., 17.
5 Stratos, *Dialogue on Choosing a Way Forward: The NWMO Draft Study Report. Summary Report* (Toronto: NWMO, 2005), 1.
6 Trudeau Foundation and Sierra Club of Canada, "Roundtable Discussion on Nuclear Waste Management" (Toronto: Trudeau Foundation and Sierra Club of Canada, 2005); United Church of Canada, Justice, Global and Ecumenical Relations Unit, *Comments of the United Church of Canada to the Nuclear Waste Management Organization on the Draft Study Report* (Toronto: United Church of Canada, 2005); and United Church of Canada, Justice, Global and Ecumenical Relations Unit, *The Response of the United Church of Canada to the Nuclear Waste Management Organization Final Report* (Toronto: United Church of Canada, 2005).
7 Assembly of First Nations (AFN), *Nuclear Fuel Waste Dialogue: Phase II Progress Report* (Ottawa: AFN, 2005); Congress of Aboriginal Peoples (CAP),

Understanding the Choices: Summary of Key Observations Regarding NWMO Discussion, Document 2 (Ottawa: CAP, 2005).

8 See http://www.nwmo.ca/help_design, accessed 13 August 2014.

9 See http://www.nwmo.ca/regional-information-sessions-conducted-in-2010, accessed 13 August 2014.

10 See http://www.nwmo.ca/communityopenhousesession, accessed 13 August 2014.

11 NWMO, *Implementing Adaptive Phased Management: 2012–2016* (Toronto: NWMO, March 2012), 2.

12 NWMO is also in ongoing discussion with Aboriginal councils and organizations, including First Nations that are located in areas surrounding the communities in the site selection process. See NWMO, *Aboriginal Policy* (Toronto: NWMO, 2014).

13 Ibid., 13.

14 Canadian Nuclear Safety Commission (CNSC), "Nuclear Power Plants," updated on 6 June 2014. http://www.cnsc-ccsn.gc.ca/eng/reactors/power-plants/index.cfm.

15 NWMO, *Choosing a Way Forward: Final Study Report*, 15.

16 Canadian Environmental Assessment Agency (CEAA), *Nuclear Fuel Waste Management and Disposal Concept: Report of the Nuclear Fuel Waste Management and Disposal Concept* (Ottawa: Minister of Public Works and Government Services Canada, 1998), 4.

17 Ibid.

18 A.M. Aikin, J.M. Harrison, and F.K. Hare, *The Management of Canada's Nuclear Wastes: Report of a Study Prepared under Contract for the Minister of Energy, Mines and Resources Canada* (Ottawa: Government of Canada, 1977).

19 Canada/Ontario, "Joint Statement on Radioactive Waste Management Program" (Ottawa and Toronto: Minister of Energy, Mines and Resources Canada and Ontario Energy Minister, 1978).

20 AECL and Ontario Hydro were directed specifically to develop a concept, and not site-specific plans, for deep geological disposal. The governments of Canada and Ontario announced in 1981 that no disposal site selection would be undertaken until after the concept had been accepted, so that no particular community would feel that it had been pre-selected without proper consultation (Canada/Ontario, "Joint Statement on the Nuclear Fuel Waste Management Program" [Ottawa and Toronto: Minister of Energy, Mines and Resources Canada and Ontario Energy Minister, 1981]).

21 AECL, *Environmental Impact Statement on the Concept for Disposal of Canada's Nuclear Fuel Waste* (Atomic Energy of Canada Limited Report AECL-10711, COG-93-1, 1994), 5.

22 Ibid.
23 CEAA, *Nuclear Fuel Waste Management and Disposal Concept*, 84–5.
24 Ibid., 2.
25 Ibid.
26 Ibid., 64–79.
27 Ibid., 70–1.
28 Natural Resources Canada, "Government of Canada Response to Recommendations of the Nuclear Fuel Waste Management and Disposal Concept Environmental Assessment Panel" (Ottawa: Government of Canada, 1998), 12.
29 Bill C-27, An Act Respecting the Long-Term Management of Nuclear Fuel Waste, 1st sess., 37th Parliament, 2002, SC 2002.
30 NWMO, *Choosing a Way Forward: The Future Management of Canada's Used Nuclear Fuel. Draft Study Report* (Toronto: NWMO, 2005), 267–71.
31 Elizabeth Dowdeswell (former president, NWMO), interview with author, Toronto, 6 June 2005 and NWMO employee, interview with author, Toronto, 6 June 2005.
32 See Judy Watling, Judith Maxwell, Nandini Saxena, and Suzanne Taschereau, *Responsible Action: Citizens' Dialogue on the Long-term Management of Used Nuclear Fuel*, Research report P/04, Public Involvement Network (Ottawa: Canadian Policy Research Networks, 2004).
33 DPRA Canada, *Final Report: National Stakeholders and Regional Dialogue Sessions* (Toronto: NWMO, 2004), 3.
34 Hardy Stevenson and Associates Limited, *Final Report: National Stakeholders and Regional Dialogue Sessions* (Toronto: NWMO, 2005).
35 Stratos, *Dialogue on Choosing a Way Forward*.
36 NWMO, *Ethical and Social Framework*, NWMO Background Papers and Workshop Reports (Toronto: NWMO, 2004).
37 David Shoesmith and Les Shemilt, *Workshop on the Technical Aspects of Nuclear Fuel Waste Management: Executive Summary*, NWMO Background Papers and Workshop Reports (Toronto: NWMO, 2003).
38 Coleman, Bright Associates and Patterson Consulting, *Development of the Environmental Component of the NWMO Analytical Framework*, NWMO Background Papers and Workshop Reports (Toronto: NWMO, 2003).
39 Global Business Network (GBN), *Looking Forward to Learn: Future Scenarios for Testing Different Approaches to Managing Used Nuclear Fuel in Canada*, NWMO Background Papers and Workshop Reports (Toronto: NWMO, 2003).
40 NWMO, *Choosing a Way Forward: Final Study Report*, 267.
41 Ibid., 267.
42 Ibid., 31.

43 See, for example, Thomas Berger, *Comments on NWMO's Consultation Process* (Toronto: NWMO, 2005); Andrew Brook (professor of philosophy and director, Institute of Cognitive Science), interview with author, Ottawa, 9 May 2005; NWMO Advisory Council member, telephone interview with author, 5 October 2005; Dave Hardy (principal, Hardy Stevenson and Associates Ltd), interview with author, Toronto, 30 September 2005; John Mutton (former mayor of Clarington and chair of Canadian Association of Nuclear Host Communities), interview with author, Clarington, ON, 7 June 2005; Norm Rubin (director of nuclear research and senior policy analyst, Energy Probe), interview with author, Toronto, 5 June 2005; and Len Simpson (former mayor of Pinawa, MB), telephone interview with author, 23 September 2005.

44 Nuclear industry spokesperson, phone interview with author, 20 October 2005.

45 For example, Kevin Kamps, "Submission of Comments to Canadian Nuclear Waste Management Organization Regarding Its 'Choosing a Way Forward: Draft Study Report'" (Washington, DC: Nuclear Information and Resource Service, 2005); Nuclear Waste Watch, *Position Statement* (Toronto: Ontario Hydro, 2004); and United Church of Canada, Justice, Global and Ecumenical Relations Unit, *Submission Two: Commentary on a United Church of Canada Ethical Lens for Viewing the Problem of Nuclear Wastes* (Toronto: United Church of Canada, 2005).

46 Anna Stanley, Richard Kuhn, and Brenda Murphy, *Response to NWMO's Draft Study Report: Choosing a Way Forward*, submission to NWMO national consultation process (Toronto: NWMO, 2005).

47 Mary Lou Harley (member of the United Church of Canada Justice, Global and Ecumenical Relations Nuclear Wastes Writing Team), response to email questionnaire from author, 4 August 2005.

48 See, for example, DPRA Canada, *Final Report*; GBN, *Looking Forward to Learn*; Sigurdson, Glenn, CSE Consulting, and Barry Stuart, *Community Dialogue: A Planning Workshop*, NWMO Background Papers and Workshop Reports (Toronto: NWMO, 2003); Hardy Stevenson and Associates Ltd, *Final Report*; Hardy Stevenson, *NWMO Community Dialogue Workshop* (Toronto: NWMO, 2005); and Watling et al., *Responsible Action: Citizens' Dialogue*.

49 NWMO, *Choosing a Way Forward: Draft Study Report*, 262–6.

50 Watling et al., *Responsible Action: Citizens' Dialogue*, 56.

51 Mary Lou Harley, response to email.

52 Dave Hardy, interview; John Mutton, interview.

53 For example, CAP, *Understanding the Choices*; Gracia Janes, "Comments on the NWMO Draft Management Plan for Nuclear Waste" (Ottawa: National

Council of Women of Canada, 2005); AFN employee no. 2, telephone interview with author, 13 October 2005; Stanley et al., *Choosing a Way Forward: Response to NWMO's Draft Study Report*; Trudeau Foundation and Sierra Club of Canada, "Roundtable Discussion on Nuclear Waste Management"; United Church of Canada, Justice, Global and Ecumenical Relations Unit, *Submission One: United Church of Canada General Comments on Nuclear Wastes and the Work of the Nuclear Waste Management Organization* (Toronto: United Church of Canada, 2004); United Church of Canada, Justice, Global and Ecumenical Relations Unit, *Comments of the United Church of Canada to the Nuclear Waste Management Organization on the Draft Study Report*; United Church of Canada, Justice, Global and Ecumenical Relations Unit, *The Response of the United Church of Canada to the Nuclear Waste Management Organization Final Report*; and United Church of Canada, Justice, Global and Ecumenical Relations Unit, *Submission Two*.

54 AFN, *Nuclear Fuel Waste Dialogue: Phase II Progress Report*; CAP, *Understanding the Choices*; and Inuit Tapiritt Kanatimi, *Final Report on the National Inuit Specific Dialogues on the Long-Term Management of Nuclear Fuel Waste in Canada* (Ottawa: ITK, 2005).

55 Soha Kneen (coordinator of the National Inuit-Specific Dialogue, Environment Department, Inuit Tapiriit Kanatami), interview with author, Ottawa, 9 May 2005; AFN employee no. 2, interview; and AFN, *Nuclear Fuel Waste Dialogue: Phase II Progress Report*.

56 NWMO established a Council of Elders in 2012 and has sought to achieve a constructive relationship with Aboriginal First Nations and organizations since launching the site selection process. See www.nwmo.ca/councilofelders, accessed 3 December 2014, and NWMO, *Aboriginal Policy*.

57 Watling et al., *Responsible Action: Citizens' Dialogue*, 56.

58 Ibid.

59 Dave Hardy, interview.

60 Berger, *Comments on NWMO's Consultation Process*.

61 NWMO Advisory Council member, interview.

62 Mary Lou Harley, response to email.

63 Stanley et al., *Choosing a Way Forward: Response to NWMO's Draft Study Report*.

64 See, for example, DPRA Canada, *Final Report*; Glenn Sigurdson, CSE Consulting Inc. and Barry Stuart, *Community Dialogue*; GBN, *Looking Forward to Learn*; Hardy Stevenson, *Final Report*; Hardy Stevenson, *NWMO Community Dialogue Workshop*; and Stratos, *Dialogue on Choosing a Way Forward*.

65 Watling et al., *Responsible Action: Citizens' Dialogue*.

66 Dave Hardy, interview.

67 Shoesmith and Shemilt, *Workshop on the Technical Aspects of Nuclear Fuel Waste Management*, 4.
68 Ibid., 4-5.
69 Watling et al., *Responsible Action: Citizens' Dialogue*.
70 Ibid., x.
71 Ibid., xi.
72 DPRA Canada, *Final Report*, 7.
73 Ibid., 25. See also Hardy Stevenson, *Final Report*.
74 DPRA Canada, *Final Report*, 35. See also Hardy Stevenson, *Final Report* and Stratos, *Dialogue on Choosing a Way Forward*.
75 See DPRA Canada, *Final Report*; DPRA Canada, *Nuclear Waste Management Organization – The Future of Canada's Used Nuclear Fuel: International Youth Congress Round Table* (Toronto: NWMO, 2004); Hardy Stevenson, *Final Report*; Hardy Stevenson, *NWMO Community Dialogue Workshop*; Stratos, *Dialogue on Choosing a Way Forward*; and Watling et al., *Responsible Action: Citizens' Dialogue*.
76 DPRA Canada, *Final Report*, 10.
77 NWMO, *Choosing a Way Forward: Final Study Report*, 23.
78 Ibid.
79 Ibid.
80 For example, Berger, *Comments on NWMO's Consultation Process*; Andrew Brook, interview; Dave Hardy, interview; NWMO Advisory Council member, interview; and Len Simpson interview with author.
81 Stratos, *Dialogue on Choosing a Way Forward*, 2.
82 Ibid., 5.
83 Ibid.
84 Ibid., 6.
85 Stanley et al., *Choosing a Way Forward: Response to NWMO's Draft Study Report*, 2.
86 AFN employee no. 2, telephone interview with author, 13 October 2005.
87 CAP, *Understanding the Choices*, 2.
88 See, for example, AFN, *Nuclear Fuel Waste Dialogue: Phase II Progress Report*; CAP, *Understanding the Choices*; Soha Kneen, interview; AFN employee no. 2, interview; and Stanley et al., *Choosing a Way Forward: Response to NWMO's Draft Study Report*.
89 Cited in Stephen Salaff, "Native Communities Refuse Nuclear Waste," www.sevenoaksmag.com, 27 October 2005; and in Murray Campbell, "Bury Nuclear Waste Underground, Group Says," *Globe and Mail*, 4 November 2005, A8.
90 Trudeau Foundation and Sierra Club of Canada, "Roundtable Discussion on Nuclear Waste Management."

91 United Church of Canada, Justice, Global and Ecumenical Relations Unit, *Submission Two*.

92 NWMO, *Choosing a Way Forward: Final Study Report*, 20.

93 Ibid.

94 NWMO, *Learning More Together: Annual Report 2011* (Toronto: NWMO, 2011), 47. The NWMO's Advisory Council has reiterated the importance of a broad public discussion on Canada's future energy supplies. See NWMO, *Moving Forward Together: Triennial Report 2008–2010* (Toronto: NWMO, 2011), 261.

95 M. Garamszeghy, *Nuclear Fuel Waste Projections in Canada – 2010 Update: NWMO TR-2010-17* (Toronto: NWMP, 2010); M. Garamszeghy, *Nuclear Fuel Waste Projections in Canada – 2012 Update: NWMO TR-2012-12* (Toronto: NWMP, 2012).

96 Mary Lou Harley, response to email; Stanley et al., *Choosing a Way Forward: Response to NWMO's Draft Study Report*; and United Church of Canada, *The Response of the United Church of Canada*.

97 NWMO, *Choosing a Way Forward: Final Study Report*, 216.

98 Ibid., 272–3.

99 NWMO, *Learning More Together: Annual Report 2011*, 36.

100 Ibid.

101 See http://www.nwmo.ca/help_design.

102 NWMO, *Learning More Together: Annual Report 2011*, 35.

103 Ibid.

104 NWMO, *Learning More Together: Annual Report 2012* (Toronto: NWMO, 2012), 44.

105 NWMO, *Moving Forward Together: Process for Selecting a Site for Canada's Deep Geological Repository for Used Nuclear Fuel* (Toronto: NWMO, 2010), 39.

106 NWMO, *Implementing Adaptive Phased Management: 2012–2016*, 21.

107 Ibid.

108 See, for example, "Saugeen Shores Shows Interest in Storing Nuclear Waste," *CBC News*, updated 11 December 2011, http://www.cbc.ca/news/canada/toronto/saugeen-shores-shows-interest-in-storing-nuclear-waste-1.1035437 and "Nuclear Waste Bid Poses Risks and Rewards for Ontario Town," *CBC News*, updated 16 October 2012, http://www.cbc.ca/news/politics/nuclear-waste-bid-poses-risks-and-rewards-for-ontario-town-1.1179870.

109 "'Secret' Meetings over Nuclear Waste Decried," *Metro*, updated 2 June 2013, http://metronews.ca/news/canada/692376/secret-meetings-over-nuclear-waste-decried/.

110 "Nuclear Waste Issue Divides Tourist Town," *TheRecord.com*, updated 3 July 2012, http://www.therecord.com/news-story/2607751-nuclear-waste-issue-divides-tourist-town/.

111 NWMO, *Choosing a Way Forward: Final Study Report*, 350.
112 Interview.
113 Ibid.
114 NWMO employee, interview, 30 September 2005.
115 Aikin et al., *The Management of Canada's Nuclear Wastes*.
116 CEAA, *Nuclear Fuel Waste Management and Disposal Concept*.
117 Ibid., 70.
118 Elizabeth Dowdeswell, interview, and NWMO employee, interviews, 6 June and 30 September 2005.
119 NWMO, *Choosing a Way Forward: Final Study*, 19.
120 CEAA, *Nuclear Fuel Waste Management and Disposal Concept*.

5. Embedded Policy Consultations and Nunavut's Official Languages

1 I say similar because Inuit have their own approach to collective decision making, which is expressed in the principles of Inuit Traditional Knowledge or *Inuit Qaujimajatuqangit*, which I discuss later.
2 For an excellent overview and analysis, see Annis May Timpson, "Reconciling Indigenous and Settler Language Interests: Language Policy Initiatives in Nunavut," *Journal of Canadian Studies* 43, no. 2 (2009), 159–80.
3 Terry Fenge and Paul Quassa, "Negotiating and Implementing the Nunavut Land Claims Agreement," *Policy Options*, July 2009: 81.
4 André Légaré, "An Assessment of Recent Political Development in Nunavut: The Challenges and Dilemmas of Inuit Self-Government," *Canadian Journal of Native Studies* 18, no. 2 (1998): 274.
5 Cited ibid.
6 Barry Dewar, "Nunavut and the Nunavut Land Claims Agreement – An Unresolved Relationship," *Policy Options*, July / August 2009: 78. See also Légaré, "Assessment of Recent Political Development in Nunavut," 275.
7 See Ailsa Henderson, *Nunavut: Rethinking Political Culture* (Vancouver: UBC Press, 2007).
8 See Jack Hicks and Graham White, "Nunavut: Inuit Self-Determination through a Land Claim and Public Government?" in *Nunavut: Inuit Regain Control of Their Lands and Their Lives* (Copenhagen: International Work Group for Indigenous Affairs, 2000). See also Henderson, *Nunavut*.
9 Dewar, "Nunavut and the Nunavut Land Claims Agreement," 79.
10 Henderson, *Nunavut*, 1.
11 Hicks and White, "Nunavut: Inuit Self-Determination," 56–7.
12 Henderson, *Nunavut*, 32.

13 During the time I was researching this case, the Legislative Assembly had nineteen seats. As of August 2013, the number of seats was increased to twenty-two.

14 *Agreement between the Inuit of the Nunavut Settlement Area and Her Majesty the Queen in Right of Canada* (Iqaluit, 25 May 1993), 1.

15 Ibid.

16 Ibid., 191.

17 Ibid., 223.

18 Hicks and White, "Nunavut: Inuit Self-Determination," 34.

19 Nunavut Bureau of Statistics, "Nunavut Quick Facts," http://www.stats. gov.nu.ca/en/home.aspx. Accessed 25 June 2014.

20 Statistics Canada, "NHS Focus on Geography Series – Nunavut," last updated 19 June 2013, http://www12.statcan.gc.ca/nhs-enm/2011/as-sa/ fogs-spg/?Lang=E.

21 Stephen Cloutier, "Protecting Inuit Language," PowerPoint presentation (Culture, Language, Elders, and Youth, Iqaluit), http://www4.uqo.ca/ sommetaet2008/documents/SCloutierpresentation.pdf, accessed 6 Sept. 2013.

22 Legislative Assembly of Nunavut, *Special Committee to Review the Official Languages Act: Final Report*, 6th Session, 1st Legislative Assembly, Rebekah Uqi Williams, chair, and Donald Havioyak, co-chair (Iqaluit, December 2003), 6. See also Statistics Canada, 2002, "2001 Census Aboriginal Population Profiles," released 17 June 2003 (last modified 30 Nov. 2005), Statistics Canada Catalogue no. 94F0043XIE.

23 Statistics Canada, 2002, "2001 Census Aboriginal Population Profiles."

24 Nunavut Bureau of Statistics, "StatsUpdate: Mother Tongue and Language Spoken Most Often at Home" (drawn from 2011 Census of Population, Statistics Canada, 24 Oct. 2012).

25 Ibid.

26 Ibid.

27 Christopher Moseley, ed., *Atlas of the World's Languages in Danger*, 3rd ed. (Paris: UNESCO Publishing), online version: http://www.unesco.org/ culture/en/endangeredlanguages/atlas, accessed on 6 Sept. 2013.

28 Nunavut Implementation Commission, *Footprints 2: A Second Comprehensive Report from the Nunavut Implementation Commission to the Department of Indian Affairs and Northern Development, Government of the Northwest Territories and Nunavut Tunngavik Incorporated Concerning the Establishment of the Nunavut Government* (Iqaluit: Nunavut Implementation Commission, 1996), 207.

29 Ibid.

30 Nunavut Implementation Commission, *Nunavut Language Policy Conference: Report and Recommendations* (Iqaluit, March 1998), 23–9.
31 Legislative Assembly of Nunavut, *Special Committee to Review the Official Languages Act: Interim Report*, 5th Session, 1st Legislative Assembly (March 2002), Rebekah Uqi Williams, chair, and Donald Havioyak, co-chair.
32 Ibid., 2.
33 Ibid., 3.
34 Ibid., 6.
35 Ibid.
36 Ibid.
37 Legislative Assembly of Nunavut, *Special Committee to Review the Official Languages Act: Final Report*, 16.
38 Ibid., 15.
39 Ibid., 16.
40 Ibid.
41 Ibid., 16–17.
42 Ibid., 17.
43 Ibid., 18.
44 Ibid., 24–32.
45 Department of Culture, Language, Elders, and Youth, *Response to Special Committee to Review the Official Languages Act Final Report, December 2003, 6th Session, 1st Legislative Assembly: Next Steps toward Made-in-Nunavut Language Legislation* (Iqaluit, May 2004).
46 Ibid., 1.
47 Ibid.
48 Ibid., 2.
49 Department of Culture, Language, Elders, and Youth, *Language Legislation for Nunavut: Consultation Paper* (Iqaluit, 2007), 2.
50 Ibid., 3.
51 Ibid.
52 See, for example, Standing Senate Committee on Legal and Constitutional Affairs, *Language Rights in Canada's North: Nunavut's New Official Languages Act. Final Report* (Ottawa, June 2009).
53 Natan Obed, director, Department of Social and Cultural Development, interview with author, 23 March 2011.
54 Participant no. 1, interview with author, 24 March 2011.
55 Natan Obed, interview.
56 Participant no. 3, interview with author, 4 May 2010.
57 Legislative Assembly of Nunavut, Ajauqtiit Standing Committee, *Interim Report* (Iqaluit, 2007), 1.
58 Ibid., 4.

59 Minister's Statement, Department of Culture, Language, Elders, and Youth, to Standing Committee Ajauqtiit (Iqaluit, 5 Dec. 2007).

60 Standing Senate Committee, *Language Rights in Canada's North*, 4.

61 Ibid., 3.

62 Ibid., 18.

63 Parliament of Canada, *Proceedings of the Standing Senate Committee on Legal and Constitutional Affairs*, 11, Evidence (Ottawa: 10 June 2009).

64 Ibid.

65 Standing Senate Committee, *Language Rights in Canada's North*, 18.

66 Government of Nunavut, *Official Languages Act*, Statutes of Nunavut.

67 Parliament of Canada, *Proceedings of the Standing Senate Committee on Legal and Constitutional Affairs*.

68 Government of Nunavut, *Inuit Language Protection Act*, Statutes of Nunavut 2008, s. 8.

69 Ibid., ss. 9 and 12.

70 Ibid., s. 16.

71 Participant no. 3, interview, 4 May 2010.

72 Natan Obed, interview with author; and participant no. 5, interview, 23 March 2011.

73 Natan Obed, interview.

74 Participant no. 3, interview, 22 March 2011.

75 Ibid.

76 Participant no. 4, interview with author, 22 March 2011.

77 Daniel Cuerrier, former director general, l'Association des francophones du Nunavut, interview, 23 March 2011.

78 Office of the Languages Commissioner, Qikiqtani Inuit Association, and Nunavut Tunngavik Inc., "Call for Immediate Action on Language" (Iqaluit, 28 October 2010).

79 Participant no. 4, interview.

80 Ibid.

81 National Collaborating Centre for Aboriginal Health, "*Inuit Qaujimajatuqangit*: The Role of Indigenous Knowledge in Supporting Wellness in Inuit Communities in Nunavut" (Prince George, BC, University of Northern British Columbia, 2009–10), 1.

82 Ibid., 2.

83 *Agreement between the Inuit of the Nunavut Settlement Area and Her Majesty the Queen in Right of Canada*, 223.

84 Ibid.

85 Kate Darling, "Sinnatuqtugiaq, faire un rêve, to dream: In Nunavut's Three Official Languages," unpublished paper (Iqaluit, 2009), 14.

86 Ibid.

87 Ibid.
88 Daniel Cuerrier, interview.
89 Participant no. 2, interview with author, 24 March 2011.
90 Participant no. 6, interview with author, 26 March 2011.
91 Legislative Assembly of Nunavut, *Special Committee to Review the Official Languages Act: Final Report*, 4.
92 Ibid.
93 See Annis May Timpson, "Rethinking the Administration of Government: Inuit Representation, Culture, and Language in the Nunavut Public Service," in *First Nations, First Thoughts: The Impact of Indigenous Thought in Canada*, ed. Annis May Timpson (Vancouver: UBC Press, 2009).
94 Participant no. 5, interview, and participant no. 7, interview with author, 24 March 2011. See also Timpson, "Reconciling Indigenous and Settler Language Interests."
95 Standing Senate Committee, *Language Rights in Canada's North*, 19–20.
96 Participant no. 6, interview.
97 Natan Obed, interview.
98 Minister of Languages, Department of Culture and Heritage, Government of Nunavut, *Uqausivut – The Comprehensive Plan Pursuant to the Official Languages Act and the Inuit Language Protection Act – 2012–2016* (Nunavut, October 2011), ii.

6. Contextual Complexity and the Importance of Deliberative Democracy

1 Leslie Malone and Tim Weis, "N.S. Now National Leader in Cutting Energy Waste," *The Chronicle Herald*, 6 August 2013, http://thechronicleherald.ca/opinion/1146251-ns-now-national-leader-in-cutting-energy-waste.
2 Pateman, "APSA Presidential Address: Participatory Democracy Revisited," 10.
3 Cohen and Fung, "The Radical Democracy Project."
4 See Warren and Pearse, eds, *Designing Deliberative Democracy*.
5 See John Gastil and Katherine R. Knobloch, *Evaluation Report to the Oregon State Legislature on the 2010 Oregon Citizens' Initiative Review* (http://www.la1.psu.edu/cas/jgastil/CIR/OregonLegislativeReportCIR.pdf) and Katherine R. Knobloch, John Gastil, Robert Richards, and Traci Feller, *Evaluation Report on the 2012 Citizens' Initiative Reviews for the Oregon CIR Commission* (http://www.la1.psu.edu/cas/jgastil/CIR/ReportToCIRCommission2012.pdf).
6 See Canadian Environmental Assessment Agency, *Nuclear Fuel Waste Management and Disposal Concept*.

7 Frank Fischer, "Participatory Governance as Deliberative Empowerment: The Cultural Politics of Discursive Space," *American Review of Public Administration* 35, no. 1 (2006): 24.

Epilogue

1 See Johnson, *Deliberative Democracy for the Future*.
2 See Genevieve Fuji Johnson, "Governing Sex Work: An Agonistic Policy Community and Its Relational Dynamics," in *Critical Policy Studies*, published online: 3 January 2015 (http://dx.doi.org/10.1080/19460171.2014.968602).

Bibliography

Abers, Rebecca Neaera. *Inventing Local Democracy: Grassroots Politics in Brazil*. Boulder, CO, and London: Lynne Rienner, 2000.

Abers, Rebecca Neaera. "Learning Democratic Practice: Distributing Government Resources through Popular Participation in Porto Alegre, Brazil." In *Cities for Citizens* edited by Mike Douglass and John Friedmann, 39–65. Chichester, UK, and New York: Wiley, 1998.

Agreement between the Inuit of the Nunavut Settlement Area and Her Majesty the Queen in Right of Canada. Iqaluit, 25 May 1993.

Aikin, A.M., J.M. Harrison, and F.K. Hare. *The Management of Canada's Nuclear Wastes: Report of a Study Prepared under Contract for the Minister of Energy, Mines and Resources Canada*. Ottawa: Government of Canada, 1977.

Andersen, Vibeke Normann, and Kasper M. Hanson. "How Deliberation Makes Better Citizens: The Danish Deliberative Poll on the Euro." *European Journal of Political Research* 46, no. 4 (2007): 531–56.

Asahi Shimbun (The Electric Daily News). "Editorial: 'Deliberative Polling' Is a Good 1st Step." 8 August 2012.

Assembly of First Nations (AFN). *Nuclear Fuel Waste Dialogue: Phase II Progress Report*. Ottawa: AFN, 2005.

Atomic Energy of Canada Limited (AECL). *Environmental Impact Statement on the Concept of Disposal of Canada's Nuclear Fuel Waste*. Atomic Energy of Canada Limited report AECL-10711, COG-93-1, 1994.

Auditor General's Office, City of Toronto. *Review of Controls over Procurement and Payment Functions at TCHC Subsidiary: Housing Services Inc*. Toronto, 9 December 2011.

Auditor General's Office, City of Toronto. *Toronto Community Housing Corporation Controls over Employee Expenses Are Ineffective: Appendix 1*. By Jeffrey Griffiths. Toronto, 7 December 2010.

Auditor General's Office, City of Toronto. *Toronto Community Housing Corporation Procurement Policies and Procedures Are Not Being Followed.* Toronto, 7 December 2010.

Avritzer, Leonardo. "New Public Spheres in Brazil: Local Democracy and Deliberative Politics." *International Journal of Urban and Regional Research* 30, no. 3 (2006): 623–37.

Baiocchi, Gianpoalo. *Militants and Citizens: The Politics of Participatory Democracy in Porto Alegre.* Stanford, CA: Stanford University Press, 2005.

Baiochi, Gianpoalo. "Participation, Activism and Politics: The Porto Alegre Experiment." In *Deepening Democracy: Institutional Innovations in Empowered Participatory Governance*, edited by Archon Fung and Erik Olin Wright, 45–76. London: Verso, 2003.

Barabas, Jason. "How Deliberation Affects Policy Opinions." *American Political Science Review* 98, no. 4 (2004): 687–701.

Benhabib, Seyla. "Toward a Deliberative Model of Democratic Legitimacy." In *Democracy and Difference: Contesting the Boundaries of the Political*, edited by Seyla Benhabib, 67–94. Princeton, NJ: Princeton University Press, 1996.

Benhabib, Seyla, ed. *Democracy and Difference: Contesting the Boundaries of the Political.* Princeton, NJ: Princeton University Press, 1996.

Berger, Thomas. *Comments on NWMO's Consultation Process.* Toronto: NWMO, 2005.

Bill C-27. An Act Respecting the Long-Term Management of Nuclear Fuel Waste. 37th Parliament, 1st sess., 2002. SC 2002.

Bohman, James. "Deliberative Democracy and Effective Social Freedom: Capabilities, Resources, and Opportunities." In *Deliberative Democracy: Essays on Reason and Politics*, edited by James Bohman and William Rehg, 321–48. Cambridge, MA: MIT Press, 1997.

Bohman, James. *Public Deliberation: Pluralism, Complexity and Democracy.* Cambridge, MA: MIT Press, 1996.

Bohman, James, and William Rehg, eds. *Deliberative Democracy: Essays on Reason and Politics.* Cambridge, MA: MIT Press, 1997.

Cabannes, Yves. "Participatory Budgeting: A Significant Contribution to Participatory Democracy." *Environment and Urbanization* 16, no. 1 (2004): 27–46.

Cabannes, Yves. *72 Frequently Asked Questions about Participatory Budgeting.* Urban Governance Toolkit Series. Quito: United Nations Human Settlements Programme, 2004.

Campbell, Murray. "Bury Nuclear Waste Underground, Group Says." *Globe and Mail*, 4 November 2005, A8.

Canada/Ontario. Minister of Energy, Mines and Resources Canada and the Ontario Energy Minister. "Joint Statement on the Nuclear Fuel Waste Management Program." Ottawa and Toronto, 1981.

Canada/Ontario. Minister of Energy, Mines and Resources Canada and the Ontario Energy Minister. "Joint Statement on Radioactive Waste Management Program." Ottawa and Toronto, 1978.

Canadian Environmental Assessment Agency (CEAA). *Nuclear Fuel Waste Management and Disposal Concept: Report of the Nuclear Fuel Waste Management and Disposal Concept Environmental Assessment Panel*. Ottawa: Minister of Public Works and Government Services Canada, 1998.

Canadian Nuclear Safety Commission (CNSC). Nuclear Power Plants. Updated 6 June 2014. http://www.cnsc-ccsn.gc.ca/eng/reactors/power-plants/index.cfm.

CBC News. "Nuclear Waste Bid Poses Risks and Rewards for Ontario Town." Updated 16 October 2012. http://www.cbc.ca/news/politics/nuclear-waste-bid-poses-risks-and-rewards-for-ontario-town-1.1179870.

CBC News. "Saugeen Shores Shows Interest in Storing Nuclear Waste." Updated 11 December 2011. http://www.cbc.ca/news/canada/toronto/saugeen-shores-shows-interest-in-storing-nuclear-waste-1.1035437.

CBC News. "TCHC Citizen Board Members Resign En Masse: Spending Shows 'Blatant Disregard': Auditor General." 3 March 2011, http://www.cbc.ca/news/canada/toronto/tchc-citizen-board-members-resign-en-masse-1.1006242, accessed 5 December 2014.

Chambers, Simone. *Reasonable Democracy: Jürgen Habermas and the Politics of Discourse*. Ithaca, NY: Cornell University Press, 1996.

"Cicle Do Op." *Portal Transparência e Acesso à Informação*. Accessed 15 August 2013. http://lproweb.procempa.com.br/pmpa/prefpoa/op/usu_doc/ciclo_op_2013_detalhado.pdf.

City of Toronto. "Infrastructure Ontario Refinancing of Toronto Community Housing Mortgages." Toronto, 6 March 2013.

City of Toronto. "Results of Tenant Election to Toronto Community Housing Corporation Board of Directors." 8 November 2007.

City of Toronto to the Toronto Community Housing Corporation. *Shareholder Direction: Joint Policy and Finance/Community Services Report 1(1) as Amended* (2001). Accessed from http://www.toronto.ca/legdocs/mmis/2011/cc/comm/communicationfile-20433.pdf.

Cloutier, Stephen. "Protecting Inuit Language." PowerPoint presentation (Culture, Language, Elders, and Youth, Iqaluit). http://www4.uqo.ca/sommetaet2008/documents/SCloutierpresentation.pdf. Accessed 6 September 2013.

Cohen, Joshua. "Deliberation and Democratic Legitimacy." In *Deliberative Democracy: Essays on Reason and Politics*, edited by James Bohman and William Rehg, 67–91. Cambridge, MA: MIT Press, 1997.

Cohen, Joshua. "Procedure and Substance in Deliberative Democracy." In *Democracy and Difference: Contesting the Boundaries of the Political*, edited by Seyla Benhabib, 95–119. Princeton, NJ: Princeton University Press, 1996.

Cohen, Joshua, and Archon Fung. "The Radical Democracy Project." *Délibération et Action Publique* (2004): 23–34.

Coleman, Bright Associates and Patterson Consulting. *Development of the Environmental Component of the NWMO Analytical Framework*. NWMO Background Papers and Workshop Reports. Toronto: NWMO, 2003.

Congress of Aboriginal Peoples (CAP). *Understanding the Choices: Summary of Key Observations regarding NWMO Discussion*. Document 2. Ottawa: CAP, 2005.

Cornwall, Andrea. "Deliberating Democracy: Scenes from a Brazilian Municipal Health Council." *Politics and Society* 36, no. 4 (2008): 508–31.

Corporate Knights. "The Carbon 50: A Report on Canada's Largest Greenhouse Gas Polluters in 2006." Investment issue, 2008. http://www.frankejames.com/pdf/CorpKnights_Carbon2008.pdf.

Darling, Kate. "Sinnatuqtugiaq, faire un rêve, to dream: In Nunavut's Three Official Languages." Unpublished paper. Iqaluit, 2009.

Delli Carpini, Michael X., Fay Lomax Cook, and Lawrence R. Jacobs. "Public Deliberation, Discursive Participation, and Citizen Engagement: A Review of the Empirical Literature." *Annual Review of Political Science* 7 (2004): 315–44.

Denki Shimbun (The Electric Daily News). "Deliberative Opinion Poll Conducted on Future Energy Choices." 7 August 2012.

Department of Culture, Language, Elders, and Youth. "Language Legislation for Nunavut: Consultation Paper." Iqaluit, 2007.

Department of Culture, Language, Elders, and Youth. *Response to Special Committee to Review the Official Languages Act Final Report. December 2003, 6th Session, 1st Legislative Assembly: Next Steps Toward Made-in-Nunavut Language Legislation*. Iqaluit, May 2004.

Dewar, Barry. "Nunavut and the Nunavut Land Claims Agreement – An Unresolved Relationship." *Policy Options*, July/August 2009: 74–9.

DPRA Canada. *Final Report: National Stakeholders and Regional Dialogue Sessions*. Toronto: NWMO, 2004.

DPRA Canada. *Nuclear Waste Management Organization – The Future of Canada's Used Nuclear Fuel: International Youth Congress Round Table*. Toronto: NWMO, 2004.

Dryzek, John S. *Deliberative Democracy and Beyond: Liberals, Critics, Contestations*. New York: Oxford University Press, 2000.

Dryzek, John S. "Deliberative Democracy in Divided Societies: Alternatives to Agonism and Analgesia." *Political Theory* 33, no. 2 (2005): 218–42.

Dryzek, John S. "Democratization as Deliberative Capacity Building." *Comparative Political Studies* 42, no. 11 (2009): 1379–402.

Dryzek, John S. *Discursive Democracy: Politics, Policy and Political Science.* Cambridge: Cambridge University Press, 1990.

Dryzek, John S. "Legitimacy and Economy in Deliberative Democracy." *Political Theory* 29, no. 5 (2001): 651–69.

Dryzek, John S., and Simon Niemeyer. "Reconciling Pluralism and Consensus as Political Ideals." *American Journal of Political Science* 50, no. 3 (2006): 634–49.

Efficiency Nova Scotia. *Be the Change: Using Energy Better Annual Report*. Dartmouth: 2012.

Elster, Jon. "The Market and the Forum: Three Varieties of Political Theory." In *Foundations of Social Choice Theory*, edited by Jon Elster and Aanund Hylland, 103–32. Cambridge, MA: Cambridge University Press, 1986.

Elstub, Stephen. "Weber's Dilemma and a Dualist Model of Deliberative and Associational Democracy." *Contemporary Political Theory* 7, no. 2 (2008): 169–99.

Fedozzi, L. *Orçamento Participativo: Reflexões sobre a experiência de Porto Alegre*. 3rd ed. Porto Alegre: Tomo Editorial, 2001.

Fenge, Terry, and Paul Quassa. "Negotiating and Implementing the Nunavut Land Claims Agreement." *Policy Options*, July 2009: 80–6.

Finhert, Desiree. "Nova Scotia Power to Pay Customers Back out of Extra Profits." 21 July 2011, http://www.news957.com/2011/07/21/nova-scotia-power-to-pay-customers-back-out-of-extra-profits/. Accessed 11 September 2013.

Fischer, Frank. "Participatory Governance as Deliberative Empowerment: The Cultural Politics of Discursive Space." *American Review of Public Administration* 35, no. 1 (2006): 19–40.

Fishkin, James. "Deliberative Polling®: Toward a Better-Informed Democracy." http://cdd.stanford.edu/polls/docs/summary/. Accessed 2 July 2012.

Fishkin, James, interviewed by Masahiro Tsuruoka. "Interview with James Fishkin: Deliberative Polling Should Be Used in Key Policy Issues like Energy." *Asahi Shimbun* (The Electric Daily News), 24 February 2012.

Fishkin, James, and Cynthia Farrar. "Deliberative Polling: From Experiment to Community Resource." In *The Deliberative Democracy Handbook: Strategies for Effective Civic Engagement in the 21st Century*, edited by John Gastil and Peter Levine. San Francisco: Jossey-Bass, 2005.

Freeman, Samuel. "Deliberative Democracy: A Sympathetic Comment." *Philosophy and Public Affairs* 29, no. 4 (2000): 371–418.

Fung, Archon. "Deliberative Democracy, Chicago Style: Grass-roots Governance in Policing and Public Education." In *Deepening Democracy: Institutional Innovations in Empowered Participatory Government*, edited by Archon Fung and Erik Olin Wright, 111–43. London: Verso, 2003.

Fung, Archon. "Survey Article: Recipes for Public Spheres: Eight Institutional Design Choices and Their Consequences." *Journal of Political Philosophy* 11, no. 3 (2003): 338–67.

Fung, Archon. "Varieties of Participation in Complex Governance." *Public Administration Review* 66 (December 2006): 66–75.

Fung, Archon, and Erik Olin Wright, eds. *Deepening Democracy: Institutional Innovations in Empowered Participatory Government*. London: Verso, 2003.

Fung, Archon, and Erik Olin Wright. "Thinking about Empowered Participatory Governance." In *Deepening Democracy*, edited by A. Fung and E.O. Wright, 3–43.

Garamszeghy, M. *Nuclear Fuel Waste Projections in Canada – 2010 Update*. NWMO TR-2010-17. Toronto: NWMP, 2010.

Garamszeghy, M. *Nuclear Fuel Waste Projections in Canada – 2012 Update*. NWMO TR-2012-12. Toronto: NWMP, 2012.

Garland, Robert. *Daily Life of the Ancient Greeks*. Indianapolis, IN: Hackett Publishing, 2008.

Gastil, John, and Katherine R. Knobloch. *Evaluation Report to the Oregon State Legislature on the 2010 Oregon Citizens' Initiative Review*. http://www.la1.psu.edu/cas/jgastil/CIR/OregonLegislativeReportCIR.pdf.

Gastil, John, Robert Richards, and Katherine R. Knobloch. "Vicarious Deliberation: How the Oregon Citizens' Initiative Review Influenced Deliberation in Mass Elections." *International Journal of Communication* 8 (2014): 62–89.

Genro, Tarso, and Ubiritan de Souza. *Orçamento Participativo: A experiência de Porto Alegre*. São Paulo: Fundação PerseuAbramo, 1997.

Global Business Network (GBN). *Looking Forward to Learn: Future Scenarios for Testing Different Approaches to Managing Used Nuclear Fuel in Canada*. NWMO Background Papers and Workshop Reports. Toronto: NWMO, 2003.

Globe and Mail. "City Hall Dissolves TCHC Board, Replaces It with One Director." 10 March 2011, http://news.nationalpost.com/2011/03/10/ford-urges-fresh-start-at-tchc/. Accessed 5 December 2014.

Goodin, Robert E., and John S. Dryzek. "Deliberative Impacts: The Macro-Political Uptake of Mini-Publics." *Politics and Society* 34, no. 2 (2006): 219–44.

Government of Nunavut. Inuit Language Protection Act. Statutes of Nunavut 2008, s. 8.

Government of Nunavut. Official Languages Act. Statutes of Nunavut, c.10.

Guild, Will, Ron Lehr, and Dennis Thomas. "Nova Scotia Power Customer Energy Forum: Summary of Results." The Public Decision Partnership, 2004.

Gutmann, Amy, and Dennis Thompson. *Democracy and Disagreement: Why Moral Conflict Cannot Be Avoided in Politics, and What Should Be Done about It.* Cambridge, MA: Harvard University Press, 1996.

Gutmann, Amy, and Dennis Thompson. *Why Deliberative Democracy?* Princeton: Princeton University Press, 2004.

Gutmann, Amy, and Dennis Thompson. "Why Deliberative Democracy Is Different." *Social Philosophy and Policy* 17, no.1 (2000): 161–80.

Habermas, Jürgen. *Moral Consciousness and Communicative Action.* Cambridge, MA: Polity Press, 1995.

Hajer, Maarten, and Sven Kesselring. "Democracy in the Risk Society? Learning from the New Politics of Mobility in Munich." *Environmental Politics* 8, no. 3 (1999): 1–23.

Hardy Stevenson and Associates Limited. *Final Report: National Stakeholders and Regional Dialogue Sessions.* Toronto: NWMO, 2005.

Hardy Stevenson and Associates Limited. *NWMO Community Dialogue Workshop.* Toronto: NWMO, 2005.

Harvard University Center for Urban Development Studies. *Assessment of Participatory Budgeting in Brazil.* Washington, DC: Inter-American Development Bank, 2003.

Henderson, Ailsa. *Nunavut: Rethinking Political Culture.* Vancouver: UBC Press, 2007.

Hendriks, Carolyn M. "When the Forum Meets Interest Politics: Strategic Uses of Public Deliberation." *Politics and Society* 34, no. 4 (2006): 571–602.

Hicks, Jack, and Graham White. "Nunavut: Inuit Self-Determination through a Land Claim and Public Government?" In *Nunavut: Inuit Regain Control of Their Lands and Their Lives.* Copenhagen: International Work Group for Indigenous Affairs, 2000.

Inuit Tapiritt Kanatimi (ITK). *Final Report on the National Inuit-Specific Dialogues on the Long-Term Management of Nuclear Fuel Waste in Canada.* Ottawa: ITK, 2005.

Janes, Gracia. "Comments on the NWMO Draft Management Plan for Nuclear Waste." Ottawa: National Council of Women of Canada, 2005.

Johnson, Genevieve Fuji. *Deliberative Democracy for the Future: The Case of Nuclear Waste Management Policy in Canada.* Toronto: University of Toronto Press, 2008.

Johnson, Genevieve Fuji. "Governing Sex Work: An Agonistic Policy Community and Its Relational Dynamics." *Critical Policy Studies*, online: http://dx.doi.org/10.1080/19460171.2014.968602.

Kamps, Kevin. "Submission of Comments to Canadian Nuclear Waste Management Organization regarding Its 'Choosing a Way Forward: Draft Study Report.'" Washington, DC: Nuclear Information and Resource Service, 2005.

Knobloch, Katherine R., John Gastil, Robert Richards, and Traci Feller. *Evaluation Report on the 2012 Citizens' Initiative Reviews for the Oregon CIR Commission.* http://www.la1.psu.edu/cas/jgastil/CIR/ReportToCIRCommission2012.pdf.

Knops, Andrew. "Delivering Deliberation's Emancipatory Potential." *Political Theory* 34, no. 5 (2006): 594–623.

Lang, Amy. "But Is It for Real? The British Columbia Citizens' Assembly as a Model of State-Sponsored Citizen Empowerment." *Politics and Society* 35, no. 1 (2007): 35–70.

Légaré, André. "An Assessment of Recent Political Development in Nunavut: The Challenges and Dilemmas of Inuit Self-Government." *Canadian Journal of Native Studies* 18, no. 2 (1998): 271–99.

Legislative Assembly of Nunavut. *Ajauqtiit Standing Committee, Interim Report.* Iqaluit, 2007.

Legislative Assembly of Nunavut. *Special Committee to Review the Official Languages Act: Interim Report.* 5th Session, 1st Legislative Assembly. Rebekah Uqi Williams, chair, and Donald Havioyak, co-chair. March 2002.

Legislative Assembly of Nunavut. *Special Committee to Review the Official Languages Act: Final Report.* 6th Session, 1st Legislative Assembly. Rebekah Uqi Williams, chair, and Donald Havioyak, co-chair. Iqaluit, December 2003.

Lehr, R.L., W. Guild, D.L. Thomas, and B.G. Swezey. "Listening to Customers: How Deliberative Polling Helped Build 1,000 MW of New Renewable Energy Projects in Texas." Golden, CO: National Renewable Energy Laboratory, June 2003.

Lerner, Josh. *Participatory Budgeting at Toronto Community Housing: Findings and Recommendations from Participatory Research with Tenants and Staff.* Evaluation report. Toronto, 2009.

Lerner, Josh, and Estair Van Wagner. "Participatory Budgeting in Canada: Democratic Innovations in Strategic Spaces." Unedited chapter in *Progressive Cities*, edited by Daniel Chavez and Einaar Braathen (2006). http://www.tni.org/archives/newpol-docs_pbcanada.

Macedo, Stephen ed. *Deliberative Politics: Essays on Democracy and Disagreement.* New York: Oxford University Press, 1999.

Maginn, Paul J. "Deliberative Democracy or Discursively Biased? Perth's Dialogue with the City Initiative." *Space and Polity* 11, no. 3 (2007): 331–52.

Malone, Leslie, and Tim Weis. "N.S. Now National Leader in Cutting Energy Waste." *Chronicle Herald*, 6 August 2013. http://thechronicleherald.ca/opinion/1146251-ns-now-national-leader-in-cutting-energy-waste.

Mansbridge, Jane, James Bohman, Simone Chambers, Thomas Christiano, Archon Fung, John Parkinson, Dennis F. Thompson, and Mark E Warren. "A Systematic Approach to Deliberative Democracy." In *Deliberative Systems: Deliberative Democracy at the Large Scale*, edited by John Parkinson and Jane Mansbridge, 1–26. New York: Cambridge University Press, 2012.

Mansbridge, Jane, James Bohman, Simone Chambers, David Estlund, Andreas Føllesdal, Archon Fung, Chistina Lafont, Bernard Manin, and José Luis Martí. "The Place of Self-Interest and the Role of Power in Deliberative Democracy." *Journal of Political Philosophy* 18, no. 1 (2010): 64–100.

McGuire, Martha. *The Toronto Community Housing Corporation Tenant Participation System: Final Evaluation Report*. Toronto Community Housing Corporation, 2006.

Metro. "'Secret' Meetings over Nuclear Waste Decried." Updated 2 June 2013. http://metronews.ca/news/canada/692376/secret-meetings-over-nuclear-waste-decried/. Accessed 27 October 2013.

Mill, John Stuart. "Representative Government." In *On Liberty and Other Essays*, edited by John Gray. Oxford: Oxford University Press, 1991.

Minister of Languages, Department of Culture and Heritage, Government of Nunavut. *Uqausivut – The Comprehensive Plan Pursuant to the Official Languages Act and the Inuit Language Protection Act, 2012–2016*. Nunavut, October 2011.

Minister's Statement. Department of Culture, Language, Elders, and Youth, to Standing Committee Ajauqtiit. Iqaluit, 5 December 2007.

Minister of Supply and Services. *Northern Frontier, Northern Homeland*. Report of the Mackenzie Valley Pipeline Inquiry 1. Ottawa, 1977.

Moseley, Christopher, ed. *Atlas of the World's Languages in Danger*. 3rd edition. Paris: UNESCO Publishing. Online version accessed 6 September 2013: http://www.unesco.org/culture/en/endangeredlanguages/atlas.

National Collaborating Centre for Aboriginal Health. "*Inuit Qaujimajatuqangit*: The Role of Indigenous Knowledge in Supporting Wellness in Inuit Communities in Nunavut." University of Northern British Columbia, Prince George, 2009–10.

National Post. "City Hall Dissolves TCHC Board, Replaces It with One Director." 10 March 2011, http://news.nationalpost.com/2011/03/10/ford-urges-fresh-start-at-tchc/. Accessed 5 December 2014.

Natural Resources Canada. "Government of Canada Response to Recommendations of the Nuclear Fuel Waste Management and Disposal

Concept Environmental Assessment Panel." Ottawa: Government of Canada, 1998.

Niemyer, Simon, and John S. Dryzek. "The Ends of Deliberation: Meta-consensus and Inter-subjective Rationality as Ideal Outcomes." *Swiss Political Science Review* 13, no. 4 (2007): 497–526.

Nova Scotia. *Seizing the Opportunity: Nova Scotia's Energy Strategy*. Vol. 1. Halifax, 2001.

Nova Scotia Department of Energy. *Renewable Electricity Plan: A Path to Good Jobs, Stable Prices, and a Cleaner Environment*. Halifax, April 2010.

Nova Scotia Department of Energy. *Renewable Energy Standard*. Halifax, 2007.

Nova Scotia Department of Energy. *Renewable Energy Standard*. NS Reg. 155/2010. Halifax, 2010.

Nova Scotia Department of Energy. *Toward a Greener Future: Nova Scotia's 2009 Energy Strategy*. Halifax, 2009.

Nova Scotia Department of Finance, Economics and Statistical Division. *Nova Scotia Statistical Review 2004*. Halifax, 2004.

"Nova Scotians Discuss Future Energy Alternatives." Center for Deliberative Democracy, Stanford University. 19 November 2004. http://cdd.stanford. edu/polls/energy/2004/ns-discuss-energy.html.

Nova Scotia Environmental Goals and Sustainable Prosperity Act, 2007, c. 7, s. 1.

Nova Scotia Finance and Treasury Board. "Nova Scotia Population Estimates as of April 1, 2013." http://www.novascotia.ca/finance/statistics/archive_news.asp?id=8736&ym=3.

Nova Scotia Power (NSPI). *Backgrounder on Key Renewable Milestones*. Halifax, 2009.

Nova Scotia Power (NSPI). *Customer Energy Forum 2004: Halifax, Nova Scotia, November 19–20, 2004. Guidebook*. Halifax, 2004.

Nova Scotia Power (NSPI). *Customer Energy Forum 2005*. Halifax: NSP, 15 October 2005.

Nova Scotia Power (NSPI). *Customer Energy Forum 2009*. Halifax, 2009.

Nova Scotia Power (NSPI). "Deliberative Polling Budget Estimates." Internal document. Halifax, 6 May 2004.

Nova Scotia Power (NSPI). "How We Make Electricity." https://www.nspower.ca/en/home/about-us/how-we-make-electricity/thermal-electricity/default-aspx, accessed 12 July 2012, and https://www.nspower.ca/en/home/about-us/how-we-make-electricity/default.aspx, accessed 19 November 2014.

Nova Scotia Power (NSPI). "New Wind Power for Nova Scotia." News release. Halifax, 19 November 2007.

Nova Scotia Power (NSPI). "Nova Scotia Power Acts on Customer Advice, Proposes $5 Million More for Conservation." News release. Halifax, 28 June 2005.

Nova Scotia Power (NSPI). *Nova Scotia Power Customer Energy Forum.* Halifax, 2004.

Nova Scotia Power (NSPI). "Nova Scotia Power Proposes Conservation and Energy Efficiency Plan." News release. Halifax, 31 January 2008.

Nova Scotia Power (NSPI). "NSPI Customer Energy Forum Expert Panels." Internal document. Halifax, 26 October 2004.

Nova Scotia Power (NSPI). "Return on Equity." http://www.nspower.ca/en/home/aboutnspower/operations/roe.aspx. Accessed 11 September 2013.

Nova Scotia Power (NSPI). "Thermal Electricity." http://www.nspower.ca/en/home/aboutnspower/makingelectricity/thermal/default.aspx. Accessed 12 July 2012 and 11 September 2013.

Nova Scotia Power (NSPI). "Who We Are." http://www.nspower.ca/en/home/aboutnspower/whoweare/default.aspx. Accessed 11 September 2013.

Nova Scotia Utility and Review Board. *Application by Nova Scotia Power Incorporated for Approval of Certain Revisions to its Rates, Charges, and Regulations.* 2006.

Novy, Andreasn and Bernhard Leubolt. "Participatory Budgeting in Porto Alegre: Social Innovation and the Dialectical Relationship of State and Civil Society." *Urban Studies* 42, no. 11 (2005): 2023–36.

Nuclear Waste Management Organization (NWMO). *Aboriginal Policy.* Toronto: NWMO, 2014.

Nuclear Waste Management Organization (NWMO). *Choosing a Way Forward: The Future Management of Canada's Used Nuclear Fuel, Draft Study Report.* Toronto: NWMO, 2005.

Nuclear Waste Management Organization (NWMO). *Choosing a Way Forward: The Future Management of Canada's Used Nuclear Fuel, Final Study Report.* Toronto: NWMO, 2005.

Nuclear Waste Management Organization (NWMO). *Ethical and Social Framework.* NWMO Background Papers and Workshop Reports. Toronto: NWMO, 2004.

Nuclear Waste Management Organization (NWMO). *Implementing Adaptive Phased Management: 2012–2016.* Toronto: NWMO, March 2012.

Nuclear Waste Management Organization (NWMO). *Learning More Together: Annual Report 2011.* Toronto: NWMO, 2011.

Nuclear Waste Management Organization (NWMO). *Learning More Together: Annual Report 2012.* Toronto: NWMO, 2012.

Nuclear Waste Management Organization (NWMO). *Moving Forward Together: Process for Selecting a Site for Canada's Deep Geological Repository for Used Nuclear Fuel.* Toronto: NWMO, 2010.

Nuclear Waste Management Organization (NWMO). *Moving Forward Together: Triennial Report 2008–2010.* Toronto: NWMO, 2011.

Nuclear Waste Watch. *Position Statement.* Toronto: Ontario Hydro, 2004.

Nunavut Bureau of Statistics. "Nunavut Quick Facts." http://www.stats.gov. nu.ca/en/home.aspx. Accessed 25 June 2014.

Nunavut Bureau of Statistics. "StatsUpdate: Mother Tongue and Language Spoken Most Often at Home." Drawn from Statistics Canada, 2011 Census of Population, 24 October 2012.

Nunavut Implementation Commission. *Footprints 2: A Second Comprehensive Report from the Nunavut Implementation Commission to the Department of Indian Affairs and Northern Development, Government of the Northwest Territories and Nunavut Tunngavik Incorporated Concerning the Establishment of the Nunavut Government.* Iqaluit: Nunavut Implementation Commission, 1996.

Nunavut Implementation Commission. *Nunavut Language Policy Conference: Report and Recommendations.* Iqaluit, March 1998.

Office of the Languages Commissioner, Qikiqtani Inuit Association, and Nunavut Tunngavik Inc. "Call for Immediate Action on Language." Iqaluit, 28 October 2010.

Papadopoulos, Yannis, and Philippe Warin. "Are Innovative, Participatory, and Deliberative Procedures in Policy Making Democratic and Effective?" *European Journal of Political Research* 46, no. 4 (2007): 445–72.

Parkinson, John. *Deliberating in the Real World: Problems of Legitimacy in Deliberative Democracy.* Oxford: Oxford University Press, 2006.

Parkinson, John, and Jane Mansbridge, eds. *Deliberative Systems: Deliberative Democracy at the Large Scale.* Cambridge: Cambridge University Press, 2012.

Parliament of Canada. *Proceedings of the Standing Senate Committee on Legal and Constitutional Affairs*, 11, Evidence. Ottawa, 10 June 2009.

Participatory Budgeting. Toronto Community Housing. Accessed on 29 July 2012 and 15 August 2013. http://www.torontohousing.ca/pb.

Pateman, Carole. "APSA Presidential Address: Participatory Democracy Revisited." *Perspectives on Politics* 10, no. 1 (2012): 7–19.

Privy Council, Commission on the Future of Health Care in Canada. *Building on Values: The Future of Health Care in Canada.* Final report. Ottawa, 2002.

The Record.com. "Nuclear Waste Issue Divides Tourist Town." Updated 3 July 2012. http://www.therecord.com/news-story/2607751-nuclear-waste-issue-divides-tourist-town/.

Rostbøll, Christian F. "Emancipation or Accommodation?: Habermasian vs. Rawlsian Deliberative Democracy." *Philosophy and Social Criticism* 34, no. 7 (2008): 707–36.

Salaff, Stephen. "Native Communities Refuse Nuclear Waste." Accessed 27 October 2005. www.sevenoaksmag.com.

Santos, Boaventura de Sousa. "Participatory Budgeting in Porto Alegre: Towards a Redistributive Democracy." *Politics and Society* 26, no. 4 (1998): 461–510.

Shoesmith, David, and Les Shemilt. *Workshop on the Technical Aspects of Nuclear Fuel Waste Management: Executive Summary*. NWMO Background Papers and Workshop Reports. Toronto: NWMO, 2003.

Sigurdson, Glenn, CSE Consulting, and Barry Stuart. *Community Dialogue: A Planning Workshop*. NWMO Background Papers and Workshop Reports. Toronto: NWMO, 2003.

Smith, Graham. *Democratic Innovations: Designing Institutions for Citizen Participation*. New York: Cambridge University Press, 2009.

Smith, William. "Democracy, Deliberation and Disobedience." *Res Publica* 10, no. 4 (2004): 353–77.

Souza, Celina. "Local Democratization in Brazil: Strengths and Dilemmas of Deliberative Democracy." *Development* 50, no. 1 (2007): 90–5.

Standing Senate Committee on Legal and Constitutional Affairs. *Language Rights in Canada's North: Nunavut's New Official Languages Act. Final Report*. Ottawa, June 2009.

Stanley, Anna, Richard Kuhn, and Brenda Murphy. *Response to NWMO's Draft Study Report: Choosing a Way Forward*. Submission to NWMO national consultation process. Toronto: NWMO, 2005.

Statistics Canada. "NHS Focus on Geography Series – Nunavut." Updated 19 June 2013. http://www12.statcan.gc.ca/nhs-enm/2011/as-sa/fogs-spg/?Lang=E.

Statistics Canada. "2001 Census Aboriginal Population Profiles." Released 17 June 2003. Statistics Canada catalogue no. 94F0043XIE. Modified 30 November 2005.

Steiner, Jürg. *The Foundations of Deliberative Democracy: Empirical Findings and Normative Implications*. Cambridge: Cambridge University Press, 2012.

Stratos. *Dialogue on Choosing a Way Forward: The NWMO Draft Study Report. Summary Report*. Toronto: NWMO, 2005.

Sunstein, Cass. "Deliberation, Democracy, Disagreement." In *Justice and Democracy: Cross-Cultural Perspectives*, edited by Ron Bontekoe and Marietta Stepaniants, 93–117. Honolulu: University of Hawaii Press, 1997.

Thompson, Dennis F. "Deliberative Democratic Theory and Empirical Political Science." *Annual Review of Political Science* 11 (2008): 497–520.

Timpson, Annis May. "Reconciling Indigenous and Settler Language Interests: Language Policy Initiatives in Nunavut." *Journal of Canadian Studies / Revue d'études canadiennes* 43, no. 2 (2009): 159–80.

Timpson, Annis May. "Rethinking the Administration of Government: Inuit Representation, Culture, and Language in the Nunavut Public Service." In *First Nations, First Thoughts: The Impact of Indigenous Thought in Canada*, edited by Annis May Timpson. Vancouver: UBC Press, 2009.

Toronto Community Housing Corporation (TCHC). *A Guide to Toronto Community Housing Tenant Elections: Tenant Participation – Shaping Our Future Together*, 1–7. Undated.

Toronto Community Housing Corporation (TCHC). *Annual Report 2012*. Toronto, May 2013.

Toronto Community Housing Corporation (TCHC). *2009 Annual Review: Tenants First – Collaboration, Cooperation, Community* (Toronto, 2009)

Toronto Community Housing Corporation (TCHC). *Community Based Business Planning in Toronto Community Housing*. 2003.

Toronto Community Housing Corporation (TCHC). *Community Management Plan 2006, 2007, 2008*. 2005.

Toronto Community Housing Corporation (TCHC). "Participatory Planning and Budgeting – Our Own Story." Presentation, Lifelong Citizenship Learning, Participatory Democracy, and Social Change Conference, Ontario Institute for Studies in Education, University of Toronto. 15–17 May 2003.

Toronto Community Housing Corporation (TCHC). *Toronto Community Housing Corporation Tenant Participation System: Final Evaluation Report*. 15 July 2006.

Toronto Community Housing Corporation (TCHC). "Participatory Budgeting – Working Together, Making a Difference." http://www.torontohousing.ca/participatory_budgeting. Accessed 4 August 2013.

Toronto Community Housing Corporation (TCHC). "Tenant Elections 2009: Tenants Vote to Shape Their Future." *Toronto Community Housing*. Published 23 June 2009. http://www.torontohousing.ca/news/20090623/tenant_elections_2009_tenants_vote_shape_their_future.

Toronto Community Housing Corporation (TCHC). "Youth Tenant Elections – Update." 17 June 2010.

"Toronto Community Housing Corporation Board of Directors." *Toronto: Agencies and Corporations*. http://www.toronto.ca/abcc/obca-community-housing.htm. Accessed 15 August 2013.

Trudeau Foundation and Sierra Club of Canada. "Roundtable Discussion on Nuclear Waste Management." Toronto: Trudeau Foundation and Sierra Club of Canada, 2005.

Tucker, Aviezer. "Pre-emptive Democracy: Oligarchic Tendencies in Deliberative Democracy." *Political Studies* 56, no. 1 (2008): 127–47.

United Church of Canada, Justice, Global and Ecumenical Relations Unit. *Comments of the United Church of Canada to the Nuclear Waste Management Organization on the Draft Study Report*. Toronto: United Church of Canada, 2005.

United Church of Canada, Justice, Global and Ecumenical Relations Unit. *The Response of the United Church of Canada to the Nuclear Waste Management Organization Final Report*. Toronto: United Church of Canada, 2005.

United Church of Canada, Justice, Global and Ecumenical Relations Unit. *Submission One: United Church of Canada General Comments on Nuclear Wastes and the Work of the Nuclear Waste Management Organization*. Toronto: United Church of Canada, 2004.

United Church of Canada, Justice, Global and Ecumenical Relations Unit. *Submission Two: Commentary on a United Church of Canada Ethical Lens for Viewing the Problem of Nuclear Wastes*. Toronto: United Church of Canada, 2005.

Valadez, Jorge. *Deliberative Democracy: Political Legitimacy, and Self-Determination Societies*. Boulder, CO: Westview Press, 2001.

Wagenaar, Hendrik. "Democracy and Prostitution: Deliberating the Legalization of Brothels in the Netherlands." *Administration and Society* 38, no. 2 (2006): 198–235.

Wagenaar, Hendrik. *Meaning in Action: Interpretation and Dialogue in Policy Analysis*. Armonk, NY: M.E. Sharpe, 2011.

Wampler, Brian. "A Guide to Participatory Budgeting." In *Public Sector Governance and Accountability Series*, edited by Anwar Shaw, 21–54. Washington, DC: World Bank, 2007.

Watling, Judy, Judith Maxwell, Nandini Saxena, and Suzanne Taschereau. *Responsible Action: Citizens' Dialogue on the Long-term Management of Used Nuclear Fuel*. Research Report P/04 Public Involvement Network. Ottawa: Canadian Policy Research Networks, 2004.

Warren, Mark. "Governance-Driven Democratization." *Critical Policy Studies* 3, no. 1 (2009): 3–13.

Warren, Mark E., and Hilary Pearse, eds. *Designing Deliberative Democracy: The British Columbia Citizens' Assembly*. Cambridge: Cambridge University Press, 2008.

Williams, Melissa S. "The Uneasy Alliance of Group Representation and Deliberative Democracy." In *Citizenship in Diverse Societies*, edited by Will Kymlicka and Wayne Norman, 124–52. Oxford: Oxford University Press, 2000.

Young, Iris Marion. "Justice, Inclusion, and Deliberative Democracy." In *Deliberative Politics: Essays on Democracy and Disagreement*, edited by S. Macedo, 151–8. New York: Oxford University Press, 1999.

Index

Aboriginal: consultations, 71, 77–9, 82; languages, 96, 107; organizations, 71, 77, 82; nations, 71, 79, 82, 90
above-ground storage, 70–1, 75, 80–2, 87
Access to Information and Privacy Protection Commissioner, 106
accommodation, 52. *See also* compromise
accountability and transparency, 11, 37, 80, 102
"accountable authorities," 85
adaptive phased management, 71–2, 76, 81–5, 88, 90, 119
adjudication, independent, 10
administration, 10, 21, 29
advisory committee, 58–9. *See also* Tenant Advisory Committee
agenda-setting, 12
Ajauqtiit, 106–7
Alberta, 88
Allocation Days (1.8 Day), 32, 34–5, 37, 118, 138
Andersen, Vibeke Normann, 19
annual business plan, 24, 30–3, 137
Annual General Meeting of the Arctic Co-operatives Ltd, 104

Application Review Committee, 34
Arctic Bay, 100, 106
Arctic College, 100, 106
Arctic Co-ops Limited, 104, 106
Arizona, 18
Arviat, 94
Asahi Shimbun, 68
Assembly of First Nations, 77, 82. *See also* Aboriginal: organizations
Association des francophones du Nunavut, 100, 102–4, 106–8
Athens (ancient), 7–8, 125
Atomic Energy Control Board (AECB), 74
Atomic Energy of Canada Limited (AECL), 70, 72, 74–5, 83, 88, 89
Attagutaaluk, Joe, 108
Auditor General of the City of Toronto, 25, 45–6
Australia, 20, 52
Avritzer, Leonardo, 20–1

Baffin Chamber of Commerce, 100, 106
Baffin/Qikiqtaaluk region, 94–5
Baker Lake, 100, 103
Ballantyne, Derek, 41, 43

Barabas, Jason, 18
Benhabib, Seyla, 11
Berger, Thomas, 79, 129
binding decisions, 19, 28, 61
Bohman, James, 11, 14–15
Brazil. *See* participatory budgeting:
    in Brazil
British Columbia, 123
Bulgaria, 52
bureaucracy, 10, 67, 114
By the People Citizen Deliberations
    Project, 53

Cabannes, Yves, 27, 29
Cambridge Bay, 100
Cameron, Bruce, 59
Canada, 3–4, 10, 21, 26, 30, 33, 44, 47–8,
    57, 64, 70–5, 77–8, 81–3, 85–8, 90–4,
    97, 100, 104, 108–9, 114–15, 119, 124
Canadian Broadcasting
    Corporation, 58
Canadian Environmental Assessment
    Agency (CEAA), 74, 124
Canadian Federation of Independent
    Business, 58
Canadian Nuclear Fuel Waste
    Management Program, 74
Canadian Nuclear Safety
    Commission (CNSC), 74
Canadian Nuclear Waste
    Management Organization
    (NWMO): and deliberative
    democracy, 3, 4, 76, 85–6, 89, 91,
    119, 123; national consultation
    process, 4, 70–9, 85–91, 119;
    recommendations, 71–2, 76, 78–9,
    81–2, 84–6, 88, 119; roundtable
    discussions, 71
Canadian Policy Research Networks
    (CPRN), 76, 79–80

CANDU, 74, 88
Cape Breton District Health
    Authority, 58
Cape Dorset, 104
Chambers, Simone, 12
Chesterfield Inlet, 100
China, 52
Chipewyan, 96, 107
Christiano, Thomas, 12
citizens: empowerment, 3, 11,
    16–18, 124; engagement, 10, 18,
    49–51, 53, 80–1, 85, 123; and equal
    opportunities, 6, 11, 13–14, 16–17,
    36, 59, 78; and government, 9–10,
    16, 18, 20, 68; and inclusiveness, 4,
    15–17, 24, 28, 48, 58, 67, 78, 84, 86–7,
    93, 104, 110, 122; mobilization,
    28; participation, 3, 10–11, 14–18,
    27–8, 53, 75–6, 123–4; and policy
    process, 3, 16–20, 50, 53, 67–8, 75–6,
    81, 85, 123–4; and public policy,
    10–11, 16–20, 27–8, 50, 53, 61, 67–8,
    75–6, 81, 123–5; and representative
    democracy, 9–10, 18, 50; and
    technologies of information, 14
Citizens' Assemblies, 8, 27, 129.
    See also popular assemblies;
    thematic assemblies
clientelism, 27
Cohen, Joshua, 9–10, 14
collective deliberation, 14, 17, 32, 37,
    51, 53, 67, 112, 118, 121, 123
Commission scolaire d'Iqaluit, 104
Commission scolaire francophone
    du Nunavut, 104, 108
Community Based Business
    Planning, 24, 42
Community Health Consultant, 35
Community Housing Unit (CHU),
    25, 30, 32–9, 40–2, 44, 135, 138;

tenant council, 31, 33, 36–7,
    40–1, 43
community participation:
    deliberative polling, 52–3, 58;
    embedded policy consultations,
    92, 95, 97–8, 100, 103–4, 108,
    110, 112–13, 116; national
    consultations, 72, 75, 79, 80, 87, 89;
    participatory budgeting, 13, 27,
    30–1, 33, 35, 37, 40–4, 118, 122
competitive representation, 9
compromise, 15, 19, 110, 113
conflict of interest, 33, 62, 119
Congress of Aboriginal Peoples, 77, 82
consensus, 15–16, 18, 51, 53, 95, 97,
    105, 112, 114, 132
conservation, 4, 56, 59–62, 65, 119
conservation plan, NSPI's, 56, 59,
    60–1, 65, 119
Conserve Nova Scotia, 119
consultation: in deliberative
    democratic theory, 6, 17, 22; in
    practice, 121, 123, 125; NWMO,
    3, 4, 70–3, 75–9, 81–9, 90–1, 119,
    123; NSPI, 51, 119, 123; Nunavut
    official languages policy, 3, 4, 92,
    99, 100, 103–6, 108, 110–11, 116;
    TCHC, 32, 42–3, 55
contestation. See deliberative
    democracy: and contestation
Cornwall, Andrea, 20
Corporate Research Associates, 56
critical theory. See deliberative
    democracy: and critical theory
Cuerrier, Daniel, 107, 111, 113
Customer Energy Forum, 3, 48, 49,
    55–6, 58, 61–4, 119; impact of, 48,
    49, 55, 60–4, 119
Customer Energy Forum
    Guidebook, 58

Daiichi Nuclear Power Plant, 68
Danish National Deliberative Poll, 19
Davis Strait. See Nunavut: borders
decision-making: collective, 5–6, 9, 28,
    32, 34, 42, 112, 152; empowerment,
    3, 5–6, 12, 16–17, 24–5, 42, 46, 48–9,
    64, 86, 118, 120, 122; hierarchical,
    23, 25, 45, 121; participation in
    collective, 6, 25, 28, 38, 42, 112, 121,
    124; principles for collective, 6, 17,
    28, 112, 152; power, 20–1, 23, 38, 41,
    45–6, 49, 64, 91, 102, 116, 120, 124
deep geological disposal, 70–2, 74–5,
    82–3, 85, 87–9, 90–1
deliberation, direct participatory, 11
deliberative democracy: and
    accessibility of information, 3, 10,
    13–14, 17, 28, 36, 38, 50, 53, 59–60,
    77–9, 123; aims, 4–8, 16–17, 51, 68,
    121; alternative to representative
    democracy, 12; and ancient Athens,
    7–8, 125; and attitude changes, 12,
    19, 48, 51; basic elements, 4–5, 12,
    85–6, 125; conception, 6–7, 11–17;
    and contestation, 11–12, 15, 20;
    context, 4–7, 12–14, 17–18, 20–1,
    23, 35–6, 41, 46, 49–50, 64, 67–8,
    86, 112, 117–18, 120–1, 123; and
    critical theory, 15; and Deliberative
    Polling, see Deliberative Polling:
    and democratic deliberation;
    empirical studies on, 4–5, 7, 18–23;
    and empowerment, 3, 7, 11, 16–18,
    41, 46, 117, 122; experiments, 18, 20,
    26; ideal, 3–4, 6–7, 12, 14, 16, 50, 117;
    information, 3, 7, 12–14, 17, 19–20,
    37, 50, 52–4, 67, 86, 117, 122–3;
    interests, 3, 5, 12–14, 16–17, 19, 21,
    25, 37, 51, 53, 64, 67, 76, 91, 117–18,
    120–2; and knowledge, 8, 13, 18–19,

41, 51, 54, 117, 123; legitimacy, 7,
16–17, 67–8, 122; limitations, 4, 25,
46, 68, 86, 112, 117–18, 120; mutual
understanding, 11, 14–15, 19, 37,
50; origins, 7–12, 26, 73; outcomes
for power relations, 5, 7, 61, 86, 118;
outputs for policy, 5, 7, 16, 22, 26,
48–9, 61, 63–4, 67, 71, 73, 85–6, 90,
117–18, 120–4; participants, 5, 7, 12,
14–21, 23, 26, 37, 41, 48, 50–4, 64,
67–8, 76, 91, 97, 110, 112, 118–23;
and party politics, 20; and policy
change, 49, 67; policy decisions,
3–4, 6–7, 12, 17, 19, 21, 41, 49–50, 54,
64, 67, 86, 117–18, 122; principles,
of inclusiveness, 3–4, 12–13, 15–16,
17, 24, 28, 32–3, 35, 38, 48, 60, 76,
105, 117, 120; —, of justice, 7, 16;
procedures, and contradictions,
46, 49, 64, 118; procedural equality,
13, 16, 17, 58, 86, 117; and public
policy, 3–6, 16–21, 23, 41, 48, 50, 64,
67–8, 76, 86, 89, 91, 97, 110, 112, 117,
119–23; reasoned opinion, 19, 48,
51; reasoning capacity, 14; scope,
11, 46, 118; theories of, 6, 12; topics,
4, 19, 51, 121, 123; and Western
Enlightenment tradition, 8. *See also*
Deliberative Polling: examples of
Deliberative Polling: agreement, 3, 51,
59; arguments, 50–1, 53, 61; bias, 59;
consensus, 16, 51, 53; consultation,
3–4, 51, 55, 119, 123; corporate
interests, 16, 51, 58, 65; criteria, 49–
50; and democratic deliberation, 3,
48–51, 54–5, 64, 67–8; diversity, 50;
educative function, 67; engagement,
49–55, 123; examples of, 19,
52–4, 56; implementing, 48–9, 67;
information 3, 19, 50–4, 58–60, 66–7;

legitimacy, 16, 67–8; moderators,
50, 53, 56, 58–9; opinions, 18–19,
48, 50–1, 54, 56, 59, 64–5, 67–8;
organizations hosting polls, 4, 48–9,
52, 55; and political equality, 50;
pre- and post-deliberation surveys,
18, 51–2, 59, 60; procedures, 16,
48–51, 57–60, 64, 67–8; public
opinion polling, 54; and public
participation, 3, 16, 18–19, 48,
50–4, 59–61, 64–8, 119, 123; public
relations, 66, 68, 119; rationale for
holding, 54; recruitment, 52, 56;
target population, 52; televising,
53; topics, 52, 123 (*see also* examples
of *above*); vis-à-vis legislative
processes, 67
democracy: Athens, 7–8, 125;
contemporary democracies, 9,
23; democratic culture, 5, 53;
representative, 9–10, 12–13;
shortcomings of, 10
democratization, 4, 20
Denmark, 19. *See also* Deliberative
Polling: examples of
Department of Culture and
Heritage, 102, 116
Department of Culture, Languages,
Elders, and Youth (CLEY),
102–6, 110
Department of Energy, Mines, and
Resources (EMR), 74
Dewar, Barry, 94
"Dialogue with the City," 20
District Education Authorities, 104
diversity: and Deliberative Polling,
see Deliberative Polling: diversity;
of opinion, 50; of participation,
35; perspectives on deliberative
democracy, 12–13, 16

"domain of governance," 4
Dowdeswell, Elizabeth, 87
DPRA Canada, 77–8, 81
Dryzek, John, 15–16, 18
due diligence, lack of, 45

Ecology Action Centre, 58, 65
Efficiency Nova Scotia, 62
Electricity Consumer's Alliance of
    Nova Scotia, 58
elite(s): commitment, 5, 21, 22, 23, 36,
    41–2, 48, 55, 64–5, 84, 87, 89, 113,
    121–2; policy elites, 4–6, 12, 17–18,
    21, 23, 41, 47–9, 64–7, 73, 87–9, 91,
    117–18, 120–1, 124; NSPI, 47–9,
    64–6; NWMO, 73, 87–9; TCHC, 41
Ellesmere Island. See Nunavut: border
Elstub, Stephen, 17–18
Emera Inc., 47, 55, 57
empowerment, 3, 5–7, 10–12, 16–18,
    24–5, 27, 38, 41–2, 46, 48–9, 64, 86,
    117–18, 120, 122, 124
energy conservation, 55, 59–62, 65, 119
energy efficiency, 47, 54, 59–62
energy policy, 21, 47–9, 54, 56, 59, 61–6,
    68, 71, 81–2, 86, 88, 90–1, 119, 121
engagement, 6, 10, 18, 42, 49–51,
    53–5, 62, 64, 80–1, 83–5, 97, 123
English, 52, 96, 99, 101–2, 109, 123
Environmental Assessment and
    Review Process, 74
equality, 3, 6, 8, 12–14, 17, 28, 38, 50,
    58–9, 60, 77–9, 86, 104, 110, 117
evaluation (TCHC), 26, 33, 36–8, 40
expert panel, 50, 53, 57–9, 123

Farrar, Cynthia, 50, 52–3
First Nations, 77, 82, 95–6
Fischer, Frank, 124
Fishkin, James, 16, 48–9, 129

Fishkin's Center for Deliberative
    Democracy, 52
francophone community. See Iqaluit
    francophone community
freedom, 6, 8–10
French, 96, 99, 101–2, 107, 109, 115
Fukushima, 68
Fung, Archon, 9, 12, 20, 122, 129

Goodin, Robert, 18
governance, collective, 10, 118
government, accountable, 10
greenhouse gases, limiting, 60
Greenpeace, 82
Guild, Will, 54, 56–8, 60
Gutmann, Amy, 11, 14–15
Gwich'in, 96, 107

Hajer, Maarten, 3
Hansen, Kasper M., 19
Hardy, Dave, 79, 80
Hardy Stevenson and
    Associates, 77
Harley, Mary Lou, 78–9
Henderson, Ailsa, 94
Hendriks, Carolyn, 20
Hobbes, Thomas, 8
host community: nuclear waste
    storage, 72, 83–5; participants in
    siting process, 84
House of Commons, 107
Huskilson, Chris, 57
Hydro-Québec (H-Q), 70

immigrants, 35
implementation (policy). See policy:
    implementation
inclusiveness, 4, 15–17, 24, 28, 32, 45,
    48, 58, 61, 66–7, 77–8, 84, 86–7, 93,
    104, 108, 122

"incompletely theorized
    agreements," 15
Indian and Northern Affairs
    Canada, 100
individuals, concerned, 54
inequalities: material, 7, 9, 14, 79;
    of opportunities, 14; and
    participation, 9, 14
information: access to, 3, 10, 13–14,
    17, 28, 36, 38, 50, 53, 59–60, 77–9,
    106, 123; technologies, 14
informational equality, 13, 50, 58–9,
    77–9
institutions, 4, 12, 17, 23, 26–7, 31, 40,
    57, 92, 109, 124
Inter-Community Housing Unit
    (ICHU), 34, 36–7; delegates, 35–6, 41
interest organizations, 11, 13, 20, 22,
    28, 58, 71, 76–8, 93, 97, 108, 120
Inuinnaqtun, 96, 98–9, 101–3
Inuit: Elders, 97–8, 112;
    organizations, 77, 82, 92–3, 95, 97,
    100, 104–5, 108, 113, 115–16, 120;
    Inuit Youth, 97, 103
Inuit Broadcasting Corporation, 106
Inuit Heritage Trust, 100
Inuit Language Protection Act, 92–3,
    106, 107, 109, 116, 120
Inuit Qaujimajatuqangit Katimajiit,
    103, 112
Inuit Qaujimajatuqangit
    Tunngaviksaliuqtiit Task Force, 100
Inuit Sign Language, 103
Inuit Tapirisat of Canada (ITC), 93
Inuit Tapirrit Kanatami, 77
Inuit Uqausinginnik Taiguusiliuqtiit
    (Inuit Language Authority), 109–10
Inuktitut, 94, 96, 98–9, 191–2, 115
investment plan, 28–9, 31, 44, 61, 65
Iqaluit, 98, 100–1, 103–4

Iqaluit Chamber of Commerce, 100,
    103
Iqaluit Deaf Nunavummiut, 103
Iqaluit francophone community, 97,
    101, 103–4, 106–8

Japan, 52, 68. *See also* Deliberative
    Polling: examples of
Johnson, Gail, 35
Joyal, Serge, 108
justice, 7, 16–17, 117, 122

Keewatin, 95
Kesselring, Sven, 3
Kitikmeot, 94–5, 100, 103, 106
Kitikmeot Chamber of Commerce, 100
Kitikmeot Elders, 103
Kitikmeot Heritage Society, 100
Kitikmeot Inuit Association, 95,
    100, 103
Kivalliq, 94–5, 100, 103, 106
Kivalliq Elders, 103
Kivalliq Inuit Association, 95, 100
Kivalliq News, 106
Kugluktuk, 94, 100, 103. *See also*
    Nunavut: borders
Kuhn, Richard, 79, 82

land cession treaty, 92–3
Language Legislation Steering
    Committee, 103, 107, 110–11
language policy, 3–4, 21, 92–3,
    97–103, 105–16, 120, 123
Languages Commissioner of
    Canada, 104
Languages Commissioner of
    Nunavut, 97, 99–100, 102–3,
    106–8, 111, 116
laypersons, 12
legitimacy, 7, 16–17, 67–8, 122

Lehr, Ron, 54, 56–8, 60
Lerner, Josh, 36–7, 42, 44
Leubolt, Bernhard, 27, 29
Lloyd, Brennain, 82
Locke, John, 8
Luscar Limited, 58

Maginn, Paul, 20
Mansbridge, Jane, 12, 14
Martin, Dave, 82
"meta-consensus," 15–16
Metis, 77, 82, 95
Métis National Council, 77
Metro Toronto Housing Corporation, 24, 26, 42, 44
Mill, John Stuart, 9
Milton, Penny, 34, 42
Minister of Culture, Languages, Elders, and Youth, 102
Minister of the Environment, 74
modernity, 9
MT&L Public Relations Limited, 56
Murphy, Brenda, 79, 82

national consultation process, 3, 72, 75, 85–6, 90
National Issues Convention, 52
Native Women's Association of Canada, 77
Natural Resources Canada, 74
Nebraska, 56
Netherlands, 19
New Brunswick, 70, 73
New Brunswick Power (NBP), 70, 75, 88
New Haven, Connecticut, 53
News/North, 106
Niemeyer, Simon, 15–16
NLCA, 93, 95, 97, 103, 113, 121
Northwest Territories (NWT), 93–4, 96

Nova Scotia, 21, 47, 57, 59, 61–8, 119, 121
Nova Scotia Department of Energy, 58–9, 63
Nova Scotia Power Corporation, 55
Nova Scotia Power Incorporated (NSPI), 4, 47–9, 55–68, 119; and Deliberative Polling, 49, 55, 64–8; and elites, see elite(s): NSPI
Novy, Andreas, 27, 29
NRCan, 74, 77, 89
NTI, 95, 104, 106, 108, 110–11, 116, 120
nuclear fuel bundles, 70
Nuclear Fuel Waste Act, 70, 75, 89, 124
nuclear waste management, 4, 72–3, 75, 77, 79, 84, 85, 87–8, 90, 123–4
Nuclear Waste Watch, 82
Nunatsiaq News, 106
Nunavummiut, 92, 103, 112, 115, 123
Nunavut: borders, 94
Nunavut Act, 93–4
Nunavut Arctic College, 100
Nunavut Association of Municipalities, 103
Nunavut Employees Union, 106
Nunavut Impact Review Board, 100
Nunavut Implementation Commission (NIC), 97–8
Nunavut Land Claims Agreement (NLCA), 93, 95
Nunavut Language Policy Conference, 98
Nunavut Legislative Assembly, 105, 107
Nunavut Literacy Council, 100
Nunavut Planning Commission, 95
Nunavut Social Development Council, 100
Nunavut Surface Rights Tribunal, 100
Nunavut Teachers' Union, 104

Nunavut Trust, 95
Nunavut Tunngavik Incorporated
    (NTI), 95, 104, 106, 108, 110–11,
    116, 120
Nunavut Water Board, 95, 100
Nunavut Wildlife Management
    Board, 95
NWMO. *See* Canadian Nuclear
    Waste Management Organization

Obed, Natan, 104–5, 110, 115
official languages: Nunavut, 96, 101–
    2, 107; Official Languages Act, 92,
    96–7, 99, 100–2, 104, 107–9, 116,
    120; policy, 3–4, 21, 92, 96, 99, 103,
    105, 108, 113, 120, 123
Official Languages Law Group, 100
on-site storage. *See* above-ground
    storage
Ontario, 43–4, 73, 74, 87–8
Ontario Hydro, 74, 89
Ontario Power Generation (OPG),
    70, 74, 88
opportunities, equal, 13
Oregon Citizen Initiative Review
    Process, 123

Pangnirtung, 100
Papadopoulos, Yannis, 20
Parkinson, John, 4, 12
participation, 3, 6, 11, 13, 14, 18–23,
    30, 33, 35–6, 38, 40–6, 52–3, 58, 59,
    64, 92, 94, 95, 103, 113, 116, 121–3;
    citizen, *see* citizens: participation;
    public, 21, 23, 27, 75, 89, 98, 100, 124;
    system, *see* Toronto Community
    Housing Corporation (TCHC):
    tenant participation system
Participatory Budget Council
    (COP), 27, 29

participatory budgeting: in Brazil,
    20–1, 26, 28–9; governance, 28–9,
    and Toronto Community Housing
    Corporation, 24–6, 30, 31–2, 36, 45,
    48, 55, 118, 122; transferability, 29–30
Pateman, Carole, 122
Pauktuutit Inuit Women's
    Association, 77
Plato, 8
policy: decision, 12, 16, 21, 23, 49,
    56, 61, 64, 87, 90, 118; elites, *see*
    elite(s): policy elites; formulation,
    67, 69, 76, 93, 99, 105, 110, 116,
    120, 123; implementation, 19, 21,
    69, 92–3; processes, 4, 6, 18, 68,
    92–3, 112–13, 117–18, 120–4, 128;
    requirements, 6, 21, 22, 26, 41, 43,
    49, 72, 121–2, 124
policymaking, 18, 69
politics, 6, 10–11, 19, 20, 23, 29, 122
pollutants, limiting, 60
popular assemblies, 27–8, 31
Porto Alegre, 21, 26–9, 31–2, 122
power relations, 7, 17, 86, 118
power structures, 5, 17, 91, 120
preferences, 17, 19, 56, 122
principles: of access to information,
    3, 10, 13–14, 17–18, 36, 38, 50, 59,
    77–9; of equal participation, *see*
    equality; of inclusion, 3, 12, 13, 17,
    28, 32–3, 35, 38, 60, 76, 105, 117,
    120; of informed deliberation, 50,
    123; of justice, 7, 16; of mutual
    reasoning, 6, 14, 17, 23, 37–8, 50; of
    procedural equality, 3, 13, 17, 18,
    38, 60, 86, 104
procedures, 3–7, 10, 13, 16–27, 31, 36,
    38, 45–6, 48–51, 57, 64, 68, 72, 78,
    86, 89–90, 102, 110, 117–18, 120–6.
    See also deliberative democracy

public consultations, 6, 76, 89, 92,
100, 103, 125
Public Decision Partnership, 56
public deliberation, 69, 91, 92
public information sessions, 78
public opinion, 51–2, 54, 56
public participation, 21, 23, 27, 75,
89, 98, 100, 124
public policy, 3–4, 6, 18–19, 50, 68,
90–1, 110, 117, 122, 126
public pressure, 5, 21–2, 26, 41, 64,
65, 121, 122
public relations, 20, 66, 68
public sphere, 11
Public Utilities Act, 55

Qikiqtaaluk, 94, 95
Qikiqtaaluk Elders, 103
Qikiqtani Inuit Association, 95, 108
Qikiqtarjuaq, 100
Quebec, 88

random digit dialling, 62
Rankin Inlet, 100, 104
RBC Dominion Securities, 58
reasoning, 3, 12, 14, 49, 76, 79;
collective, 80; mutual, 23, 50;
public, 59, 60
Redfern, Madeline, 106
regional budget forums, 28
regulatory context, 6
renewable energy, 54, 60, 62–3,
65, 119
Renewable Energy Services, 58
Renewable Energy Standard, 63
representatives, 10, 13, 28, 29, 31–7,
40–1, 93–4, 97, 103–4, 108, 116; and
responsiveness, 10
resources, redistribution of social
and economic, 12

rights: civil, 9, 10, 27; equal, 6, 9;
fishing, 94; Inuit, 95, 99, 112, 121;
language, 106, 107, 109; treaty, 82
Rostbøll, Christian, 15

Sanikiluaq, 100
Seaborn, Blair, 74
Seaborn panel, 75, 88–9
self-government, 94
Senate, 107–8, 114
shared interests, 15–17, 23, 28, 59,
76, 118
Sierra Club, 58, 71, 82
Slavey, 96, 107
Smith, Graham, 27, 29
social capital, 17
social housing, 4, 21, 24, 26, 30, 33,
42–6, 121, 127
Social Housing Reform Act, 42–3
Socrates, 8
Souza, Celina, 21
speakers of Inuinnaqtun, 103
Special Committee of MLAs, 99–101,
114
stakeholders, 18, 66–7, 72, 80–1, 93,
99–101, 103, 106–8, 110
Standing Senate Committee on Legal
and Constitutional Affairs, 107
Stanford University, 52
Stanley, Anna, 79, 82
structures: hierarchical, 23. *See also*
decision-making: hierarchical
Sunstein, Cass, 15

Taloyoak, 103
technical experts, 18
Tedesco, Ralph, 56
telephone survey, 56, 68
Tenant Advisory Committee, 32, 35;
tenant councils. *See* Community

Housing Unit (CHU): tenant council
Tenant Participation System, TCHC's, 24, 30–3, 37, 40–3, 46; and deliberative democracy, 37; and TCHC decision-making, 38, 46
tenant representatives, 36
thematic assemblies, 27, 28, 29
Thomas, Dennis, 54, 56–8, 60
Thompson, Dennis, 11–12, 14–15
Thompson, Ken, 35
Toronto, 26, 40, 42, 44, 121, 127
Toronto Community Housing Corporation (TCHC), 3, 4, 24, 25, 26, 30–46; Application Review Committee, 34; board of directors, 30, 34, 41–2, 44; budgeting, see participatory budgeting: TCHC; CEO, 30, 34; decision making, 25; hierarchy, 38; mismanagement within, 25; participation system, see Tenant Participation System, TCHC's
Toronto Housing Company, 24, 26, 42
Toronto Stock Exchange, 55
traditional knowledge, 77
Trudeau Foundation, 82
Tungavik Federation of Nunavut (TFN), 93–4

unilingual Government of Nunavut employees, 103
United Church of Canada, 71, 78, 82
United Kingdom, 52
United Nations Educational, Scientific and Cultural Organization, 96
United States, 48, 49, 52, 54
United Way, 58
Utility and Review Board of Nova Scotia (UARB), 48, 61–2, 119

values, 11, 16–17, 50, 56, 67, 78, 82, 93
Van Wagner, Estair, 36–7, 42, 44
Vermont, 56
voters, 19, 33, 94, 123; turnout, 10

Wagenaar, Hendrik, 19
Wampler, Brian, 29
Warin, Philippe, 20
Warren, Mark, 4, 12
waste management plan, 88
Whale Cove, 104
women, 8–9
Workers' Compensation Board, 104
Worker's Party (Brazil), 26–7
Wright, Erik Olin, 20

Young, Iris Marion, 13

Studies in Comparative Political Economy and Public Policy

1 *The Search for Political Space: Globalization, Social Movements, and the Urban Political Experience* / Warren Magnusson
2 *Oil, the State, and Federalism: The Rise and Demise of Petro-Canada as a Statist Impulse* / John Erik Fossum
3 *Defying Conventional Wisdom: Political Movements and Popular Contention against North American Free Trade* / Jeffrey M. Ayres
4 *Community, State, and Market on the North Atlantic Rim: Challenges to Modernity in the Fisheries* / Richard Apostle, Gene Barrett, Peter Holm, Svein Jentoft, Leigh Mazany, Bonnie McCay, and Knut H. Mikalsen
5 *More with Less: Work Reorganization in the Canadian Mining Industry* / Bob Russell
6 *Visions for Privacy: Policy Approaches for the Digital Age* / Edited by Colin J. Bennett and Rebecca Grant
7 *New Democracies: Economic and Social Reform in Brazil, Chile, and Mexico* / Michel Duquette
8 *Poverty, Social Assistance, and the Employability of Mothers: Restructuring Welfare States* / Maureen Baker and David Tippin
9 *The Left's Dirty Job: The Politics of Industrial Restructuring in France and Spain* / W. Rand Smith
10 *Risky Business: Canada's Changing Science-Based Policy and Regulatory Regime* / Edited by G. Bruce Doern and Ted Reed
11 *Temporary Work: The Gendered Rise of a Precarious Employment Relationship* / Leah Vosko
12 *Who Cares?: Women's Work, Childcare, and Welfare State Redesign* / Jane Jenson and Mariette Sineau with Franca Bimbi, Anne-Marie Daune-Richard, Vincent Della Sala, Rianne Mahon, Bérengère Marques-Pereira, Olivier Paye, and George Ross
13 *Canadian Forest Policy: Adapting to Change* / Edited by Michael Howlett
14 *Knowledge and Economic Conduct: The Social Foundations of the Modern Economy* / Nico Stehr
15 *Contingent Work, Disrupted Lives: Labour and Community in the New Rural Economy* / Anthony Winson and Belinda Leach
16 *The Economic Implications of Social Cohesion* / Edited by Lars Osberg
17 *Gendered States: Women, Unemployment Insurance, and the Political Economy of the Welfare State in Canada, 1945–1997* / Ann Porter
18 *Educational Regimes and Anglo-American Democracy* / Ronald Manzer
19 *Money in Their Own Name: The Feminist Voice in Poverty Debate in Canada, 1970–1995* / Wendy McKeen

20 *Collective Action and Radicalism in Brazil: Women, Urban Housing, and Rural Movements* / Michel Duquette, Maurilio Galdino, Charmain Levy, Bérengère Marques-Pereira, and Florence Raes

21 *Continentalizing Canada: The Politics and Legacy of the Macdonald Royal Commission* / Gregory J. Inwood

22 *Globalization Unplugged: Sovereignty and the Canadian State in the Twenty-first Century* / Peter Urmetzer

23 *New Institutionalism: Theory and Analysis* / Edited by André Lecours

24 *Mothers of the Nation: Women, Family, and Nationalism in Twentieth-Century Europe* / Patrizia Albanese

25 *Partisanship, Globalization, and Canadian Labour Market Policy: Four Provinces in Comparative Perspective* / Rodney Haddow and Thomas Klassen

26 *Rules, Rules, Rules, Rules: Multi-Level Regulatory Governance* / Edited by G. Bruce Doern and Robert Johnson

27 *The Illusive Tradeoff: Intellectual Property Rights, Innovation Systems, and Egypt's Pharmaceutical Industry* / Basma Abdelgafar

28 *Fair Trade Coffee: The Prospects and Pitfalls of Market-Driven Social Justice* / Gavin Fridell

29 *Deliberative Democracy for the Future: The Case of Nuclear Waste Management in Canada* / Genevieve Fuji Johnson

30 *Internationalization and Canadian Agriculture: Policy and Governing Paradigms* / Grace Skogstad

31 *Military Workfare: The Soldier and Social Citizenship in Canada* / Deborah Cowen

32 *Public Policy for Women: The State, Income Security, and Labour* / Edited by Marjorie Griffin Cohen and Jane Pulkingham

33 *Smiling Down the Line: Info-Service Work in the Global Economy* / Bob Russell

34 *Municipalities and Multiculturalism: The Politics of Immigration in Toronto and Vancouver* / Kristin R. Good

35 *Policy Paradigms, Transnationalism, and Domestic Politics* / Edited by Grace Skogstad

36 *Three Bio-Realms: Biotechnology and the Governance of Food, Health, and Life in Canada* / G. Bruce Doern and Michael J. Prince

37 *North America in Question: Regional Integration in an Era of Economic Turbulence* / Edited by Jeffrey Ayres and Laura Macdonald

38 *Comparative Public Policy in Latin America* / Edited by Jordi Díez and Susan Franceschet

39 *Wrestling with Democracy: Voting Systems as Politics in the Twentieth-Century West* / Dennis Pilon

40 *The Politics of Energy Dependency: Ukraine, Belarus, and Lithuania between Domestic Oligarchs and Russian Pressure* / Margarita M. Balmaceda

41 *Environmental Policy Change in Emerging Market Democracies: Central and Eastern Europe and Latin America Compared* / Jale Tosun

42 *Globalization and Food Sovereignty: Global and Local Change in the New Politics of Food* / Edited by Peter Andrée, Jeffrey Ayres, Michael J. Bosia, and Marie-Josée Massicotte

43 *Land, Stewardship, and Legitimacy: Endangered Species Policy in Canada and the United States* / Andrea Olive

44 *Copyfight: The Global Politics of Digital Copyright Reform* / Blayne Haggart

45 *Learning to School: Federalism and Public Schooling in Canada* / Jennifer Wallner

46 *Transforming Provincial Politics: The Political Economy of Canada's Provinces and Territories in the Neoliberal Era* / Edited by Bryan M. Evans and Charles W. Smith

47 *Comparing Quebec and Ontario: Political Economy and Public Policy at the Turn of the Millennium* / Rodney Haddow

48 *Ideas and the Pace of Change: National Pharmaceutical Insurance in Canada, Australia, and the United Kingdom* / Katherine Boothe

49 *Democratic Illusion: Deliberative Democracy in Canadian Public Policy* / Genevieve Fuji Johnson